THE PALMETTO STATE

THE PALMETTO STATE

The Making of Modern South Carolina

JACK BASS *and* W. SCOTT POOLE

The University of South Carolina Press

© 2009 University of South Carolina

Published by the University of South Carolina Press
Columbia, South Carolina 29208

www.sc.edu/uscpress

Manufactured in the United States of America

18 17 16 15 14 13 12 11 10 09   10 9 8 7 6 5 4 3 2 1

LIBRARY OF CONGRESS CATALOGING-IN-PUBLICATION DATA

Bass, Jack.
    The Palmetto State : the making of modern South
Carolina / Jack Bass and W. Scott Poole.
        p. cm.
    Includes bibliographical references and index.
    ISBN 978-1-57003-814-3 (cloth : alk. paper)
    1. South Carolina—History.   2. South Carolina—
Race relations—History.   3. South Carolina—Politics
and government.   4. South Carolina—Social
conditions.   I. Poole, W. Scott, 1971–   II. Title.
    F269.B269 2009
    975.7—dc22
    2008054777

Portions of this book have been adapted, with permission,
from *Porgy Comes Home*, by Jack Bass (Columbia, S.C.:
R. L. Bryan, 1972).

This book was printed on Glatfelter Natures, a recycled
paper with 30 percent postconsumer waste content.

CONTENTS

ILLUSTRATIONS

ACKNOWLEDGMENTS

The origin of this book is a column, written in 2002 by Will Moredock for the *Charleston City Paper*, noting the fortieth anniversary of the publication of my book *Porgy Comes Home*. Moredock wrote that the book "documents the quiet revolution that changed South Carolina between World War II and 1970." It seemed to me that this revolution has continued to shape the state in those forty years, and the story needed updating.

The idea of updating that volume morphed into a much longer narrative, a story of the Palmetto State that begins with the first European settlers. I subsequently invited W. Scott Poole, a younger historian and author who teaches South Carolina history and directs the joint graduate history program at the College of Charleston and the Citadel, to join me as coauthor. Scott and I have worked together since then to produce a book that will provide a solid understanding of and introduction to the state's history and development into the twenty-first century.

The emphasis the University of South Carolina Press has given in recent decades to publishing books about the state has significantly expanded the knowledge and understanding of South Carolina and its development. We are grateful for the press's attention to our book, with special mention of acquisitions editor Alexander Moore's role in shepherding this book to publication and project editor Karen Beidel's cheerful understanding and attention to detail.

Our special thanks are extended to Director Allen Stokes and to Beth Bilderback at the South Caroliniana Library of the University of South Carolina for their helpful support.

Special appreciation also goes to James R. Morris Jr., whose guidance, broad knowledge, and introductions led to numerous excellent sources, including officials and industry leaders important in the new economy that began taking off in 1970 in South Carolina. He symbolizes the many scholars and interviewees who gave of their time and insight.

The libraries and librarians of the College of Charleston provided excellent reference help. Their dean, David Cohen, read the manuscript and provided valuable insights.

Joi Mayo and Kate Jenkins, students in the master's program in history at the College of Charleston, assisted in the indexing of the volume, and their help is gratefully acknowledged.

Scott expresses his thanks to Beth Phillips for her love and support and his delight that their courtship and wedding interfered with the completion of this book. He also acknowledges his thanks and appreciation to his parents, Joan and Clarence Poole, for giving him a South Carolina childhood in the best sense of the phrase.

I would like to express my special appreciation to my wife, Nathalie Dupree, for her love, special support, and excellent copyediting. I also want to acknowledge my parents, Esther and Nathan Bass, of blessed memory, who brought forth their youngest child to grow into maturity as a native South Carolinian.

Scott and I dedicate this book to our parents.

JACK BASS

INTRODUCTION

South Carolinians began their fourth century looking not behind, but ahead. Yet, as William Faulkner observed, especially about the South, "The past is never dead. It's not even past."

After vigorous statewide debate in 2000 over the Confederate battle flag and whether it symbolized heritage or hate, the legislature moved it from the State House dome, where it had flown for almost four decades, to a flag-pole on the capitol grounds. A small step, perhaps, but important symboli-cally—a turn from the legends of "heritage" and toward historical truth. Its presence remained sufficiently provocative for the state NAACP that it launched a boycott.

A significant factor in the flag's removal from the dome came in a state-ment signed by more than one hundred historians in the state. They docu-mented beyond doubt that the direct cause of the Civil War, so devastating for this state, was not the idea that a state had the right to determine its destiny. The issue was slavery. That historical truth cut down any attempt at a moral argument by flag proponents.

Then came the stunning revelation by Essie Mae Washington-Williams after the death of Senator Strom Thurmond, a complicated and iconic politi-cal figure who many identified as a symbol of allegiance to the state's racial past, that she, an African American, was his daughter. Her announcement was followed by a full acceptance of her by his South Carolina family. The addition of her name to those of his other children on a State House monument to Thurmond signaled acceptance of something new by the state as a whole.

Recognition began to develop that the legacy of good manners had pro-vided both a veneer of civility and a cover of silence over a historic range of matters related to race and poverty that remained unaddressed. This develop-ing recognition in itself reflected change and signaled a state in transition.

Not long before his death, author and philosopher James McBride Dabbs recalled that it was the traditional South Carolina emphasis on manners that first got him involved in civil rights. He was referring to 1944, when Governor

Olin D. Johnston convened a special session of the legislature after federal courts threatened South Carolina's whites-only primary.

In an attempt to circumvent a Supreme Court decision, Johnston called the legislature into special session to pass bills that would allow the state Democratic Party to regulate the primary as a private club of whites. (Johnston would later receive strong black support as a U.S. senator with a liberal record on economic issues.)

"I knew they couldn't succeed," Dabbs recalled. "You couldn't set up a gentlemen's club. It was impossible; you knew they would get you sooner or later." He wrote a letter of protest that was published in South Carolina's largest newspaper, the *State* in Columbia. "What really motivated me," Dabbs continued, "what really got me was such bad manners, talking publicly about taking the vote from Negroes. I knew we had mistreated the Negro, but my mother taught me to be polite. This was very impolite, I thought, and I said so. South Carolina still has a good deal of this."[1]

What is new is the opening up of discussion about issues once considered taboo. Charles W. Joyner, a South Carolina native and one of the outstanding historians of the South—he holds doctorates in both history and folklore—has observed, "We South Carolinians—black and white—have a thing about history. That's what visitors first notice about us. We look to the past with nostalgia and to the future with hope; for memory without hope is unbearable, and hope without memory is impossible. Our history is a long tragic legacy of black and white harnessed together in slavery and segregation, in guilt rather than innocence, in defeat rather than victory, embodying more failure than success. Some of it is so painful that it hurts. And our fierce almost unbearable incomprehension leaves us terrified and touchy. Some of the lessons of our history are inspiring, but more of them—and the most important of them—are cautionary. Ours is a history rich in experience."[2]

In 1958 Dabbs published his autobiographical *Southern Heritage*, a book that calmly talked about race relations with a reasoned plea for social justice. It was a time of emotional, massive resistance to desegregation. In a television interview that year with newsman Mike Wallace, the host asked if Dabbs feared being physically harmed.

"Oh no, I'm a member of the aristocracy of damn fools," Dabbs replied gently to his baffled host. Dabbs puffed on his pipe and continued, "I say what I believe and folks around shake their heads and say, 'Don't pay any attention to Dabbs; he's a damn fool.'"

A one-time college English professor who returned in midlife to Rip Raps plantation, his ancestral home in Sumter County, Dabbs displayed in his writings and philosophy a keen insight into the similarities of all southerners, rather than their racial differences. The southerners' sense of place and their feeling for history were themes he developed fully. Before he died in May 1970, the monthly publication *South Today* called him "one of the South's great voices of common sense and poetic insight."

Not long before his death, he observed, "I think whites learned something that the everyday experience of Negroes taught them. . . . History is in his heart. He suffered history. History is not just a playground; it could run smack over you. And it didn't have much regard as to how you felt about it. You might like or not like it. You might feel innocent, but you still got run over. The South knows this."[3]

The day after Dabbs died, a small-town merchant in a nearby county with a population more than 60 percent black drove a visitor around town, past the new classrooms under construction at the private, segregated Robert E. Lee Academy. "Things will never be the same here," he reflected. He drove through the heart of the black section of town, past the segregated black high school that would become the town's junior high school for everyone in the fall. His daughter would attend the private academy as a ninth grader. "I just don't want the disruptions," he said, "but next year maybe she'll be back in the public high school."[4]

Near the private academy was a yarn plant, the newness of the luster of the brick exterior indicating that it had been in operation only a few years. Past the academy was a stand of young pine trees, planted where cotton had grown a few years earlier. An abandoned tenant shack stood as testimony to a desperate black family's flight to the promised land of the North, often from the frying pan into the fire. Other shacks remained that weren't abandoned, signaling families often desperate with poverty and yet hopeful and striving for dignity and a dream of equality.

Near the black section of town, wooden frame houses with faded paint stood, white children scurrying around the yards. Their parents would not have money for the tuition in the fall for the private school.

The issue of schools dominated the 1970 fall campaign for governor. The Democratic candidate, Lieutenant Governor John C. West, who as a state senator once had his life threatened by the Ku Klux Klan, was a racial moderate who said education should be kept out of partisan politics. For South Carolina to prosper, he said, the state must continue to combat the problems of poverty, illiteracy, and ignorance that for so long have shackled it. His opponent, Republican congressman Albert W. Watson, said he would not "surrender" to court desegregation orders without a fight.

After the Supreme Court desegregation decision in 1954, *Brown v. Board of Education,* South Carolina's leaders correctly read the meaning of the extremism of Arkansas, Mississippi, and Alabama. "They saw both its futility as regards integration and its danger as regards the economic future of the state," Dabbs wrote in his 1964 book, *Who Speaks for the South?* He added, "It is true, there has been, and there is, mean legal and economic infighting in South Carolina; but violence itself, even the suggestion of violence, is quickly condemned."[6]

South Carolina fought integration every step of the way, the state's political leaders reflecting the mood of the people. But a few days before Harvey Gantt broke the color line by enrolling at Clemson University in January 1963, outgoing Governor Ernest F. "Fritz" Hollings told the legislature: "As we meet, South Carolina is running out of courts. If and when every legal remedy has been exhausted, this General Assembly must make clear South Carolina's choice, a government of laws rather than a government of men. As determined as we are, we of today must realize the lesson of one hundred years ago, and move on for the good of South Carolina and our United States. This should be done with dignity. It must be done with law and order."[7]

Gantt enrolled a few days later without disruption, less than four months after the violence in which two were killed and scores injured when James Meredith was admitted to the University of Mississippi after Governor Ross Barnett called for defiance. Gantt, who after graduation would remain in the South as an architect in Charlotte, North Carolina, where he was elected mayor, observed while at Clemson, "If you can't appeal to the morals of a South Carolinian, you can appeal to his manners."[8]

Greenville had opened 1970 by successfully achieving a transition to a fully unitary school system, with busing that resulted in a roughly 80-20 white-black ratio in every school. In this Piedmont city pulsing from the impact of gleaming new industrial plants and commercial growth, a plain-faced, white grandmother leaving a textile mill shift talked that fall about people being laid off work and going on "short time." She also complained about racial problems in her grandchild's school and then talked about the governor's race. She said she was for West because Watson "talks about the schools, but there ain't nothing he can do about it, and we're going to have to live with it."[9] Her remarks reflected the power of law to effect change.

Southern politics traditionally have revolved around personalities, but this 1970 governor's election clearly was based on the joined central issues of race and education. In no state had the politics of color prevailed longer than in South Carolina. That grandmother's expression of resignation about racial integration illustrated a break with the past. West won the election with 52 percent of the vote. He was the fourth in succession of a line of progressive governors.

Four decades after Gantt's enrollment at Clemson, however, historian Dan Carter described what had developed in the state as an "unfinished transformation." He cited a single statistic that tells much. In the decade of the 1990s per capita income among black South Carolinians rose from 48 percent that of whites to 53 percent. At this rate of increase it would take roughly another century to overcome the effects of past discrimination.[10]

The forward thrust of developing a genuine biracial culture that appeared so promising three decades earlier had lost momentum after a backing away from civil rights by the U.S. Supreme Court. But South Carolinians old and new—northern migrants, Latinos, and a significant handful of well-educated natives who had left the South and now returned home as part of an expanded black middle class—debated such issues as identity and the meanings of memory.

In *Slaves in the Family* Edward Ball traces his prominent South Carolina family's history to rice planters owning hundreds of slaves and connects some of the descendants of the planters and the slaves as blood relatives today. Most of the state's African American population includes a mix of numerous African tribal groups with degrees of white ancestral connections. Interracial marriage by the twenty-first century, though uncommon, had become a recognized reality.

The mix of European and African influences in shaping the state's folk culture can be found in music, literature, art, religion, and food. Soon after the twenty-first century opened, Joyner wrote of the simultaneous need to confront "the tragic failures of our history" and "to embrace both our marvelous diversity and the essential unity underlying it."[11] A third of a century earlier, James McBride Dabbs had observed, "I don't care if whites like Negroes or Negroes like whites, but the question is how much they are alike. And by golly, you come to break it down, point after point; they're almost like two peas in a pod."

The past that traditional South Carolinians still feel in their bones includes so much. Foremost there is the element of race that dates to the state's first permanent European settlers who brought chattel slavery with them, but also the decades of dominance by planters and "King Cotton" that helped bring on the Civil War and the total defeat and devastation following the war's loss. There are the myths and realities of Reconstruction and the romanticism of the "Lost Cause" as well as the legally designated inferiority and disenfranchisement of

African Americans—sanctioned by the U.S. Supreme Court–that followed. There is the out-migration of hundreds of thousands of residents (mostly African Americans) and the Depression. There is a reviving economy that got support from the New Deal and federal defense during World War II and the civil rights revolution's impact in expanding both the workforce and the market for goods and services while opening the state to new ideas; and most recently there is the attraction of the state's natural beauty and its developing cultural facilities to people from "off" who have added new spice to the cultural mix.

As Faulkner observed, the past is still the lens through which the southerner looks to navigate the future.

| 1 |

THE BEGINNING

Although earlier European settlements on today's South Carolina coast had failed, Stephen Bull wrote on September 12, 1670, to his patron in England, Lord Ashley, "Wee conceive this to be as healthful A place as ever was settled . . . there is a lande sufficient here for some thousands of People where they may make very brave and happy settlements."[1]

The Kiawah Indian chief Cacique had directed the settlers to Albemarle Point on the Ashley River, the site of today's major state historical park known as Charles Towne Landing. In exchange for guns to protect themselves from the rival Westos from across the Savannah River, the Kiawah befriended the English, providing them supplies and other help. This site provided the launch for the state's first permanent European settlers. It turned out to be less healthy and less safe than first believed, and in 1680 the settlers moved across the Ashley to today's Charleston peninsula, building a palisade wall around the settlement for protection—the only English walled city in what would become the United States.

More than a century and a half earlier, other Europeans—from Spain—had landed on the South Carolina coast, confronting native peoples who called their land Chicora. Those earliest Europeans left behind a record of treachery, mistreatment, and devastating new diseases. In 1521, after a Spanish expedition from the Caribbean anchored on the coast near present-day Beaufort, crew members enticed friendly Indians aboard, held them captive, and sailed back to the Caribbean. There they sold the captives as slaves.

One of these ships, however, wrecked at sea. Its survivors included a captive who learned Spanish, became a Christian, and two years later traveled to Spain. Given the name Francisco Chicora, he spent time with and influenced the royal family. His stories, some of which got into print, led to Charles V's approving an exploration and a settlement north of present-day Florida. This time the Spanish brought African slaves with them.

In 1526 Chicora served as interpreter and guide for the first Spanish settlement, San Miguel de Gualdape, probably near present-day Georgetown, South Carolina. Once back among his native people, Chicora quickly abandoned the Spaniards. Their settlement became the first European colony anywhere in what today is the United States. It survived less than a year. In the earliest of many slave revolts in what would become South Carolina, Indians and Africans rose up against the Spanish. Only a starving one-fourth of the original six hundred settlers made it back to Spain.

In 1540 Hernando de Soto led an expedition across the South that crossed through South Carolina. At a major Indian settlement near present-day Camden, an Indian headwoman welcomed the Europeans as if they were visiting dignitaries. De Soto responded by taking her hostage, together with her female court, when he moved northward into North Carolina.

In 1562 France settled a short-lived colony on Port Royal Sound, a name given by the French leader Jean Ribaut, at the site of what would someday

Spanish settlement map. In 1577 Spain placed a settlement on Santa Elena Island near Beaufort. This settlement had a baroque church, a fort, and about sixty houses. Ten years later it would be abandoned. The place name survives today as St. Helena Island. *History of South Carolina Slide Collection*, B-06 become Parris Island Marine Recruit Depot. After the French colony failed, the Spaniards returned. By 1570 they had established a model Spanish town with more than three hundred people, including women and children. This colony suffered, however, from an absence of effective leadership. When food became scarce, the colony's raids on Indian settlements ultimately led to open warfare. In 1587, after Sir Francis Drake's English explorations along the South Atlantic coasts and his assault on St. Augustine, Spain abandoned its settlements north of Florida.

Although the remaining native population on the South Carolina coast seemed to regain their lands after the first European assault, the Spanish legacy included new diseases, such as typhus fever, that wiped out much of the native population. Native Carolinians had managed, nevertheless, to repel the Europeans seeking land, labor, and mastery. They would not return for almost a century.

The English political philosopher John Locke helped draft the original Fundamental Constitutions for Carolina before the settlement in 1670 that established Charleston. The provision for religious liberty exceeded anything existing in seventeenth-century Europe. Another provision provided specifically for chattel slavery. Although none of the five drafts were ever adopted, many of the basic principles became fully accepted and influenced the earliest development of the colony. Only Roman Catholics were excluded from the free practice of their religion, a reflection of the politics of Restoration England. A provision that settlers believe in God covered Jews as well as Christians. Capitalist-minded Quakers and Huguenots were welcomed in a colony looking for settlers and economic development.

Three black slaves landed with the first fleet of Englishmen, thus introducing into the permanent settlement the issue that would dominate much of the economic, social, and political life of South Carolina's next three hundred years.

South Carolina developed as the only English colony in North America where slavery had been entrenched from the very beginning. Although the earlier colonists of Virginia had first experimented with slavery early in the seventeenth century, it was the hard- and high-living English planters on the Caribbean island of Barbados who perfected the oppressive system of chattel slavery in the 1630s. Their system became the model for the Carolina settlement, and sons of Barbadian planter families—seeking new lands and new staple crops—became a significant part of the original Charles Town settlement.

Locke had written his document of governance for his patron, Lord Anthony Ashley Cooper, the Earl of Shaftesbury, who emerged as the leader of the colonization effort as one of eight entrepreneurial English aristocrats. Known as the Lords Proprietors, all had loyally supported Charles II in his days of war and exile. As a reward after the Restoration, Charles gave them a grant of land that would be named "Carolina" after "Carolus," the Latin version of his name.

These eight noblemen included some of England's most daring men. Many of their names remain familiar today. Present-day South Carolina counties are named for Sir John Colleton, Lord Berkeley, and the Earl of Clarendon. The Berkeley County seat of Monck's Corner apparently was named for General George Monck, Duke of Albemarle. Traditional Charlestonians still say, with mock solemnity, that Charleston is located where the Ashley and Cooper rivers meet to form the Atlantic Ocean.

The grant of Carolina included all the land between Virginia and a point in Florida sixty-five miles south of St. Augustine and extending to the Pacific Ocean. Captain William Hilton sailed from Barbados in 1663 to find a location for a settlement by wealthy Barbadians. Although his voyage produced no settlement, publication of his glowing account helped the proprietors in securing settlers. Hilton Head Island, today an upscale subtropical resort and retirement center, was named for him.

Most of the Lords Proprietors already had strong Caribbean connections. Ashley Cooper, in addition to a Caribbean plantation, also held a financial interest in the Royal Africa Company, the major English financial concern involved in the transatlantic slave trade. Moreover some of South Carolina's most prominent families, including the Draytons and the Middletons, can trace their lineage directly to Barbadian settlers. The first Africans in the colony had been slaves in Barbados. Some historians refer to South Carolina as "the colony of a colony" because of the strong Barbadian influence.[2] Barbadian architectural influence is also found in Charleston, especially the single houses—a single room wide with their downstairs and upstairs piazzas, or porches, to catch the breezes.

PRESENT-DAY SOUTH CAROLINA roughly resembles an equilateral triangle, with roughly a 200-mile base resting upon the Atlantic Ocean and the apex 236 miles to the northwest on the crest of the Blue Ridge Mountains. South Carolina acquired most of its mountain strip in 1772 when North Carolina made an equitable settlement of an earlier boundary error to the east that was caused by faulty surveying.

The state that grew from these colonial beginnings divides geologically and geographically into two regions. This division is marked by a fall line,

Charleston Powder Magazine and St. Philip's Protestant Episcopal Church (left). The St. Philip's congregation was the first Anglican congregation in the settlement of South Carolina. The current structure was built in 1838 and has had numerous restorations since, including a 1993–94 renovation. John C. Calhoun is among the South Carolina notables buried in the churchyard. Library of Congress, Historic American Buildings Survey, South Carolina, 10-CHAR, 114-1

a sandy belt that runs from Augusta northeastward through Columbia to the North Carolina line near Cheraw. In the early days of settlement the fall line marked the point where streams became navigable, and it marked a rough political and cultural boundary between lowcountry and upcountry. In the centuries to come these two sections would vie for control in state politics and, just as frequently, unite against outside threats to a common way of life.

In granting official toleration to all groups that "solemnly worship God," Locke's original Fundamental Constitutions of Carolina opened the colony to settlers who practiced a tradition that dissented from the Anglican form of worship. England fought wars with Spain and France, two of the great Catholic powers of Europe, almost once a generation in the early modern period. Englishmen worried throughout the seventeenth century about Romish plots against their liberties at home. After the Restoration most Englishmen equated the practice of Catholicism with political treason. South Carolina would not have an active openly Catholic congregation until after the American Revolution, with the founding of St. Mary of the Annunciation in Charleston in 1789.

Most of the first English settlers in Carolina were members of the Church of England. One of the first churches built in the new colony was St. Philip's, built on the Charleston peninsula in 1680 on the present site of St. Michael's. In 1707 the Anglican Church became the established church in Carolina.

Clergy received stipends funded by the colonial government, and church parishes functioned as voting districts. Although the Anglican Church would be disestablished in South Carolina during the American Revolution, its Episcopal form, developed after adoption of the Constitution, would continue to have a profound cultural influence in the South Carolina lowcountry.

Most white settlers unaffiliated with the Church of England adhered to some variant of the Reformed tradition. French Huguenots seeking religious freedom were among the early settlers of the colony. A group of Puritans from Dorchester, Massachusetts, founded a Congregational church in 1696 in today's Dorchester County, leaving behind the county name before moving to Georgia. "The White Meeting House" on today's Meeting Street had been established in 1681 in Charleston as the primary congregation for those of Calvinist and Congregationalist persuasion. Theological disagreements led to splits in this congregation and the founding of First Scots Presbyterian and Charleston's Unitarian congregation, the first of its kind in the American South. The original church is today's Circular Church, a vibrant and politically progressive congregation at the original Meeting Street site in downtown Charleston.

By 1700 Charleston's first Baptists had organized a congregation. Like most English Baptists of the time, this congregation followed closely the teachings of John Calvin on election and predestination. Influenced by American revivalism in the early nineteenth century, the Southern Baptist tradition departed from its Reformation roots. Today the First Baptist Church of Charleston calls itself "the mother church of the Southern Baptist Convention."

Dissenters who made up the so-called left wing of the Reformation also came to Carolina. Quakers, persecuted throughout much of the British Atlantic world, made Carolina home in the late seventeenth century. By the middle of the eighteenth, a large Quaker community lived in what is today Newberry County, and a small but prominent group settled in Charleston. Most Quakers, largely because of their opposition to slavery, left South Carolina by 1808, but the original members of two prominent South Carolina families, the Ladsons and the Elliotts, were Quaker.

Jews arrived in the colony before 1700. Francis Salvador, a member of the Provincial Congress of South Carolina in 1775, became the first Jew ever to hold public office in the Western Hemisphere. Although the Jewish population in the state remains less than half of 1 percent, Charleston was home to the largest Jewish population of any American city as late as 1820. Participation by Jews in public affairs would continue in the tradition set by Salvador. Columbia, the state capital, elected two Jewish intendants (mayors) before the Civil War.

Francis Salvador plaque. Francis Salvador, a member of the Provincial Congress of South Carolina in 1775, was the first Jew ever to hold public office in the Western Hemisphere. © Images by Joseph, Charleston, S.C.

ONLY A TINY REMNANT exists of the original Indian settlers. The Catawba, who possess a reservation in York County, have tribal status now recognized by the federal Bureau of Indian Affairs. In 2005 the descendants of both the Pee Dee and Waccamaw Indians received official recognition from the state of South Carolina. A small group of Kusso-Natchez (Edisto) remain in Dorchester County, and some Santee descendants lived near the town of Santee.

The names of many original Indian tribes remain preserved in South Carolina. Rivers include the Catawba, Pee Dee, Wando, Congaree, Saluda, Santee, Waccamaw, Combahee, Edisto, Keowee, and the wild Chattooga that links South Carolina, North Carolina, and Georgia. Cherokee County was once part of the lower Cherokee nation. Oconee County is named for a mountain in the Cherokee nation. Kiawah Island near Charleston is named after the tribe whose leader welcomed the first English settlers.

THE FIRST KNOWN RICE grown in South Carolina was on the Charleston peninsula in the 1690s. It was initially an experimental crop grown by a few entrepreneurs, but by the 1720s thousands of West Africans familiar with the crop had been brought to the colony to provide both the skills and hard labor necessary to build dikes and convert tens of thousands of acres of tidal marshes into rice fields. During that time rice replaced the deerskin trade and other early economic experiments as the primary product for export.

Slave labor quickly became the economic engine driving the colony. By 1708 enslaved Africans outnumbered whites. Chattel slavery shaped everything from law to land ownership. The earliest colonial land policy insured both the marginality of the small farmer and the centrality of plantation slavery.

In the first fifty years of colonial existence, the fierce independence of the Barbadian settlers caused the financial hopes of the Lords Proprietors to dim. White settlers, many with an aristocratic temperament linked to a strong entrepreneurial impulse, quickly gained control of the profitable deerskin trade. By 1719 the Lords Proprietors had lost control of the colonial governorship, and a decade later South Carolina became a royal colony, with the king appointing the governor.

Land ownership became more common after King George II authorized colonial governor Robert Johnson in 1730 to grant fifty acres to white men for every dependent man, woman, and child—white or black, slave or free. From 1731 to 1738 more than a million acres were added to the tax books by feverish land speculation, with planters importing 15,600 slaves. Between 1720 and 1740 a total of 40,000 enslaved Africans came into the colony.

Meanwhile the colony had survived such major crises as a war with the Yamassee Indians and a showdown with pirates. The Yamassee War of 1715 had almost wiped out the English settlement. White settlers survived only with the help of their Cherokee allies to the north. Piracy became a serious problem with the end of Queen Anne's War in 1713 and the sudden unemployment of hundred of "sea dogs." The hanging of forty-nine pirates in Charleston in 1718 is recorded on a stone marker at White Point Gardens near the Battery in Charleston. The marker tells of the hanging of Stede Bonnet—the so-called Gentleman Pirate who had once been a respectable sugar planter in the Caribbean—and his crew.

The refusal of Africans to submit meekly to the slave system had represented the major challenge for the first generations of South Carolina whites. Escape to the frontier or into Spanish-controlled Florida became a common occurrence in the early eighteenth century. Spanish authorities encouraged this practice as a way to strike back at the hated English. In 1733 Governor Antonio de Benavides of Florida declared that slaves who adopted the Catholic faith and worked in St. Augustine for four years would become free. Before 1740 the Spanish had a settlement and a fort north of St. Augustine made up of armed African militia, almost all of them former slaves from South Carolina.

TO BE SOLD on board the Ship *Bance-Ifland*, on tuefday the 6th of *May* next, at *Afhley-Ferry*, a choice cargo of about 250 fine healthy

NEGROES,

juft arrived from the Windward & Rice Coaft. —The utmoft care has already been taken, and fhall be continued, to keep them free from the leaft danger of being infected with the SMALL-POX, no boat having been on board, and all other communication with people from *Charles-Town* prevented.

Auftin, Laurens, & Appleby.

N. B. Full one Half of the above Negroes have had the SMALL-POX in their own Country.

Slave sale. By the 1730s Africans came into Charleston by the thousands, twenty thousand between 1720 and 1740 alone. Fears of small-pox, as illustrated by this advertisement, led to their quarantine on Sullivan's Island before sale. *History of South Carolina Slide Collection*, B-31

In September 1739 resistance reached its apex with the Stono Rebellion. A group of about twenty African slaves seized weapons near the western branch of the Stono River south of Charleston and began a march they hoped would take them to the safety of Florida. As their numbers grew, the Africans made no attempt to hide themselves. Martial tunes played on captured fife and drums joined with shouts of "Liberty!"

Leaving a swath of destruction and violence in their wake, the Africans burned and plundered plantations, taverns, and shops. Whites were killed with little regard for age or gender, but at least two were spared because of their reputation for kindness to slaves.

In a dramatic moment the carriage of Lieutenant Governor William Bull crossed paths with the insurrectionists. Bull ordered his driver to get him back to Charleston posthaste, where he called out all available white militia. The white militia and the rebels fought a pitched battle near Jacksonborough, between Charleston and Beaufort. The better-armed and better-trained militia defeated and captured many of the slaves. Roughly forty whites and sixty blacks died in the melee. Others escaped in groups into the woods, where they continued to harass outlying white settlements for many months.

White response to the rebellion proved swift and brutal. Travelers on the Old Post Road between Charleston and Beaufort (U.S. Highway 17 essentially follows this route today) would have seen the heads of the rebels placed on pikes up and down the route.

Many scholars view the Stono Rebellion as a significant turning point in South Carolina's history. The "Negro Act" of 1740 significantly narrowed the lives of African slaves while encouraging white planters to follow a policy that combined paternalism and repression. This method of control characterized white supremacy in South Carolina into the mid–twentieth century.

Stono increased white fears of the black majority. The state legislature levied a duty on slave imports that briefly slowed down the African trade. In order to attract more white immigrants, Governor Nathaniel Johnson had already proposed a plan for nine townships that would bring structure and organization to South Carolina's frontier.

In the 1730s and 1740s about eight thousand Germans, mostly German-Swiss, settled into the present Lexington, Calhoun, Orangeburg, and Newberry counties, bringing with them the Lutheran Church. From the descendants of these settlers emerged today's Lutheran Theological Southern Seminary in Columbia, the denomination's only seminary in the South. Another group of Germans settled in Charleston. In 1759 they founded St. John's Lutheran Church, still an active congregation on Archdale Street. In the decade before the Revolutionary War, these Germans established a vibrant community of artisans and merchants. German Palatines from upper Bavaria and parts of southwestern Germany came in the 1760s, many as indentured servants who were forced to settle along the Savannah River just above Augusta, Georgia, as a line of defense against the hostile Indian frontier.

About 1840 a large colony of Welsh Baptists from Pennsylvania were granted a tract of a thousand square miles on the Pee Dee River. Their descendants, whose names include Lewis, Rowland, Wilds, Evans, Ellerbe, Griffith, Gillespie, Greenwood, Jones, Pawley, and James, spread throughout South Carolina.

Although a group of Scots-Irish colonists settled in the Williamsburg Township in 1736, the major Scots-Irish movement in South Carolina began fifteen years later. These settlers, originally attracted to William Penn's colony, had pushed south in the search for surplus land. Their path from Pennsylvania went through the Shenandoah Valley of Virginia in the 1730s, into North Carolina the next decade, and then in the 1750s into the present South Carolina counties of Lancaster, York, Chester, and Chesterfield—all named after communities in Pennsylvania. By 1775 an estimated forty thousand Scots-Irish had settled throughout the South Carolina upcountry, bringing the Presbyterian Church with them.

The Scots-Irish were actually Scotsmen, whom the British government around 1600 had begun moving into Ulster in northern Ireland. The rebellious

Irish were never subdued, and the Ulster Scots by 1700 had begun to experience economic hardship as well as political and religious difficulties. They had never intermarried with the Roman Catholic Irish, who bitterly resented their presence. In South Carolina a Scots-Irishman was described as one who came to keep the Ten Commandments and everything else he could get his hands on. They also were known for family feuds and a fondness of whiskey and as significant contributors to the South's general bellicosity.

By the middle of the eighteenth century, the Piedmont had become primarily an area of small farmers, whose chief products were cattle and grain. Fiercely independent Calvinists, their devotion to duty and dedication to entrepreneurialism as a moral obligation made them ideal frontiersmen. Their entrepreneurial habits would soon make them ideal slaveholders. By the beginning of the nineteenth century, the Scots-Irish love of profit and the development of the cotton gin had helped transform the Piedmont into a plantation region.

Other Scottish settled in Charleston. In addition to names introduced by *Mc* and *Mac,* others range from Caldwell, Calhoun, Reed, and Logan to Deas, Buchanan, Gleaton, and Pringle.

The heavy migration of Scots-Irish resulted in a white majority in the 1770s in South Carolina that lasted until the 1820 census. A third of the European colonists were Scots-Irish or Scottish, the highest percentage of any colony. Although English settlers dominated the lowcountry, their 37 percent of the white population was smaller than that of any colony except Pennsylvania. Another 12 percent of the state's European immigrants were Irish, and 9 percent were Welsh—a total of 90 percent from today's Great Britain. The remaining European colonists were German, French, Swedish, and Dutch. No other colony received as high a percentage of French immigrants, overwhelmingly Huguenot Protestants seeking religious freedom. Many of their descendants achieved prosperity, influence, and social standing.

The enormous expansion of the white population in South Carolina's backcountry led to conflict with the Cherokee Indians, one of the largest Indian tribes in the colonial Southeast. The expansion of white settlements into Cherokee lands soured their relationship with the English, as did their indebtedness to the wily white Indian traders who crisscrossed the region. Local folklore in the upstate still reflects the anxiety of those times.

At Issaqueena Falls in northern Oconee County, one can still hear the sad tale of the legendary Indian maiden who threw herself from the falls after an unhappy love affair with one of these traders. An official current version inscribed on a state marker there, however, instead tells of Issaqueena hiding

Located in northwestern Greenville County, Caesar's Head had been a sacred site for the Cherokee. This postcard picture was taken in 1910 after the site had become a popular site for hikers. *History of South Carolina Slide Collection,* A-26

on a ledge just below the overhang of today's Issaqueena Falls as the Cherokee raiders searched for her, then riding a horse to Fort Ninety-Six to warn David Allen, a silversmith, of the impending Cherokee raid. They later married and by one account moved to Alabama, where they happily lived for many years.

A few hundred yards away from those falls is the Stumphouse Mountain railroad tunnel, the remains of a nine-year project to link Charleston to the Midwest by railroad. The tunnel was scheduled for completion in 1861, but the Civil War intervened. The 25-foot high, 17-foot wide, and 1,600-foot long tunnel through solid granite was abandoned after the war. Roughly a hundred yards off Highway 28 north of Walhalla, visitors receive a spectacular view of the falls and beyond.

Dissatisfaction erupted into open warfare in 1754 after Britain and France began the Seven Years' War, also known as the War for Empire. In North America the conflict became known as the French and Indian War. The Cherokees had initially allied with British forces, but they withdrew from that alliance after British soldiers in Virginia executed braves for alleged desertion. In response Cherokee war bands raided white settlements all along the southeastern frontier, including South Carolina.

Between 1759 and 1762 South Carolina mounted three separate expeditions against the Cherokee. In the summer of 1761 Lieutenant Colonel James Grant of the British regular army commanded a destructive campaign that drove the Cherokee into the upper northwestern tip of what is now South Carolina.

But jealousy exposed conflict between colonial South Carolina and British authority. Thomas Middleton came close to meeting Colonel Grant in a duel over what Henry Laurens later called "a serious quarrel on a very silly subject."[3] Grant had supposedly been too easy on the Indian enemies and allegedly slighted the fighting abilities of local troops in comparison to British regulars.

Christopher Gadsden of Charleston, a successful merchant who owned one of the largest wharves on the Charleston peninsula, become embroiled in this controversy and helped to publicize it. His political views and fiery temperament made him a thorn in the side of the British colonial government. In 1762, after Gadsden was elected to the Colonial Assembly, the royal governor of South Carolina refused to allow him to take his seat, supposedly because of a technical violation in election procedure. In truth Governor Thomas Boone was carrying out a new British mandate of the 1760s: assert royal authority over the North American colonies and remind them of their ultimate obedience to the Crown. Gadsden presented a tantalizing target.

British efforts to strengthen control over their colonies produced furor in New England and Virginia. The economic depression made the combination of taxation and mercantilism favoring British firms especially burdensome. In South Carolina, however, rice planters on the coast benefited from British rule. Meanwhile white settlers in the backcountry, rather than being angry at British laws that barely affected them, felt outrage at the colonial legislature in Charleston and its unresponsiveness to upcountry issues, such as the lack of courts. To rustic backcountry farmers, King George seemed less of a tyrant than the wealthy rice planters and Charleston merchants who dominated the assembly.

Christopher Gadsden led a delegation to the Stamp Tax Congress in New York in 1765. After returning home, he addressed a crowd that gathered under a large oak, known afterward as the Liberty Tree. It became the site of many future meetings, where Gadsden organized the small craftsmen who as the Sons of Liberty became the core of support for the cause of independence.

The plantation and mercantile elites came slowly to support if not independence, at least some adjustment of relations with Britain. Henry Laurens, a descendant of Huguenot settlers, became disenchanted with British policy after 1767. He had made a fortune in the slave trade and other shipping ventures, but British customs officials that year seized some of his ships, offending one of England's closest friends in South Carolina. Laurens later served as the president of the Continental Congress and became the only American ever imprisoned in the Tower of London.

Why did elites, seemingly so conservative in instinct and practice, move in the direction of independence? One explanation is that many saw it as an issue of honor, that what they perceived as their rights as Englishmen were being violated. The historian Robert Olwell, in his book *Masters, Slaves and Subjects*, suggests that the fears of these elite whites were aroused by rampant rumors that the British intended to ignite a slave rebellion in South Carolina.[4]

Lord William Campbell, the colony's last royal governor, wrote in the summer of 1775 that white South Carolinians believed that "14,000 stands of arms were aboard the Scorpion, the sloop of war I came out in," for the purpose of arming a slave rebellion. Although such stories were unsupported by evidence, Laurens wrote that all was "fear and zeal with delirium" that summer.[5]

Fear that the British intended to use every means available to suppress the colonies led white South Carolina to support the Declaration of Independence when it was proclaimed in July 1776. Four South Carolinians—Arthur Middleton, Edward Rutledge, Thomas Lynch Jr., and Thomas Heyward Jr.—signed it. Gadsden presented the declaration to South Carolina's new Provincial Congress along with a copy of Tom Paine's *Common Sense* and the banner, thereafter called the Gadsden Flag, with a coiled rattlesnake prepared to strike and emblazoned with the words "Don't Tread on Me."

During the 1670s and 1770s white South Carolinians had proudly shaped a set of social and cultural institutions. In their devotion to a premodern concept of liberty, they saw little irony in their equal devotion to chattel slavery. They rebelled against loss of their rights as Englishmen. For them liberty came to mean that native whites should rule the land. They threw off proprietary rule when it undercut their independence. In the 1760s many South Carolinians reacted assertively when the king and his ministers attempted to assert the Crown's prerogative. In the two decades that followed they would fight a war for their concept of liberty and help forge a new American nation.

2

THE AMERICAN REVOLUTION

On June 28, 1776, nine British ships attempting to enter Charleston Harbor bombarded Fort Sullivan on Sullivan's Island on the northern flank of the city's harbor. Colonel William Moultrie commanded patriot forces manning the fort, whose soft, spongy palmetto log walls absorbed the shock of British cannonballs without shattering. In the first major victory by American patriots, British forces were repulsed.

In commemoration South Carolina proclaims itself the Palmetto State, and a palmetto tree is depicted as the main symbol on the state flag. The state seal, struck the same year as the battle, depicts a palmetto tree rising triumphant over a fallen oak, symbolizing British naval power. The present Jasper County was named for Sergeant William Jasper, who in the midst of battle risked his life to replace the flag at what would soon be called Fort Moultrie in honor of the commander during the battle.

The battle of Sullivan's Island represents the only major battle in South Carolina during the first phase of the American Revolution, which was fought primarily in the northern colonies over the next two years. In 1778, however, the British began shifting their attention to the southern colonies. Savannah fell in 1779. The siege of Charleston ended in May 1780 with victory for the British and the capture of an army of six thousand. Roughly five thousand slaves, most of them following their Loyalist masters, joined the British forces.

After a smashing victory by the British at Camden three months later, the revolution appeared wiped out. South Carolina and Georgia were under British control, and it was predicted that North Carolina, too, would soon surrender. So serious was this defeat that America's French allies considered a separate peace with Britain. Meanwhile a number of patriot leaders in Charleston, including Christopher Gadsden, were imprisoned in the dungeon of the

Provost Guard, a building later to become the Exchange and today is a museum at the corner of East Bay and Broad streets. Many of these leaders, including Gadsden and three of the state's signers of the Declaration of Independence—Arthur Middleton, Edward Rutledge, and Thomas Heyward Jr. (Thomas Lynch Jr. had drowned in a ship accident earlier)—would soon be sent to Florida and the sweltering dungeons of British-controlled St. Augustine. Throughout the rebellious colonies those who signed the Declaration had become special targets of the British forces.

Although all seemed lost for the patriot cause, South Carolina soon became a center of unorganized resistance that flared after Lord Charles Cornwallis attempted to crush the Carolinians into submission by ordering the execution of all who had violated their paroles by taking up arms against the king. Cornwallis, promoted to lieutenant general, had become commander in the South after his role in the siege of Charleston and the decisive British victory in the battle of Camden.

In the following months, however, further British blunders and excesses fueled the opposition. Until 1780 the German and Scots-Irish settlers showed little concern about the war. Loyalist sentiment for the British had been strong throughout the upcountry. The only early fighting on land in South Carolina had been between patriot and Loyalist militias in the upcountry, including the battle of Ninety Six in November 1775. Some 1,800 British Loyalists attacked 600 Continentals. After two days of fighting and light casualties, the two sides agreed to a truce.

Cornwallis, however, told his men to take "the most vigorous measures to extinguish the rebellion."[1] He then unleashed Banastre Tarleton, soon called "Bloody Tarleton," to pacify resistance in South Carolina. Tarleton, known both for his brutality in combat and for his flaming shock of bright red hair, commanded a unit of infantry and cavalry immediately recognizable by their bright green uniforms. He had made his reputation in South Carolina after the fall of Charleston when he chased the Virginia cavalry of Colonel Abraham Buford one hundred miles to Waxhaws in present-day Lancaster County. Tarleton hunted down the fleeing Americans and attacked them from all sides. His men terrified the raw recruits, who attempted to surrender, shooting and sabering more than a hundred of them, including some attempting to wave the white flag.

Tarleton continued to pursue his scorched earth policy in the upcountry. He burned many of its Presbyterian churches to the ground, calling them "sedition shops" because of their reputation for revolutionary sentiment. Presbyterian ministers responded with strong sermons denouncing the British that helped shift sentiment among the Scots-Irish. A bitter civil war erupted in the upcountry between families of Loyalist and patriot sentiment. Chaos and violence, rather than order and restored British rule, swept the upcountry.

Cornwallis also failed to solidify his gains in the lowcountry. Conflicting British proclamations suggested that paroled American prisoners who had surrendered at Charleston might be forced to fight in the British army. In response General Andrew Pickens—operating throughout the Savannah River basin—and others took up arms again. Colonel Isaac Hayne, a lowcountry planter who had surrendered with his militia unit after the fall of Charleston, reacted to the threat of conscription by reorganizing and rearming his troops. He also committed a series of atrocities against Loyalists. Hayne, whom the British executed in Charleston in the summer of 1781, became a patriot and martyr for the American cause.

Generals Thomas Sumter and Francis Marion, known respectively as the "Gamecock" and the "Swamp Fox," also organized forces that harassed the British. Sumter and Marion counties are named for them. Sumter had kept a neutral stance throughout much of the war until after the British burned his plantation. Fleeing to the upcountry, he told one group of prospective recruits, "With me it is liberty or death!" Marion's hit-and-run, partisan raids in the rural lowcountry, with some armed blacks among his forces, provided an early example of modern guerrilla warfare.

The South Carolina Loyalists suffered a major defeat in upper South Carolina after British colonel Patrick Ferguson marched into the Piedmont and gave the independent men the choice of taking an oath to the Crown or receiving "fire and sword" from his hand. These needless threats caused hundreds of leathery frontiersmen, known as the Over the Mountain Men, to swarm down from Virginia, North Carolina, and Tennessee. They destroyed Ferguson's force of 1,100 Tories on October 7, 1780, at the battle of Kings Mountain in today's Cherokee County. Local tradition still encourages upcountry children to throw a stone on the grave of Ferguson, who along with most of his men died in the battle.

Historians of the period now recognize that battle as one of the turning points of the Revolution. Cornwallis and his army had advanced into North Carolina heading northward as the southern force in a pincer movement with General Henry Clinton aimed at George Washington's main Continental army. Ferguson's defeat at Kings Mountain forced Cornwallis to return to South Carolina before the end of the year.

Three months later, at the battle of Cowpens in Cherokee County on January 17, 1781, Tarleton lost three-fourths of his men in a pitched battle against a combined force of American militiamen and Continental soldiers. This battle became one of the most important of the American Revolution, forcing Cornwallis to pursue the patriot forces into the interior, a move that began the course of events that led twenty months later led to the ruin of Cornwallis at Yorktown. The surrender there of a weakened Cornwallis to George Washington virtually ended the war.

The sites for the battles of Kings Mountain and Cowpens, now preserved by the National Park Service, have become two of the most popular visitor attractions in the upcountry. Kings Mountain National Military Park attracts more than a half-million visitors annually. It lies at the southern terminus of the developing Overmountain National Historic Trail, a 330-mile part of the National Trail System that commemorates the route of the patriot army as it marched from Virginia through Tennessee, North Carolina, and South Carolina to Kings Mountain. By 2005 approximately 30 miles of the corridor were accessible to visitors.

Cowpens, designated a national battlefield in 1972, was attracting more than 200,000 visitors annually as the twenty-first century began. Several thousand reenactors and spectators participated in 2006 at the battle's 225th anniversary celebration.

Another upcountry National Park Service facility, the Ninety Six National Historic Site, was created in 1974 to interpret and preserve an area of unique historical significance. Ninety Six derived its name from traders in the 1700s who believed the location was ninety-six miles from Fort Prince George, the British garrison across the Keowee River from the lower Cherokee Nation's capital of Keowee at the base of the Blue Ridge Mountains. The National Park Service facility interprets colonial frontier life and the early relationship with Native Americans, and it details the site's significance during the southern campaign of the Revolutionary War.

The role South Carolina played in winning the American Revolution was historically crucial. R. L. Barbour's 2002 tour guide, *South Carolina's Revolutionary War Battlefields*, documents 254 battles and engagements in South Carolina, more than in any other state.

African Americans fought on both sides of the American Revolution in South Carolina. In Charleston slaves built the siege walls around the city. A few slaves joined Marion's band, often because of the promise of freedom. In Columbia the African American presence in Marion's band is included in a painting prominently mounted in the State House. Slaves by the thousands escaped into British lines, and in 1782 recently freed men donned the British uniform to fight as the Black Dragoons. These former slaves carried a banner emblazoned with the word *Liberty* into battle against the patriots.

The British army evacuated Charleston in December 1782. Close to five thousand former slaves left South Carolina with them, as did many white Loyalists who feared retribution for their support of the Crown. Many of these Loyalists later settled either in London or the Caribbean. Only a small number of the slaves who left with the British attained freedom; most went with their Loyalist masters to new homes in Jamaica or British-controlled Florida. Many of the men of the Black Dragoons took to the swamps of the Savannah River, and not until 1786 did militia from South Carolina and Georgia combine to wipe out these resisters.

The disorder of the Revolutionary years continued throughout the 1780s. In Charleston class conflict erupted as the artisans, the city's white working class, fought a losing battle to prevent the incorporation of the city. Many believed, correctly as it turned out, that the new intendant and city council would be dominated by lawyers, planters, and merchants. The place of the white working class in Charleston society can be seen in an unsuccessful petition to the state legislature in the late 1780s, claiming that city government in Charleston had become "an engine of oppression."[2]

After the Revolution rifts between upcountry and lowcountry also continued in the controversy over the ratification of the United States Constitution in 1787–88. Federalists, who favored a constitution that would create a strong central government, resided mostly in the lowcountry and were large planters and merchants. Democratic-Republicans, who hoped the central government would remain weak, were mostly small farmers and planters centered in the upcountry.

The lowcountry prevailed as Britain's former colonies formed "a more perfect union" in 1788 with the ratification of the Constitution. South Carolinians made notable contributions to the new nation's guiding document. John Rutledge, Charles Pinckney, Charles Cotesworth Pinckney, and Pierce Butler represented the state in Philadelphia. Although reflecting more the interests of elite Charleston rather than the state as a whole, the group made several notable contributions to the founding document. Charles Pinckney initiated the discussions on behalf of a provision that "no religious test shall ever be required" to hold any office in the United States government. South Carolina's long history of religious toleration lay behind Pinckney's initiative. Butler spoke in favor of the provision that would allow ratification after approval from nine of the thirteen states. All four delegates signed the final document.

Earlier, on June 25, 1778, when the Articles of Confederation were being considered by Congress, the delegates from South Carolina had moved to amend the fourth article by inserting the word "white" between the words "free" and "inhabitants." It would have meant that the privileges and immunities of general citizenship would have been limited to white persons. Delegates rejected it overwhelmingly, with only South Carolina and one other state approving it.

The United States Constitution, ratified a decade later, retained that article without significant change: "The citizens of each state shall be entitled to all privileges and immunities of citizens in the several states."

South Carolinians also insisted that slavery remain untouched by federal law, its existence recognized implicitly by the Constitution. John Rutledge made the North's acceptance of slavery in the South a prerequisite for the southern states entering the compact. The South Carolina delegation joined other southern leaders in insisting the slave trade have an extended life until 1808 and that three-fifths of the black population be included in the count on which members of the U.S. House of Representations would be apportioned.

The convention that ratified the Constitution in South Carolina met in Charleston in May 1788. Over objections from the upcountry, South Carolina became the eighth state to ratify. Upcountry leaders, many of whom were quickly becoming wealthy planters, objected primarily to the constitutional compromise to end the international slave trade in 1808.

Although the upcountry leadership lost the battle over the Constitution, their growing influence had been recognized in 1785 by the lowcountry's acquiescence in replacing Charleston as the state capital with the planned city of Columbia. The new capital was laid out where the Broad and Saluda rivers join to form the Congaree, almost in the geographic center of the state. Columbia's wide streets, so laid out because of the contemporary belief that the malaria problem in Charleston was related to that city's narrow passageways, help give Columbia a modern look today. The burning of the city by General Sherman's forces in the Civil War—a matter some still consider unsuited for levity but that others refer to wryly as the city's first federal urban renewal program—also enhanced the appearance of modernity.

Despite the new capital in the heart of the state, the political structure remained substantially unaltered. A new state constitution in 1790, which retained a considerable property qualification for voting, left the upcountry—with four times the white population as the lowcountry—with minorities in both houses of the legislature. That body operated as a ruling committee of the landed gentry of both regions for the next seventy years, providing for an aristocratic republic in South Carolina.

Growing wealth in the upcountry also altered the economic balance between the two sections. The invention of an efficient cotton gin by Eli Whitney in 1793 profoundly affected South Carolina. Cotton, and with it slavery, spread across the Piedmont, and South Carolina in 1804 reopened the slave trade for a few years because of the demand for labor. In four years, before the constitutional deadline ending slave importation in 1808, South Carolina imported as many new African slaves as had come to the colony between 1720 and 1740, close to forty thousand. Many of these new Africans went to the new cotton fields on the Sea Islands near Beaufort, and thousands of others to the short-staple cotton fields of the upcountry, where small farmers as well as great planters became slave masters. Slavery spread quickly throughout the upcountry, where small entrepreneurs could put in a crop of cotton with minimal start-up costs, unlike the expense involved in growing rice.

The shared commitment to slavery united the elite classes of both sections. When the South Carolina College, which would later become the University of South Carolina, was founded in 1801, its role was conceived in part as a means to lessen the antagonisms between upcountry and lowcountry by

South Caroliniana Library Reading Room. The South Caroliniana Library was completed in 1840 as the first freestanding academic library in the United States. The building was designed by Robert Mills, a prominent architect of the nineteenth century who also designed the Washington Monument. The South Caroliniana Library houses book, photograph, and manuscript collections that continue to serve as an important resource for scholars studying South Carolina and American history. *History of South Carolina Slide Collection*, I-9 bringing together the future leaders of the state. Lowcountry leaders saw the establishment of the college as a means of indoctrinating an appreciation of tidewater values among the upcountry youth.

As the most influential cultural institution in the South Carolina upcountry, Willington Academy in the old Abbeville district near present-day McCormick provided a classical education to students from throughout the state as well as to those from other states. Presbyterian clergyman Moses Waddel taught ancient Greek and Latin and honed the oratorical skills of students, who went on to become political leaders in the state and region. Students, sons of the Charleston elite as well as upcountry farm boys with ability, boarded with local farm families. Top students entered Princeton and Yale with advanced standing, and many of lesser means pursued further study at South Carolina College. Famous graduates included four pre–Civil War governors of South Carolina, three U.S. senators from the state, nine members of Congress from Georgia, and two from Alabama. Impetus for the school came initially from Calvinist-minded French Huguenot settlers in the area, and the name "Willington" came from their being "willing to" join with local Presbyterians to establish the new school.[3]

Charleston lawyer Henry W. DeSaussure candidly commented, "We of the lower country know that the power of the State was thence forward to be in the upper country, and we desired our future rulers to be educated men." A twentieth-century writer has described educated South Carolinians in that age as having "a Roman reverence for slavery."[4]

An amendment to the 1790 state constitution, known as the Compromise of 1808, represented the alliance of upcountry and lowcountry elites. Political power subsequently began to shift: a majority of South Carolina's nineteenth-century governors would come from the upcountry, as did the state's most powerful political leader, John C. Calhoun.

The lowcountry did continue, however, to have a profound influence in state government. Eighteen lowcountry parishes, remnants of the Anglican Church organization, remained as election districts with heavy, nonvoting slave populations. For example, St. Stephen Parish and its 226 white inhabitants had three representatives and one senator, the same as upcountry Edgefield and its 9,785 whites. With property qualifications requiring ownership of five hundred acres of land and ten slaves for the lower house and double that for senators, control of the all-powerful General Assembly remained in the hand of wealthy slaveholders until 1865. The Compromise of 1808 really meant a certain class, rather than a particular region, would control state government until the end of the Civil War.

3

AN ERA OF DECLINE

During the first two decades of the nineteenth century, South Carolina prospered. Charleston trailed only New York in the value of its imports in 1816. The national Panic of 1819, however, dealt South Carolina an economic blow from which it never recovered.

Other developments in the following decades diminished the state's status. Cotton's westward expansion not only greatly increased total cotton supply and reduced prices, but after 1820 more than 200,000 whites—40 percent of all whites born in South Carolina—and 170,000 slaves moved west before the Civil War to the cotton regions of Alabama, Mississippi, Louisiana, and the new state of Texas.

Charleston, the nation's fifth largest city in 1800—behind New York, Boston, Philadelphia, and Baltimore—ranked only twenty-second in 1860. British actress Frances Anne "Fanny" Kemble fondly recalled a visit to Charleston in an otherwise fiercely antislavery journal in which she described her life as the wife of a Georgia planter. Published first in London in 1863 a few months after President Lincoln issued the Emancipation Proclamation, *Journal of a Residence on a Georgian Plantation in 1838–1839* would move England away from support of the Confederacy. On an 1838 visit over Christmas to the slowly declining city, she wrote in her journal: "In walking about Charleston, I was forcibly reminded of some of the older country towns in England. . . . The appearance of the city is highly picturesque . . . a little gone down in the world, yet remembering still its former dignity. . . . Charleston has an air of eccentricity, too, and peculiarity."[1]

South Carolina remained a majority black state and the only one in which a majority of whites owned slaves. More than 98 percent of the population was born in the state. Religion reinforced the status quo, and it also allowed South

Charleston in 1853 was enjoying a recent boom in rice exports in the decade before secession. This bird's-eye view of the city was published in *Harper's Illustrated Weekly*, 1853. *History of South Carolina Slide Collection*, F-26

Carolina gentlemen to consider the state as the peak of a superior southern civilization.

Slavery's significance in antebellum South Carolina made religion a biracial phenomenon. Slaves, sometimes against their will, sometimes willingly, accompanied their masters to revival meetings. The architecture of most South Carolina churches featured a "slave gallery" or some other special section for slaves. By the 1830s many white churches actually had a majority black membership. This circumstance was especially true in Methodist and Baptist congregations but could also be seen in other churches, especially in the lowcountry. By 1860, for example, Johns Island Presbyterian Church had 60 white members and 510 black members.

Slaves embraced Christianity, but not necessarily the Christianity of their masters. South Carolina ministers preached a very conservative version of the Christian message, one that emphasized obedience to social superiors as the basis of a truly Christian society and underscored the apostle Paul's quote about a slave following his master.

Slaves sometime openly rejected this version of the Gospel message. Charles Colcock Jones, a Presbyterian frequently called upon by lowcountry planters to preach to their slaves, once watched helplessly as an entire congregation stood up and walked out in the middle of one of his sermons about duties to masters.

A similar impulse led the black Methodists of Charleston to form their own congregation in 1818. Black "members" of white congregations had no role in church governance. Conflict over this issue, in this case a desire by whites to build a shed over the black cemetery, led about four thousand black members to leave the white-controlled Bethel Methodist Church and form their own congregation. This congregation, the forerunner of today's Emanuel African Methodist Episcopal (AME) Church on Calhoun Street, faced constant harassment from white authorities.

The law required blacks to have a white person present in order to hold services, which couldn't be held in the evenings. They couldn't teach classes such as reading and writing—a violation of state law if taught to slaves. Such offenses resulted in arrests of a number of blacks.

Whites felt anxious over the independence of these black Methodists. In 1822 a leader in the congregation named Denmark Vesey was accused of planning what would have been the largest slave insurrection in the history of North America. What happened next remains historically controversial.

All copies of the final official report, privately published by some of the judges (transcripts of the "trials"—more like interrogations—remain at the South Carolina Department of Archives and History in Columbia), were ordered destroyed, but one brought home from the Beaufort area by a Union soldier during the Civil War ended up in the possession of a brother of Harriet Beecher Stowe. He had it archived at Harvard University. It stated that Vesey, a former slave, after winning a city lottery had purchased his freedom from the sea captain who had treated him almost like a son after buying him as a child. (He actually purchased his freedom from Captain Vesey's wife.) The report said Denmark Vesey inspired his followers by reminding them of the biblical book of Exodus, which tells of God freeing the oppressed Jews.

What happened next is unclear. The story of a plot was overheard in June 1822 at the docks by two enslaved black house servants. They revealed what they had heard to their masters, who notified authorities. Retribution came swiftly.

Other blacks, both slave and free, were jailed and threatened with hanging if they did not confess. White leaders became convinced Vesey and his co-conspirators planned to seize the city of Charleston, kill all white citizens in the city, and then commandeer some of the ships at anchor in the harbor and make their way to Haiti, the first free black republic in the Western Hemisphere. Rumors spread quickly that thousands of blacks were ready to strike and that weapons and poisons (to be put into the city wells) were hidden away for this purpose. No such weapons were found. (In fact Charleston was second only to New Orleans as a destination for mulatto refugees who had fought on the side of the losing planters in the Haitian revolution at the end of the eighteenth century. They and their descendants lived as "free persons of color" in Charleston. Many of them became slave owners, in some cases a free man technically owning his slave wife. During the Civil War and Reconstruction, they would join with the freedmen.)

A series of secret trials followed. Vesey and many others never heard testimony or saw the evidence against them, much of it coerced through torture. By the twenty-first century, Vesey came to be remembered by many as a freedom fighter, with an artist's representation of him hanging as a portrait in the Gaillard Municipal Auditorium in Charleston. Others viewed him as a terrorist who would have massacred whites had his uprising succeeded.

A powerful two-person play written by Charleston stage director Julian Wiles and staged during Piccolo Spoleto in 2007 presented Vesey and his former owner debating what happened. Wiles researched at some length in the Department of Archives and History and found material that undermined the official account; his Vesey character points out that no whites were ever molested or injured and that the evidence against him was coerced from slaves whose screams he heard in jail while they were being whipped and tortured.

The one fact on which there is agreement is that Vesey and thirty-four others were executed in July 1822 in the largest mass hanging in U.S. history. Although no whites had been killed or molested, by order of the South Carolina legislature, authorities that fall razed the Hampstead church to the ground. Another new law required black seamen, even if free, coming into Charleston on ships to be imprisoned while in the city.

The Vesey conspiracy had alerted white South Carolina to the anger that seethed beneath their slaves' apparent subservience and furthered an inward retreat from outside influences. Just two years before, in 1820, a national controversy over whether slavery could be extended into the young nation's western territories had raised the ire of white South Carolina. Although the Missouri Compromise (allowing Missouri to enter the Union as a slave state) could be seen as generous, it angered defenders of slavery. Why should the South's institution not be allowed anywhere in the growing United States? Could slaveholders not take their property to any part of the Union?

White Charleston responded by building a guardhouse on today's Marion Square to serve as a headquarters for rallying troops against any future slave uprising. In 1844 the guardhouse became the South Carolina Military Academy —the Citadel.

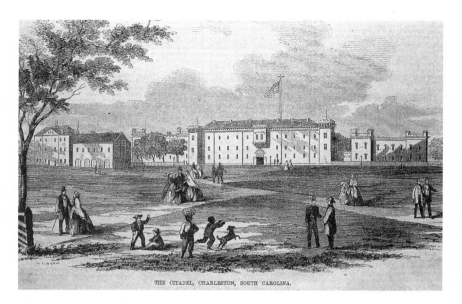

The Citadel was founded in 1844 at the site of a military fortification built to protect the city of Charleston in the event of a slave uprising. This picture shows the military school in 1853. *History of South Carolina Slide Collection*, I-21

THE HISTORIAN JAMES HAW has written that South Carolina antebellum leaders, "unable to admit that slavery rested ultimately on material greed incompatible with their ideal, created an image of a superior southern civilization on which South Carolina was the highest example. Their idea of selfless public service was the highest example."[2] The belief that theirs was a superior culture led them to consider attacks on slavery as a relic out of step with advancing concepts of freedom as attacks on the state's honor. This element limited the ability to compromise. The interaction of all these influences produced radical behavior by the planter elites and their urban allies that was leading the state confidently and blindly down the road to a confrontation with history. South Carolina in the nineteenth century, the historian Ira Berlin has written, became a slave society rather than simply a society that held slaves.[3]

Sensitive visitors at the time saw something quite horrific. Harriet Martineau, an English visitor to South Carolina in the early nineteenth century, never forgot the slave pens and auction blocks of Charleston. Martineau remembered the streets surrounding the Exchange Building, on East Bay Street, as "the most infernal sight I ever beheld."[4] Martineau especially remembered the image of a mother, her two mulatto children grappling her in terror as they were sold apart. (In the first decade of the twenty-first century, the Old Slave Mart museum on Chalmers Street worked to commemorate the suffering of that period.)

In the interior of the state, speculators bought slaves in the Upper South and sold them farther South. South Carolina's old Edgefield District included eight such firms. The slaves were transported by forced march overland in a coffle, traveling about twenty miles a day, and then placed in pens and auctioned like cattle. The slave Charles Ball, sold by his master in Maryland circa 1805 and marched to South Carolina for resale, left a vivid account of his experience:

> The women [two of them pregnant] were merely tied together with a rope, about the size of a bed cord, which was tied like a halter around the neck of each; but the men, of whom I was the stoutest and strongest, were very differently caparisoned. A strong iron collar was closely fitted by means of a padlock round each of our necks. A chain of iron, about a hundred feet in length, was passed through the hasp of each padlock. . . . We were handcuffed in pairs . . . and the poor man to whom I was thus ironed wept like an infant when the blacksmith with his heavy hammer fastened the end of the bolts that kept the staples from flipping from our arms.[5]

The practice of hiring out, in which non-slaveholding farmers and artisans leased the use of slaves from their owners, ensured that almost all whites in the state gained an economic advantage from the institution. The boom in cotton and the revitalization of the rice economy in the early nineteenth century had focused the minds of planters and merchants on the prices of slaves and of staple crops. But reaction to growing antislavery sentiment in the American North and the capitals of Europe worked to develop a siege mentality in the South's premier slave state.

The fate of Charleston's culture of the mind provides an example. Charleston had a flourishing intellectual culture in the eighteenth century. The Charleston Library Society, incorporated in 1755, functioned as both a subscription lending library and a center for lectures, public readings, and debates. The Charleston Museum, America's premier museum of natural history in the eighteenth century, grew out of the city's large number of botanists, geologists, and marine scientists. At least four bookstores operated in Charleston during the antebellum period, with Robert Wells's store on East Bay Street the largest bookstore south of Philadelphia.

This vibrant intellectual life began to wither as the values of the slaveholding class replaced free intellectual inquiry. Some eighteenth-century southerners had argued that slavery represented a necessary evil. Now, with the morality of slavery under attack, South Carolina's political and religious leaders began defending the institution as a positive good. Rather than producing books on the natural sciences and medicine, the state's intellectuals wrote proslavery pamphlets and tracts. A few, like Charleston novelist William Gilmore Simms, did so while lamenting the low state of intellectual life in the state.

THE BIBLE PLAYED an important role in the proslavery argument, in part because the Bible played an increasingly important role in the lives of South Carolinians. In the early nineteenth century a series of regional evangelical revivals swept across the state. The Baptists and Methodists flourished in this context. Both emphasized a transformative conversion experience, one often accompanied by great emotional outpourings. One observer of an early up-country revival noted that participants behaved "as though they were struck by lightning, speechless and motionless; and when they somewhat recovered, they could be heard shrieking bitterly and supplicating God for mercy and grace."[6]

BY THE 1830s Methodism had more adherents, black and white, than any other religious tradition in South Carolina. The Baptist Church closely followed. While these churches flourished, other South Carolina religious traditions remained important. The Presbyterianism, the church of the Scottish and the Scots-Irish, remained strong. James Henley Thornwell, a Presbyterian divine who briefly served as pastor of Columbia's First Presbyterian Church, subsequently directed the Columbia Presbyterian seminary and served for a time as president of South Carolina College. Thornwell became known nationally as a leader among the "Old Side" Presbyterians, the most conservative version of nineteenth-century Presbyterianism.

He also helped develop and became a spokesman for the theory of slavery as morally and theologically a positive good. Slavery, he believed, had helped bring the Gospel to the "savages" and also ensured that society would be well ordered and properly hierarchal. Thornwell saw abolition as one of many modern heresies, connected to both feminism and socialism.

Roman Catholicism gained strength in the antebellum period, following a century of repression. Bishop John England, the first bishop of South Carolina, gave the church both intellectual and social respectability in the 1820s and 1830s. England believed (as did Alexis de Tocqueville) that Roman Catholicism could prosper amid the republican institutions of the United States. England became a national voice for this progressive position within Catholicism, with which many in both Europe and the United States disagreed. In 1829 England also founded a religious order native to South Carolina, the Sisters of Mercy.

The daughters of many of the state's planter elite received their early education at the highly respected convent school run by the Ursuline sisters in Columbia. The Sisters of Mercy ran similar institutions, as well as orphanages and hospitals, in Charleston. In the 1850s Bishop Patrick Lynch, the third bishop of Charleston, joined in shaping the proslavery argument. During the Civil War Lynch served as a Confederate emissary to the Vatican.

Judaism continued to prosper in Charleston. In 1820 about 700 Jews lived in South Carolina, more than in any other America state. New York was second with 550. Although most Jews in the state, like most Roman Catholics, lived in Charleston, Columbia elected two Jewish intendants (mayors) before the Civil War. In 1840 Kahal Kadosh Beth Elohim (Holy Congregation House of God) became America's first and premier Reform synagogue. Charleston would also have the first distinctively Ashkenazic, or eastern European, synagogue in the United States when Brith Shalom formed in the mid-1850s. Many propertied Jews in South Carolina became slaveholders, like other elites in the state, but few were planters. Those South Carolina Jews who held slaves represented a small part of the total percentage of slaveholders and a minority within the Jewish community itself, many of whom were struggling immigrants. Collectively they owned fewer slaves than did free persons of color, the term for free blacks.

Little religious friction developed among the varied religious groups in the state. This was in part because Protestants represented the overwhelmingly numerical majority, and neither Jews nor Catholics represented a significant voting bloc. But more important, white unity over the issue of slavery mattered far more than religious and ethnic differences.

IN THE TWO DECADES FOLLOWING Vesey's failed insurrection, white South Carolina took the lead in the defense of slavery and the sectional controversy. They turned inward against the world of ideas, a reaction to fear and anxiety of a possible slave revolt at home and the stirrings of abolitionist agitation in the North.

John C. Calhoun's career best illustrates the state's role in this period. A graduate of Yale with a first-rate education as a lawyer, he had served two terms in the state legislature before election at age twenty-eight to the U.S. House of Representatives in 1810. There he became known for his support of strong nationalist policies, including a strong military and improvements to roads that would connect the nation. An outspoken hawk in the War of 1812, Calhoun joined many other southern political leaders in anger against British interference with American trade in the Atlantic.

RELIGIOUS DIVERSITY TOOK ROOT EARLY IN
SOUTH CAROLINA AND REMAINS A SIGNIFICANT
PART OF THE STATE'S CULTURE.

One of the few remaining original Presbyterian houses of worship, the Old Stone
Church was built in the early nineteenth century and is two miles from the campus
of Clemson University. *History of South Carolina Slide Collection*, J-10

Pilgrim Holiness Church at Winnsboro Mills. This is one of the many churches built
on land donated by mill owners, who believed that religion encouraged good work
habits. *History of South Carolina Slide Collection*, I-85

St. Philip's Protestant Episcopal Church, the original Anglican church in the Carolina colony, was built in the 1680s on the site of today's St. Michael's at the corner of Meeting and Broad streets in Charleston. In 1711 it was moved to its current location on Church Street. This photograph shows the current structure, built in 1835. The Dock Street Theatre is visible in the left foreground. *History of South Carolina Slide Collection*, I-66

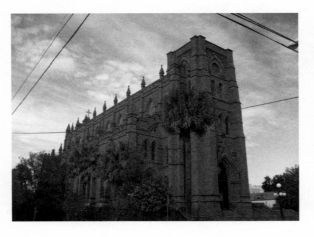

The Cathedral of St. John the Baptist, the seat of the Roman Catholic Diocese of Charleston, was completed in 1888. It sits on the site of the Cathedral of St. John and St. Finbar, which was built in 1852 and destroyed in Charleston's Great Fire of 1861. Photograph by Beth Phillips

Its name in Hebrew meaning "Holy Congregation House of God," the Kahal Kadosh Beth Elohim Synagogue was founded in 1749. The current structure was built in 1841. KKBE is the first Reform congregation in the United States and the second-oldest synagogue. Since World War II, it has been the oldest Reform synagogue in the world. KKBE Records, MSS 1047, College of Charleston Special Collections; special thanks to John White

The Circular Congregational Church had its origins in the Reform Meeting House that gave Meeting Street its name. The current structure dates to 1870. Historic American Buildings Survey, South Carolina, 10-CHAR, 91-4

Charleston's First Baptist Church is described as the "Mother Church of the Southern Baptist Convention." The congregation itself predates the SBC, having emerged during early colonial times as part of the missionary efforts of New England Baptists. Historic American Buildings Survey, South Carolina, 10-CHAR, 70-2

Emanuel African Methodist Episcopal Church. Rev. Richard Cain, an important Reconstruction leader who served in Congress, reorganized Charleston's Emanuel AME Church, which was dismantled in 1822 after the Vesey conspiracy. The current structure was built on Calhoun Street in 1891. Photograph by Beth Phillips

First Scots Presbyterian Church. This congregation emerged from an amicable separation from the Independent Meeting House in Charleston (later Circular Church) in 1731. Governed according to the precepts of the Church of Scotland, First Scots celebrates Scottish Heritage Sunday in September. Historic American Buildings Survey, South Carolina, 10-CHAR, 110-3

The Central Mosque of Charleston on upper King Street comprised in 2008 about one hundred families who practice the Sunni Muslim faith, the largest branch of the Islamic religion. Central Mosque was founded in 2006. It is located next to the Fresh Cut Barbershop, a gathering place for the largely African American neighborhood. The congregation is made up of people with diverse ethnic and national heritages, including Arabs, Indians, Russians, Pakistanis, Egyptians, and Africans. There are about five thousand practicing Muslims in contemporary South Carolina. Photograph by Beth Phillips

"Silent Churches" of Charleston. This photograph captures both the Unitarian Church of Charleston and St. John's Lutheran Church on Archdale Street. These are known as the "silent churches" because their church bells were melted down for use as ammunition during the Civil War and never replaced. The Unitarian Church is the first Unitarian congregation in the South (1772), and St. John's is the oldest Lutheran congregation in the city (1816). Historic American Buildings Survey, South Carolina, 10-CHAR, 197-1

St. Mary's Roman Catholic Church. St. Mary's Church dates to 1788 and is the oldest Roman Catholic church in North Carolina, South Carolina, or Georgia. This church functioned as the cathedral of the state's first bishop, John England, until the building of the Cathedral of St. John the Baptist. The interior was frescoed, and stained glass windows were added, in the 1890s. Historic American Buildings Survey, South Carolina, 10-CHAR, 97-2

Visit of Pope John Paul II. Pope John Paul II visited South Carolina in September 1987. A large ecumenical service was held in USC's Williams-Brice Stadium. *History of South Carolina Slide Collection*, B-214

He resigned from Congress in 1817 to serve as secretary of war under President James Monroe. After campaigning for president in 1824 in a crowded field, the forty-two-year-old Calhoun emerged as a consensus second choice. He was elected vice president under John Quincy Adams after a contentious election that was decided by the House of Representatives. As vice president—first to Adams and then, after the 1828 election, to Andrew Jackson—Calhoun emerged as South Carolina's political strongman, with the capacity to reward friends and punish enemies.

In 1824 white southerners felt they had yet another reason for anger. Congress passed a protectionist tariff, placing an import tax on foreign manufactured goods. Carolina planters interpreted this as purely sectional. They even saw it as antisouthern legislation. As an agricultural region, the South depended on the import of manufactured goods. A worldwide fluctuation in agricultural prices, with economic repercussions in the United States that created the Panic of 1819, had created anxiety among planters about their economic health.

By the late 1820s influential planters saw the tariff as part of a growing conspiracy to change their way of life. Robert J. Turnbull authored a pamphlet called *The Crisis* that viewed the tariff as part of a larger plan by the North and West to destroy slavery. Thomas Cooper, the president of South Carolina College, went so far as to suggest that the time had come "to calculate the value of the Union."[7]

Meanwhile another tariff act raising rates 20 percent had been passed in the U.S. Senate in 1828. Calling it the Tariff of Abominations, South Carolina leaders entered a new phase of radicalism. Although the crisis that followed led to a compromise that gave the South relief from the Tariff of Abominations, it also forced Calhoun to reveal himself as the author of the nullification argument, which unwittingly and to his distress was expanded by South Carolina's more radical defenders of slavery to claim a state's right to withdraw from the Union. Within the state the psychological impact of these developments produced radical behavior by the planter elite and their urban associates that only intensified, with some calling for a nullification convention.

Calhoun feared that this growing radicalism meant he would lose control of his home state, destroying his hopes for the presidency. In a bid in 1828 to strengthen the South's position for attacking the tariff Congress passed that year, which protected northern manufacturers while raising prices of goods in the South, Calhoun anonymously published a tract at home in South Carolina, *Exposition and Protest*, that advanced a theory of state sovereignty that would allow a state to nullify a federal law. He developed the idea of nullification in which an individual state could meet in convention and vote to nullify any law that encroached on its sovereignty or violated the Constitution. His argument, however, included a provision requiring a nullifying state to accept the law if three-fourths of the states later affirmed it. He never intended for his theory of nullification to become a case for secession. By 1830 the state had divided between Nullifiers, who wanted a nullification convention to oppose the federal law, and Unionists, who believed that nullification represented the path to disunion.

In the summer of 1831 white South Carolinians felt further besieged and frightened by the Nat Turner rebellion in Virginia, in which Turner—acting on a "vision from God"—led his fellow slaves in killing fifty-five white people in Southampton County. Also that summer Calhoun protégé George McDuffie made a fiery speech in Charleston advocating both nullification and secession. It electrified the audience.

Although Calhoun's goal had been to provide a political weapon to redress grievances, not promote disunion, he came out forcefully for nullification in order to retain control. By 1832 the Nullifiers had the upper hand in state politics. Candidates who ran as Nullifiers swept into office and gained control of the legislature. Governor James Hamilton's support for nullification ensured these victories. Hamilton had been the mayor of Charleston during the Vesey conspiracy a decade earlier and directed the trials related to it.

Calhoun, his political link to President Andrew Jackson now ruptured, resigned as vice president in December 1832, near the end of his term, after election by the legislature to an open seat in the U.S. Senate. The new legislature called for a nullification convention, which on February 1, 1833, declared the 1828 and 1832 tariffs void. Jackson minced no words in responding to South Carolina.[8] He made it clear that he considered nullification to be nothing less than treason.

Political leaders in other southern states, even in Mississippi and others later known for their states' rights radicalism, urged South Carolina to back down. One Tennessean remarked that if "Old Hickory" Jackson gave the order, the men of the state would assemble on the Blue Ridge Mountains and "piss enough to float the whole nullifying crew of South Carolina into the Atlantic Ocean."[9] But Calhoun played a key role in the Senate in negotiating a revised tariff, one acceptable to the South. He became firmly convinced that nullification had forced Congress to back down.

In South Carolina, however, the Nullification Crisis had spawned a whole generation of men who "calculated the value of the Union" and decided it not worth preserving. Meanwhile, in 1832, in the midst of the crisis, William Lloyd Garrison had begun publication of the *Liberator*, the flagship publication of the American Anti-Slavery Society. Garrison believed in immediate abolition, that slavery was a moral evil that must end quickly. Many white South Carolinians incorrectly viewed radical abolition as the dominant viewpoint in the northern states.

A strong cadre of agitators developed in South Carolina in the 1830s. Robert Barnwell Rhett of the lowcountry represented the most extreme example, using his newspaper, the *Charleston Mercury*, to warn of the dangers faced by slaveholders in the United States. Some smaller newspapers in the upcountry did the same. William King Easley of Pickens District used his editorship of the *Keowee Courier* to promote a sense of southern identity in his readers.

Calhoun, endowed with a superior, penetrating mind and an apparent absence of humor, intrigued Harriet Martineau. In her 1838 book, *Retrospect of Western Travel*, she characterized him as "the cast iron man, who looks as if he had never been born and never could be extinguished. . . . he is wrought like a piece of machinery, set going vehemently by a weight and stops while you answer; he either passes by what you say, or twists it into suitability with what is in his head."[10]

Anxiety over the safety of slavery within the Union reached new heights in the 1840s as the United States won its war with Mexico and brought new territory into the Union. Southerners feared that if these new lands were organized as free states, the balance of power in the federal government would tip in the North's favor.

Calhoun, and much of South Carolina's legislative delegation, had opposed the war with Mexico. Calhoun feared that it would degenerate into a protracted guerrilla conflict that would pull in the European powers and would reopen the issue of slavery. But Calhoun's concerns did not prevent more than a thousand South Carolinians from joining the "Palmetto regiment" that fought in the war with Mexico. The regiment, honored today with a monument on the State House grounds, placed the first flag on the walls of Chapultepec and suffered a casualty count more than three times that of comparable units.

His presidential hopes still alive, Calhoun resigned from the Senate in 1843 to run as an independent candidate. After his campaign faltered he accepted an offer in March 1844 from President John Tyler to fill a vacancy as secretary of state, in which capacity he participated in the final negotiations for annexing Texas. Six months after Tyler's term expired in 1845, Calhoun returned permanently to the Senate.[11]

Before he died in 1850, Calhoun lamented the conflict between North and South. In some of his final words to the Senate, he raised the possibility that the differences between the regions were irreconcilable.

Although secession had been discussed in South Carolina for almost three decades by the 1850s, outright secessionists remained a small political faction. James L. Orr of Anderson County urged South Carolina to take a more active role in the national Democratic Party. Orr believed that nothing endangered slavery more than an excessive sectionalism that would leave the slaveholding South politically isolated. Benjamin F. Perry of Greenville represented Unionist sentiment in the legislature.

The sun seemed to have set for such ardent secessionist leaders as Rhett in the early 1850s. Several events, however, changed their fortunes. In 1854 Congress debated whether Kansas and Nebraska, territories with large enough populations to organize as states, would enter the Union as free or slave states. Senator Stephen Douglas of Illinois proposed the notion of popular sovereignty. The settlers themselves could decide, in a popular referendum, whether to allow slavery.

"Bleeding Kansas" became the unintended consequence of this policy. As abolitionists from New England moved into Kansas territory, proslavery radicals from nearby Missouri and the Deep South also left to settle in Kansas and engage in literal battle for slavery. A number of young militiamen from South Carolina moved to Kansas, including organized groups from Edgefield and Beaufort. By 1856, South Carolinians had drawn blood for the defense of slavery.

Violence also made its way in 1856 to the floor of the Senate, where Congressman Preston Brooks of Edgefield assaulted Massachusetts senator Charles Sumner and battered him into a coma with a gutta-percha cane. Sumner had made a speech titled "The Crime against Kansas," which Brooks believed insulted the honor of his Edgefield relative, aged senator Andrew Pickens Butler (on whose plantation lived a young slave boy who would become the grandfather of Essie Mae Washington-Williams, daughter of Strom Thurmond).

Before Congress could vote on a resolution censuring Brooks, the fiery congressman resigned his seat. His Edgefield constituents promptly reelected him almost unanimously. He received replacements for his broken cane from dozens of admirers from South Carolina and around the South. A bust of Brooks today occupies an alcove on the stairway of the Caroliniana Library at the University of South Carolina, a historical reminder of an impetuous past.

What remained of Unionism in South Carolina withered during the events of 1857 to 1860. The Supreme Court's 1857 *Dred Scott* opinion seemed to strengthen southern intransigence. The Court's 7–2 decision kept the controversy at white-hot heat with the opinion of Chief Justice Roger Taney that even free black people in the United States had "no rights a white man was bound to respect."[12]

In 1859 South Carolina's James H. Hammond would declare to fellow members of the U.S. Senate that "Cotton is King." And King Cotton, it was left unsaid, demanded slave labor.

In the fall of 1859 the abolitionist John Brown, already a leader in the violence in Kansas, led a guerrilla raid on the federal arsenal at Harpers Ferry, Virginia. Brown hoped to ignite a slave revolt that would spread throughout the South. Following his capture (and subsequent hanging), the story circulated that a map had been found in Brown's belongings with large red Xs over spots where slave insurrections would be likely. South Carolina had been covered with Xs.

In this heated atmosphere the 1860 presidential election loomed. The Democratic Party, which held its convention in an anxiety-ridden Charleston, split over the issue of slavery. The Republicans, a new political party formed in 1854 (its 1856 presidential candidate, John C. Frémont, was an alumnus of the College of Charleston and had become an abolitionist), nominated an Illinois lawyer named Abraham Lincoln.

Lincoln did not support the immediate abolition of slavery, advocating only that it not be allowed to spread into the West. But that was enough for white South Carolina to identify him with John Brown and William Lloyd Garrison. Robert Barnwell Rhett actually hoped for Lincoln's election, believing it would rend the Union and lead to the creation of a southern nation.

Sectional controversy allowed Lincoln to win the 1860 election, with four candidates splitting the vote. Lincoln received less than 40 percent of the popular vote. He did not even appear on the ballot in South Carolina. By the time of the Civil War, slavery was important in every South Carolina county, and every upcountry county except Anderson had at least one slaveholder who owned a hundred or more slaves. By 1860 almost half of the white families in South Carolina owned slaves, almost twice the rate of the South as a whole. Even the upcountry Pickens District, which includes today's Pickens County and mountainous Oconee County, had an African American population that accounted for 30 to 35 percent of the total population.

The Secession Convention met in December 1860 at the First Baptist Church of Columbia. After one meeting the convention adjourned and moved to Charleston, both because of a rumored outbreak of smallpox and, perhaps more important, because secessionist fervor ran strongest in Charleston. There, on December 20, 1860, the convention voted unanimously to secede from the Union.

Charleston lawyer James Louis Petigru, a strong Unionist, told his friend Rhett, "South Carolina is too small to be a republic and too large to be an insane asylum." Few white South Carolinians shared his views as celebrations broke out all over the state. In Washington thirty-six-year-old South Carolina congressman Lawrence Keitt interrupted a dinner party when receiving the news by exclaiming, "South Carolina has seceded! South Carolina has seceded! I feel like a boy let out of school!"[13]

| 4 |

CIVIL WAR AND RECONSTRUCTION

On the night of December 26, 1860, Colonel Robert Anderson moved about seventy-four United States soldiers from Fort Moultrie on Sullivan's Island to a still-incomplete fort, Fort Sumter, in the middle of Charleston Harbor. Anderson had informed his superiors that he could not hope to defend the land-bound Fort Moultrie, open to attack from secessionist forces on three sides.

Anderson's move angered secessionist leaders, though South Carolina's new governor, Francis W. Pickens, waited until April 1861 to respond. During that time delegates from throughout the Deep South met in Montgomery, Alabama, and formed the Confederate States of America. In the early morning darkness of April 12, Confederate forces in Charleston Harbor opened fire on Fort Sumter.

South Carolina, the first state to secede, opened the first battle of the American Civil War. The barrage on Fort Sumter launched a four-year war that became the bloodiest in American history. South Carolina suffered more than twenty-three thousand military deaths during the Civil War, which was more than one-third of the white male population subject to military service in 1860. But in the first days of the conflict, many secessionist leaders boastfully predicted how quickly the North would be defeated. Governor Pickens, a former American ambassador to Russia, said that he would drink all the blood that would be spilled, so insignificant would it be.

In late 1861, however, reality struck Confederate South Carolina in the form of an amphibious invasion of its southeastern coast. The largest armada of the nineteenth century, along with about twelve thousand federal troops, seized Beaufort and its adjacent islands connected by Port Royal Sound. Beaufort's planter elite fled to Charleston and into the upcountry, attempting, and usually failing, to take their slaves with them. Thousands of slaves on the rice planta-tions of the Combahee River and the sea-island cotton plantations of St. Helena and Hilton Head islands suddenly became free, by force of arms if not by law.

By 1862 General David Hunter, a committed abolitionist, served as supreme commander of the region. Teachers, nurses, and missionaries from New England, New York, and Philadelphia came to the region to teach the former slaves basic literacy and the tenets of American democracy. The efforts by these abolitionists would become known as the "Port Royal experiment" or, as the historian Willie Lee Rose termed it, a "rehearsal for Reconstruction."[1]

Two of these northern missionaries, Ellen Murray and Laura Towne, opened a school at the meeting place of a Baptist congregation known as the Brick Church on St. Helena Island. Under their leadership this school would educate generations of children from the Sea Islands. It was named the Penn School for William Penn, the Quaker leader and founder of Pennsylvania.

Many of the northern teachers who came to Port Royal misunderstood the Gullah culture of the Sea Islands and perceived themselves as civilizing the freed people. Laura Towne expressed shock when she first saw "the ring shout," a common style of African American worship in which worshipers moved in a circle to the rhythmic sound of clapping hands, pounding feet, and shouted exclamations of fervor. Towne, and other well-meaning northerners, felt that these Gullah traditions had to be eliminated for the freed people to become fully American. Penn Center continues to operate today, now as an institution to preserve rather than annihilate the Gullah culture and heritage. During the civil rights era, Penn Center served as a quiet retreat for Martin Luther King Jr., a place for him to write.

During the Union occupation enslaved people from all over the low-country took the initiative in securing their freedom by fleeing to the Port Royal region. Robert Smalls, an enslaved boatman aboard the Confederate steamer *Planter*, led a daring and justly famous escape from Charleston Har-bor in May 1862, turning the steamer over to a Union naval squadron blockad-ing the city. After another daring action, Smalls became the first African American ship's captain in the U.S. Navy and fought in a number of Civil War naval engagements. He later served four terms in the U.S. House of Represen-tatives from South Carolina.

The Port Royal experiment took a new turn in the spring of 1862 when General Hunter attempted to raise a black regiment to serve in the Union army. A few hundred freedmen enlisted, some under duress, and Hunter dis-banded this early effort before the end of the summer, in part because of lack of support from Washington.

Hanging of Amy Spain. African American men joined the Union army ranks while black women, in and out of slavery, often acted as spies, nurses, and scouts. Amy Spain, a Darlington County slave who spied for Union forces, was hanged in 1865 in front of the county courthouse. *History of South Carolina Slide Collection*, B-112

Abraham Lincoln had, however, announced his intention to issue the Emancipation Proclamation, which he did on January 1, 1863. His announcement in 1862 revived the effort to arm the Port Royal freedmen. The First South Carolina Volunteers, also called the First S.C. African, became a reality that fall and served under Colonel Thomas Wentworth Higginson of Massachusetts. Consisting primarily of former South Carolina slaves, the First South Carolina became the first federally authorized black regiment in a Union army in which approximately 180,000 black troops ultimately served.

The two years after secession had gone poorly for Confederate South Carolina. Soon after the fall of Port Royal, the Great Fire of 1861 ripped through Charleston and destroyed 540 acres of the city, including such landmarks as Circular Congregational Church, the Cathedral of St. John and St. Finbar, and even Institute Hall, where the Ordinance of Secession had been signed.

In the summer of 1862 Confederate forces defending Charleston managed to fend off a poorly coordinated Union attack on James Island. This victory raised hopes, but Charleston remained surrounded by Union forces. Each major battle of the Civil War created more grieving parents, widows, and orphans in the state. Just before his death on March 3, 1863, James Louis

Petigru wrote, "The war makes itself felt very near us." Throughout the state, observers commented on how many women they saw wearing the black veil of mourning.

South Carolina troops served in both major Confederate armies, most of them in the Army of Northern Virginia and a smaller number in the Army of the Tennessee. By the midpoint of the war, the state achieved close to full enlistment of its white male population of military age. Although some deserted and hid out in the "dark corner," along the Blue Ridge Mountain in the state's western corner, South Carolina became the only Confederate state without at least one white Union regiment.

Notable South Carolina Confederates included Wade Hampton III, a tall, strapping heir to the Hampton fortune, who took command of Robert E. Lee's cavalry after the death of the famous Jeb Stuart in 1864. Some of the state's leading secessionists were killed in combat. Lawrence Keitt, the former congressman, died at Cold Harbor in 1864. Maxcy Gregg of Columbia, another fire-eater, died at the battle of Fredericksburg in 1862. His final words were "I yield my life cheerfully, fighting for the independence of South Carolina."[2]

On the home front white women and others ineligible for military service did their part for the war effort. Several Charleston churches gave their bells to be melted into ammunition. Two of them next to each other on Archdale Street, one Lutheran and one Unitarian, never replaced them and remain known as the "silent churches." Women from all over the state raised money to help build an ironclad gunboat to defend Charleston. Known officially as the CSS *Palmetto State*, it would be popularly known as the "Ladies Boat." On February 17, 1864, Confederate forces launched the first successful submarine attack about two miles off Sullivan's Island, sinking the Union ship *Housatonic*. The *Hunley*, named for its Alabama inventor, never made it back to port. The *Hunley* would be heard from again more than a century later, raised from the Atlantic Ocean floor amid much fanfare—and a bit of controversy.

White-hot devotion to the cause failed to reverse the course of the war. In July 1863 news came of two Confederate disasters. Robert E. Lee's army came to grief at Gettysburg, and Vicksburg fell to Union forces in the West—a loss of the South's last stronghold on the Mississippi River. By August 1863, Union forces had taken a number of the small islands and sand spits that ringed Charleston Harbor, using them as artillery emplacements to bombard the city.

During that summer the famous attack by the black Fifty-fourth Massachusetts on Battery Wagner had failed, with the regiment taking heavy casualties. The charge of the Fifty-fourth would be commemorated in the 1989 film *Glory*. Despite the failure of the attack, black troops had proven their ability

Written by Charles Joyner and signed by 116 South Carolina historians, this statement—issued on March 31, 2000—fully explains the central role of slavery in the state's secession from the Union.

One of the most visible, and most controversial, symbolic icons of our history in South Carolina is the so-called "Confederate battle flag." It flies over the State House in Columbia, as it has done since 1962, when it went up as part of the observance of the Civil War Centennial. To some South Carolinians it is a symbol of their heritage. To other South Carolinians it is a symbol of slavery and racism. What any object "symbolizes" can be slippery. It is especially so in this case because the rectangular banner atop the State House is neither the flag commissioned by the Confederate government to serve as its official symbol nor the flag under which Confederate troops made war against the United States. It neither adorned the Confederate capitols in Montgomery or Richmond nor fluttered atop any state capitol within the Confederacy. The rectangular battle flag that flies over the State House in Columbia was never the official flag of either of the two great military arms of the Confederacy, the Army of Tennessee and the Army of Northern Virginia, under which virtually all South Carolina Confederate soldiers served.

The crux of the present controversy is not in the flag itself but in conflicting interpretations of the meaning of the Civil War. Some South Carolinians deny that the Civil War was fought over slavery, maintaining that it was fought over the rights of the states to control their own destinies. Slavery, they believe, was incidental.

But when South Carolina delegates walked out of the 1860 Democratic National Convention in Charleston as a prelude to secession, their spokesman William Preston minced no words in declaring that "Slavery is our King; slavery is our Truth; slavery is our Divine Right." And a few months later when the signers of the South Carolina Ordinance of Secession issued their Declaration of the Causes of Secession, they specifically referred to the "domestic institution" of slavery. They objected that the free states have "denounced as sinful the institution of slavery." They charged that the free states had "encouraged and assisted thousands of our slaves to leave their homes; and those who remain have been incited by emissaries, books, and pictures, to hostile insurrection."

Moreover, in 1861, as President and Vice President of the Confederate States of America, Jefferson Davis and Alexander H. Stephens each candidly acknowledged that their new nation was created for the specific purpose of perpetuating slavery. In an address to the Confederate Congress in April of 1861 Davis declared that "a persistent and organized system of hostile measures against the rights of the owners of slaves in the Southern States" had culminated in a political party dedicated to "annihilating in effect property worth thousands of dollars." Since "the labor of African slaves was and is indispensable" to the South's production of cotton, rice, sugar, and tobacco, Davis said, "the people of the Southern States were driven by the conduct of the North to the adoption of some course of action to avert the danger with which they were openly menaced."

In a speech in Savannah, Stephens made it even clearer that the establishment of the Confederacy had "put to rest forever all the agitating questions relating to our peculiar institutions—African slavery as it exists among us—the proper status of the negro in our form of civilization. This was the immediate cause of the late rupture and present revolution." He added that the Confederacy was "founded upon" what he called "the great truth that the negro is not equal to the white man; that slavery, subordination to the superior race, is his natural and moral condition."

Running successfully for governor of South Carolina in the critical election of 1860, Francis W. Pickens left little doubt of his support for disunion and even war to perpetuate slavery. His sentiments were echoed by his old friend Edward Bryan, who declared in the campaign, "Give us slavery or give us death!" Pickens committed his state—and ours—to a ruinous course. "I would be willing to appeal to the gods of battles," he defiantly declared, "if need be, cover the state with ruin, conflagration and blood rather than submit." These are not interpretations by historians; they are statements made at the time by Confederate leaders explaining what they were doing and why.

After the war had been lost, and the Lost Cause was in need of justification, Davis and Stephens backed away from their original statements, casting the cause of the war in the context of "states rights." Their revisionist interpretation, in which slavery became not the cause but merely the "question" resolved on the field of battle, still misleads many South Carolinians. The historical record, however, clearly shows that the cause for which the South seceded and fought a devastating war was slavery.

to stand toe to toe with whites in combat. The Confederates who defended Battery Wagner, however, would soon abandon the position as untenable. Across the harbor Charleston came under almost constant bombardment from the summer of 1863 until the city surrendered in February 1865. Few major battles, however, took place in the state.

Meanwhile General William T. Sherman's famous march through Georgia had opened the way for what would be the most destructive leg of his campaign, the march into South Carolina. Leaving Savannah untouched in January 1865, Sherman's troops spoke openly and cheerfully of the destruction they planned to bring to "the mother of traitors" and "the hell-hole of secession."

On February 17 Sherman's forces entered Columbia after shelling the granite capitol building from across the Congaree River. The bombardment left behind shell marks still visible today, marked by bronze stars. In a night of chaos that followed, much of the city was burned to the ground.

Although Sherman earned much hatred for Columbia's destruction, his actual role in the burning of the city remains unclear. Union soldiers, drunk from the liquor they found stored in the city's many warehouses, frightened citizens and looted at will. Although many Union officers and men tried to restore order, a third of the city was destroyed, leaving bitter memories. Fleeing Confederate cavalry set fire to the bales of cotton that sat stacked on Main Street to keep them out of Yankee hands. In his memoirs Sherman summed up his attitude, saying he had never ordered the burning of Columbia and had never been sad over the burning.[3]

When Charleston surrendered on February 18, fleeing Confederate forces burned stockpiles of cotton and rice and blew up much of the harbor defenses, including the ironclads. Symbolic legend claimed that as the gunboat *Palmetto State* exploded, the smoke from its ruin formed a perfect palmetto tree in the sky and then evaporated, like the hopes of the South. The harsh reality of defeat was already beginning to be covered with romance and legend.

White South Carolina faced the end of the Civil War with a volatile combination of fear and defiance. The bitterness felt toward Sherman and the Union high command that had pounded Charleston to ruins for two years only grew as the results of the war became clear. On the night of February 18, African American soldiers from the 121st United States Colored Troops entered Charleston singing the abolitionist hymn "John Brown's Body."

Although uncertain what might become of them with the war's end, whether they might be tried for treason or perhaps even summarily shot, Confederate leaders showed little remorse. General Wade Hampton in May 1865 offered himself and his remaining troops as a cavalry escort for the

Columbia in ruins, 1865. The destruction of Columbia resulted from a variety of factors, including Yankee drunkenness and the Confederates' setting scores of cotton bales on fire on a windy night. The results are seen here, in a view from the State House grounds. *History of South Carolina Slide Collection,* B-103

Charleston in 1877. This photograph of Charleston, taken twelve years after the fighting ended, still shows the devastation wrought by the Civil War. *History of South Carolina Slide Collection,* F-27

fleeing Jefferson Davis and his cabinet, which held its final meeting in upcountry Abbeville. Hampton apparently hoped that Davis would continue the struggle south of the border, launching raids from Mexico against the United States. Martin Witherspoon Gary, a Confederate cavalry general from Edgefield, also refused to accept the war's obvious outcome. Upon hearing of the surrender of the Lee's army at Appomattox Courthouse, Gary cursed and told his troops that "South Carolinians never surrender."[4] Gary would be heard from again.

Black South Carolinians, meanwhile, responded to the defeat of the Confederacy with jubilation. African American soldiers found themselves greeted with cheers and song as they occupied Charleston. Many of the city's most prestigious addresses, elegant planter homes along South Battery and Tradd Street, presented a battered remnant of their former glories. Some of these urban estates became quarters for Union soldiers. In some cases the former slaves took up residence in the homes of their former masters.

The war's painful outcome for white South Carolinians included more than twenty-three thousand lives lost and the financial loss of four hundred thousand slaves, for whom the war's end meant freedom—a combination of circumstances that would lead South Carolinians to struggle for generations.[5] Many South Carolinians feared that the end of slavery, a system of racial control as much as a method for controlling wealth-creating labor, meant revolution. Rumors circulated in 1865 that the Fourth of July would signal a massive uprising and all whites would be murdered. When that day came and went without incident (other than the freed people's jubilant celebrations of freedom), a new rumor had it that January 1, 1866, Emancipation Day, would mark the beginning of war between the races.

Freed African American people, while not planning a bloody revenge as whites feared, did assert their new status. The white residents of the ironically named upcountry town of Union complained to the local federal commander that he must act against certain freedmen who had become "obnoxious characters in the community." They mentioned one freedman in particular, known simply as Brandon, who wore a pistol on his hip "in a manner calculated to threaten the peace of the community." Sergeant Prince Rivers, who with the First South Carolina occupied the town of Anderson following the war, marched down the aisle of the local First Baptist Church one Sunday morning, dressed in full military regalia. The tall and striking soldier seated himself in the front pew, a spot traditionally reserved for local elites.[6]

White South Carolina men, hardened by combat in one of the nineteenth century's bloodiest conflicts, refused to accept the verdict of history. A white insurgency exploded across the state. Guerrilla units, mostly the broken fragments of Confederate regiments, sought to intimidate freed people and African American regiments stationed near the Berkeley County hamlet of Pineville. Two white officers of the First South Carolina were assassinated by former Confederates in the first year of "peace." In another occurrence Lieutenant Jerome Thurman, one of the regiment's white officers, had been asked by a citizen of Walhalla to take an evening stroll. This "courtesy" turned out to be a trap, and Thurman was murdered by his evening caller and fellow insurgents.[7]

These Confederate insurgents, essentially seeking home rule and the preservation of white supremacy, found the political situation increasingly favorable. Andrew Johnson of Tennessee, who became president after the assassination of Lincoln, showed no desire to punish white secessionists for their role in secession or to protect the rights of the freed people. Confederate veterans received pardons freely, along with an immediate return of their voting rights.

Presidential Reconstruction in South Carolina meant a return of the state's ruling white elite. White leaders drew up a new constitution to their liking, and the South Carolina legislature passed a series of acts known as the Black Codes. These draconian laws restricted employment opportunities of freed people, who theoretically could only work as agricultural workers or domestics. Other codes limited movement, property rights, and the legal privileges of former slaves. South Carolina whites sought to revive the slave system, in fact if not in name.

Republicans in Congress, meanwhile, consolidated their power, gaining the upper hand over President Johnson, who had barely survived impeachment by his Republican enemies. In 1867 Congress passed the Reconstruction Acts. They required South Carolina and its sister states in the South to draw up new constitutions, and most important, these new state constitutions would include the right to vote for all males, regardless of color. Moreover these acts would have teeth, with voting rights protected by the presence of federal troops.

Black South Carolinians seized the new opportunity offered them by Congressional Reconstruction, what many whites in the South would refer to as Radical Reconstruction. The freedmen in South Carolina registered to vote in overwhelming numbers. One study has found that more than 90 percent of eligible blacks were registered to vote in 1867. By 1870 virtually all black men in South Carolina went to the polls.[8]

The 1868 Constitutional Convention reflected this new electorate. Its delegates consisted of 124 members, 76 black and 48 white men. Although the white southern myth of Reconstruction suggested that the new constitution had been drawn up by illiterate former slaves and white carpetbaggers from

RADICAL MEMBERS
OF THE S?. C.A. LEGISLATURE.

South Carolina General Assembly in 1868. This composite photograph shows the 1868 Reconstruction legislature with fifty African Americans and thirteen whites. This photo would later be used by Ben Tillman in his effort to create a new state constitution disenfranchising African American voters. *History of South Carolina Slide Collection,* B-116

the North, the story is far more complicated. A number of native whites participated in the convention. Most of the African American delegates had at least some level of literacy; some had received solid educations in the North or in Europe. Many had been free persons of color before the war. Many of the carpetbaggers were former Union soldiers or philanthropists from the North interested in bringing democracy to the South rather than filling their own pockets. Some were interested in both.

Together this diverse group created the state of South Carolina's first truly democratic constitution. All men would have the right to vote, with no qualification of property, heritage, or race. Although women would receive the right to vote only after ratification of the Nineteenth Amendment in 1920, the 1868 state constitution did include the state's first divorce law, granting women some autonomy over their property and personal destinies.

A provision requiring the state of South Carolina to fund public education, the first such act in the state's history, clearly represented the most long-lasting achievement of the 1868 document. Known for its cogency of thought and practicality, this constitution would remain in force in South Carolina for almost two decades after whites regained political power in 1877.

In the decade after the Reconstruction Acts, black South Carolinians exercised real political power. Eight of the twenty-two African American members of Congress from the former Confederate states during the Reconstruction era came from South Carolina, more than from any other state. Joseph H. Rainey of Georgetown, who took his seat in December 1870, became the nation's first black congressman, serving four terms. Born a slave, he fled to Bermuda early in the Civil War and opened a successful barber shop there before returning to South Carolina after the war. He was soon joined in Washington by Robert C. DeLarge, Alonzo J. Ransier, Richard Cain (who established many African Methodist Episcopal churches in South Carolina), and Robert Elliott. Robert Smalls won election to Congress four times in the 1870s and 1880s. Thomas E. Miller served less than six months in 1890–91, and George W. Murray served from 1893 to 1897, after which no blacks represented South Carolina in Congress until the election of James E. Clyburn in 1992.[9]

Voter registration among African American men remained high throughout the period. Black women in the state, though unable to vote, gave evidence of a strong political consciousness by holding mass meetings, joining Republican clubs, and in some cases urging, or insisting, that their husbands vote.

The period also created social and economic opportunities. In Edgefield, for example, African Americans became attorneys, clerks, business partners with whites, bakers, and shopkeepers even as widespread white violence, including murder, occurred throughout the county. Blacks attended the University of South Carolina, and the Reconstruction government opened a law school there.

But most white South Carolinians, overwhelmingly as dedicated to white supremacy as ever, simply refused to accept their changed situation. Although they had lost the war, they demonstrated a determination to win the peace. Martin W. Gary's post-Appomattox comment that "South Carolinians never surrender" defined this attitude. Nowhere does this sentiment appear more clearly that in the white celebration of "the Lost Cause."

Soon after the end of the war, Confederate veterans met to commemorate their battlefield role, and local communities made plans to raise monuments to Confederate heroes. In 1870 a monument to the Confederate soldier was placed in Columbia's Magnolia Cemetery. After the collapse of Reconstruction, whites moved the monument to a position in front of the State House, symbolizing their return to power. There it remains.

The Lost Cause developed over time into a romanticized, nostalgic activity. This was not the case immediately following the war. Men celebrated the experience of battle still fresh in their memory. The first Confederate veteran "reunion" in South Carolina occurred in upcountry Walhalla as early as 1866. Federal authorities, recognizing the political import of such an event, sent cavalry patrols to break up the proceedings.

Whites throughout the South, stripped of their honor by defeat on the battlefield, faced how to cope with newly freed blacks, who in South Carolina were a majority. Whites believed a distant government in Washington was implementing policies that threatened the established social order, one based on local control and racial deference. Washington was invoking federal legal power that both protected the freedmen and strengthened the Republican Party.

Following the Reconstruction Acts the Ku Klux Klan became the primary embodiment of the Lost Cause in South Carolina. Former Confederates dressed as the vengeful spirits of their dead comrades to terrorize and intimidate blacks before the 1870 elections. Blacks refused to be intimidated, continuing to vote in large numbers. In October 1870 the Klan went on a rampage the day after the Republican Party won elections in Laurens County, destroying freedmen's homes and murdering thirteen people, some of them newly elected African American officials.

In Union county perhaps as many as five hundred masked Klansmen assaulted the local jail and lynched eleven black prisoners. In York County almost the entire white male population belonged to the Klan. In some South Carolina counties, during the worst of the Klan terror in late 1870 and early 1871, African American families took to the woods each night to avoid the inevitable assault of night riders.

In March 1871 York County Klansmen led by a former Confederate major took James Rainey, a former slave serving as an officer in the all-black militia and a supporter of the Republican Party, from his home at night. They savagely beat him and then murdered him by hanging him from a tree. The Klan continued its rampage of beatings, whipping members of the black militia and their families.

In October 1871, exactly a year after the explosion of violence in Laurens, the Grant administration declared nine upcountry South Carolina counties to be "in a condition of lawlessness" and sent federal troops to arrest both the leaders and rank and file. Many Klansmen fled South Carolina. More than one hundred were convicted in federal court and sentenced to jail in York County. Many of the acts to which the indicted Klansmen confessed—including murder, rape, burglary, and arson—shocked the nation. U.S. Attorney General Amos T. Ackerman, who directed the investigations and the prosecutions, later noted that the investigations had "saddened him" as they "revealed a perversion of the moral sentiments among the Southern whites which bodes ill to that part of the country for this generation."[10]

Despite the successful prosecutions, many by confession, before majority black juries under the Enforcement Act of 1870 and the Ku Klux Klan Act of

1871, the federal judiciary ruled narrowly rather than broadly in extending constitutional and federal protection to the freedmen and their families.

White defiance remained even after the legal proscription of the Ku Klux Klan. Beginning in 1872 whites organized themselves into rifle clubs or gun clubs. In large part the clubs represented a rebirth of the Confederate army. Many white South Carolina men even joined rifle clubs made up of the same men they had served with in their Confederate regiments, and in a few cases they served under the same officers.

In response African American leaders and their Republican allies prepared to meet the white terror. Immediately after the end of the war, many black Civil War veterans helped organize home guard units to protect their communities. During Reconstruction the state government incorporated these units into the state militia (whites refused to serve in the militia with blacks). Though poorly funded and poorly equipped, the Republican-controlled militia provided some measure of defense for the freed people, especially in those lowcountry counties with an African American majority.

Reconstruction-era political cartoon. This 1872 political cartoon focused on fraud and corruption in the Republican administration of Governor Franklin J. Moses. Corruption was widespread in 1870s America, and in South Carolina both Conservative Democrats and Republicans were in involved in fraud to win elections and in graft once in office. *History of South Carolina Slide Collection*, B-118

The Republican Party continued its political domination of the state until the middle of the 1870s, though growing gradually weaker after 1870. By 1875 serious divisions based on race and class existed within the party, amid charges of corruption and lack of responsiveness to the black electorate. Meanwhile most South Carolina whites remained politically and culturally united, especially under the banner of the Lost Cause and the desire to end Reconstruction. Calling themselves Conservative Democrats or simply Conservatives, white leaders, mostly former Confederate generals, plotted their return to power.

In 1876 whites united behind Wade Hampton as the Conservative candidate for governor. Although a symbol of the Lost Cause, Hampton sought also to appeal to black voters, promising to continue the most progressive reforms of Reconstruction, including voting rights and free schools. Some of Hampton's own supporters disagreed with this approach, including Martin Gary. He advocated a program of violence and fraud, which had proven successful in the Mississippi Plan in 1875, as the best method for ending "radical rule" and restoring conservative white dominance. Gary looked with disgust on Hampton's willingness to speak to black audiences, saying that, for his part, he would rather "sing psalms to a dead mule."[11] Most of this dissension remained private, as Gary and others united behind their best chance to take back the reins of power.

In Edgefield the rifle clubs formed the nucleus of Gary's Redshirts, armed mounted horsemen wearing shirts dyed red with the juice of wild berries. Their initial formation in late spring of 1876 involved 1,600 red-shirted men riding out of the grounds of Oakley Park, Gary's impressive Edgefield home that today remains as a well-maintained Redshirt shrine. Leading them riding sidesaddle was seventeen-year-old Douschka (Russian for "Little Darling") Pickens, the daughter of Civil War governor Francis Pickens of Edgefield, who was born in 1859 when her father was ambassador to Russia.

Determined to return white control to South Carolina, Gary's Redshirts sowed terror throughout the Edgefield District. The organization spread to other parts of the state. In July a local dispute in then majority-black Hamburg (today's North Augusta) began on the Fourth of July when two young white men in a buggy insisted that the reluctant local black militia company break ranks during a parade and let them through. It ended four days later in a massacre.

Former Confederate general Matthew Calbraith Butler ostensibly came to Hamburg as a lawyer for the two men, but his clear intent was to disarm and punish the militia for being uppity. More than two hundred men, many with firearms, joined him. After Prince Rivers, by now the local judge, ruled that

Butler and his men lacked legal authority to disarm the militia and that if there were any trial of the militia captain it would be a court-martial, Butler secured a cannon from a friendly unit in Augusta and returned. Roughly twenty-five militiamen, with little ammunition, barricaded themselves and some local black officials in a blockhouse armory. Butler's men began firing, one of them getting killed by return gunfire, and after four rounds of cannon fire, the militiamen chose to surrender. One tried to escape and was killed. Five blacks were executed on the spot and three severely wounded. Others, told to run, were shot in the back.

The Hamburg Massacre became widely publicized, with those from the North seeing it as a savage reminder of the white South's commitment to white supremacy and whites in the South seeing it as an expression of white resolve.

One of the Redshirt units present at Hamburg, the forty-man Sweetwater Sabre Company, was led by twenty-eight-year-old Benjamin Ryan Tillman. This future governor participated actively in the violence. As violence against blacks in the Edgefield District intensified, Tillman's unit was selected to execute black state legislator Simon Coker of Barnwell. On September 19, informed he had only a few minutes to live, Coker replied, "Here is my cotton house key; I wish you would please send it to my wife and tell her to have our cotton ginned and pay our landlord rent just as she can." Asked if there was anything else, Coker said he would like to pray and dropped to his knees in prayer.

Tillman described what happened next: After a few moments one of his men said, "You are too long. . . . The order 'aim, fire,' was given with the negro still kneeling." In writing about this incident, Tillman continued, "It will appear a ruthless and cruel thing to those unacquainted with the environments. . . . The struggle in which we were engaged meant more than life or death. It involved everything we held dear, Anglo-Saxon civilization included."[12]

Hampton ran a two-tier campaign. In addition to his pledge to protect the rights of freedmen, his campaign also organized a brigade of mounted black Redshirts. (One member of the brigade was assaulted in a Columbia neighborhood by a group of African American women. They expressed their political feelings by stripping the man of all his clothes and leaving him naked in the street.)

But at the same time he approved units of black Redshirt supporters, Hampton also allowed implementation of rule 12 of Gary's thirty-three-rule "plan of the Campaign." Rule 12 declared, "Every Democrat must feel honor bound to control the vote of at least one negro, by intimidation, purchase, keeping him away or as each individual may determine how he may best accomplish it."[13] Gary's all-white Redshirt supporters spread the use of violence, intimidation, and fraud beyond the confines of Edgefield.

On election day 1876 these elements prevailed. African American voters in Edgefield County appeared at their courthouse to find it surrounded by Redshirts, prepared to do them violence. Their objective was to overthrow the Reconstruction government led by Republican governor Daniel Chamberlain, who as state attorney general had prosecuted the York County Klansmen. Stuffed ballot boxes in bloody Edgefield exceeded by more than two thousand the voting-age population in the county according to the 1870 census. The inflated Edgefield vote provided Hampton's margin of victory.

Fraud occurred throughout South Carolina's 1876 governor's race. In both Laurens and Aiken counties Hampton also received a larger number of votes than there were registered voters. Both sides claimed victory, and the state of South Carolina for a brief time had two men claiming to be governor and two slates of candidates claiming control of the State House.

National events proved decisive for the outcome of South Carolina's contested election. The presidential election, a race between Democrat Samuel Tilden and Republican Rutherford B. Hayes, had been close, largely due to voting irregularities in the South. South Carolina was one of three states with contested electoral votes. Southern political leaders agreed to throw their support to Hayes if this would ensure the end of Reconstruction. In the so-called Compromise of 1877, Republicans sold black civil rights for the presidency while whites in the South surrendered their traditional loyalty to the Democratic Party for the cause of white supremacy.

Without the support of federal bayonets, the Reconstruction government in South Carolina collapsed. Wade Hampton assumed the governorship. South Carolina's first experiment with biracial democracy was quickly coming to an end.

The years between the fall of Reconstruction and the rise of "Pitchfork" Ben Tillman in the 1890s have been referred to as the "Bourbon" era because, like the return of Bourbon dynasty in France after Waterloo, former Confederates and South Carolina's antebellum elite returned to power. The Bourbon regime would be marked by parsimonious state spending, an overwhelming focus on agriculture as the state's central economic engine, and the gradual repeal of all the changes wrought during Reconstruction.

Governor Hampton, knowing his government would be carefully scrutinized by Washington, initially appointed some Republicans, blacks and whites, to office. After a few years, however, black political leaders, those who had not been driven from office in 1876, soon found themselves the target of

Beaufort became the center of a large Emancipation Day celebration that brought African Americans from around the Southeast. The military cemetery there, where numerous African American soldiers were buried, made Beaufort the perfect location for the celebration. This photograph was taken in the 1890s. *History of South Carolina Slide Collection,* G-25

investigations for alleged fraud and corruption. A series of show trials ruined credibility and political careers of men such as state treasurer Francis Cardozo, an able and well-educated man who had presided over a surplus in the state treasury.

With Democrats firmly in control of the election machinery in the state, blacks found it difficult to find an official to register them to vote. In what became the nation's first literacy test for voting, South Carolina in 1882 adopted the "eight-box law." Instead of a single ballot for the state's eight constitutional officers, separate ballots and ballot boxes were provided for each office. Illiterate white voters casting a ballot for governor or for attorney general could confidently get advice from a white election official to the proper box for dropping in his ballot. Illiterate black voters understood they would have to guess the proper ballot box, which meant misplaced ballots would not be counted. Other fraudulent devices were also used, allowing full white rule by a 40 percent minority in the 1880s.

Bourbon rule, however, would prove short lived. A severe, worldwide agricultural crisis had caused crop prices to drop. South Carolina farmers lost their land at an alarming rate. Both white and black farmers fell into tenantry and sharecropping.

The Bourbons, who had little understanding of how the lives of most South Carolina farmers had changed since antebellum days, did little to deal with the crisis. At a time when farmers needed strict homestead provisions that would shield them from land loss, the Bourbons instead passed legislation that funded more agricultural demonstrations at the state fair.

They would be unprepared for the political earthquake that would hurl them out of office in the 1890s. Most of them had never heard of the one-eyed farmer from Edgefield, Benjamin Ryan Tillman.

5

THE TILLMAN ERA

Ben Tillman rose to political prominence on a wave of dissatisfaction with the Bourbons. Tillman came from a well-to-do Edgefield family that had owned close to fifty slaves before the war and managed to hold onto their land afterward. As a boy he would sit outdoors and read the classics. But young Tillman, born in 1847, did not serve in the Civil War, due both to his age and to a painful disease that left one eye sightless.

Although not a war veteran, Tillman became fully acquainted with violence in 1876. So closely did he associate himself with and participate in the violent white insurgency of '76 that he would later claim to have invented the Redshirt.

Tillman began his public political career in the mid-1880s. He spoke at small county agricultural societies and won the hearts of many small farmers with his tirades against the uncaring Bourbon regime. In 1886 he spoke at the State Farmers Convention in Columbia, calling for a state agricultural college, reform of what he called "land butchery" (the failure to fertilize cotton lands properly), and the closing of the Citadel. He presented the last initiative as a way to rid the state of what he considered the last vestiges of its useless, aristocratic past.

Tillman, a popular speaker, told the rough-handed farmers that the Citadel was no more than a "dude factory." He told them the Bourbons cared more about what they had done on faraway battlefields in the 1860s than what down-and-out farmers did in their tired fields of the 1880s.

The Tillman movement might still have come to nothing had it not been for the death of John C. Calhoun's aged son-in-law, Thomas G. Clemson. Clemson, a supporter of agricultural reform, left a little more than eight hundred acres to the state along with much of his personal fortune, with proviso that the state use it to build an agricultural college in the upcountry. The will named Tillman as one of seven self-perpetuating life trustees who would remain forever a majority on the board of trustees. (By the twenty-first century that provision had repeatedly blocked all efforts to create a unified state system of public higher education, such as those existing in neighboring Georgia and North Carolina.)

Clemson College, which opened to students in 1893 when Tillman was governor and was renamed Clemson University in 1963, was the product of this bequest, and it had a startling effect on South Carolina politics. The Bourbons, who had acquired the reputation of doing little, found themselves confronted by Tillman, who had achieved the reputation among his followers of being able to do much. Tillman soundly defeated his Bourbon opponent in the state governor's race of 1890 and served until 1894.

Although Governor John P. Richardson Jr. in 1889 signed the bill establishing Clemson, credit for Clemson went largely to Tillman and his movement, especially after Governor Tillman rejected federal funds from the Morrill Act that encouraged the building of agricultural colleges throughout the nation.

Clemson College was founded in the 1889 with the support of Ben Tillman and his farmer's movement. Like many agricultural colleges of the era, Clemson originally had a corps of cadets. This photograph was taken in 1910 of Tillman Hall and Bowman Field. *History of South Carolina Slide Collection*, I-25

Given the racial demographics of South Carolina, accepting the funds would have required that two-thirds of the money go to black students at Claflin College. Tillman expressed concern that black South Carolinians would forget who their friends were if educational funds came to them from outside sources.

Tillman continued to control state politics after he left the governor's mansion and became a U.S. senator in 1895. With senators still elected by the legislature (the Seventeenth Amendment of the Constitution changed it to election by popular vote in 1913), and state representative William Thurmond from his home county of Edgefield as floor manager, Tillman defeated incumbent Bourbon icon Wade Hampton in a vote by the legislature. (Thurmond's son, James Strom Thurmond, would become governor and set records as both the oldest and longest-serving member of the U.S. Senate.)

At the beginning of Tillman's Senate career, he earned the nickname "Pitchfork Ben" when, during a stump speech in Winnsboro, he called President Grover Cleveland "an old bag of beef" and promised to go to Washington with a pitchfork to "prod him in his old fat ribs." A popular speaker on the national Chautauqua circuit, he remained a senator until his death in 1918, strengthening South Carolina's reputation for political radicalism. He told the Senate in 1900, "We of the South have never recognized the right of the negro to govern the white man and we never will."[1] The days of genteel Bourbon supremacy had passed, and indeed the Civil War generation had largely passed away.

Crude, profane, and a demagogue on the issue of race, Tillman defended lynching, the ultimate weapon for controlling blacks, especially after they lost the political right to vote or serve as jurors and had been reduced again nearly to bondage. In terrifying language he articulated that classic fear of the white South—black male sexuality. Tillman told the Senate in 1902, "Whenever the Constitution comes between me and the virtue of the white women of the South, I say to hell with the Constitution!" He vividly described a mythical southern woman raped by a black man, "her chastity taken from her and a memory branded on her brain as with a red-hot iron to haunt her night and day as long as she lives." Then, arguing that such a rapist had "put himself outside the pale of the law, human and divine," he raged, "Kill, kill, kill!"[2]

Tillman's rough-and-tumble rhetoric deeply influenced the style of South Carolina politics into the twentieth century, as did his twin themes of class envy and white supremacy. In 1908 Ellison D. Smith, known as "Cotton Ed," swept into the U.S. Senate, winning a seat that he retained until 1944, through a combination of praise for the cotton farmer and vigilance for his interests in Washington, venomous campaign rhetoric against African Americans, and a gift for symbolic showmanship. Wearing a cotton boll in his lapel, Smith rode

Benjamin Ryan "Pitchfork Ben" Tillman, reactionary on matters of race and appearing to be progressive on matters related to the interests of small farmers, upended the state's politics when he became governor of South Carolina in 1890. Courtesy South Caroliniana Library, University of South Carolina, 7500–2.

about the state on the back of a wagon stacked high with cotton bales and delivered speeches in praise of "our sweetheart," cotton.

DEVOTION TO COTTON had taken on a new form in South Carolina by the time of Cotton Ed. Until the Civil War, South Carolina's nineteenth-century economy was dominated by cotton production that depended overwhelmingly on slave labor. The slave-based economy amounted to a house of cards blown away by the war, which transformed South Carolina from the wealthiest southern state to the most devastated. The cash value of slaves alone, $400 million ($9.7 billion in 2005 dollars) before the war, had vanished. And land values plunged by more than two-thirds.

After the war, in South Carolina as in much of the rest of the South, cotton remained the main cash crop. Trial and error led to systems of sharecropping and tenancy. The former slaves had no money or capital and had been kept illiterate by law, and the only work that most knew was farm labor. In reality sharecroppers—whether black or white—were laborers whose wages were paid with a share of the crop. Often failing to earn enough to meet loans for living expenses, they fell into perpetual debt and poverty under laws passed to protect the interests of the property owner. Some former slaves, who had learned management skills while supervising others on plantations, obtained land after the war that they farmed successfully.

Farm laborers in Mount Pleasant. Laborers return from a day of picking cotton in 1870. "Head-toting" is a practice derived from African culture. *History of South Carolina Slide Collection*, H-01

Fishermen, Isle of Palms. The labor of African Americans in South Carolina was not limited to agricultural work. In the lowcountry African Americans worked as fishermen, boatmen, and dockworkers, both as enslaved and as free people. This picture shows African Americans on the Isle of Palms in 1899, using a traditional African method of surf fishing with nets. *History of South Carolina Slide Collection*, D-81

The crop-lien system, in which farmers borrowed money from merchants for operating and living expenses and gave a mortgage with a lien on the crop as security, caused thousands of mostly white farmers to lose their land in the 1880s because of either a bad crop or a fall in cotton prices. They experienced downward mobility, becoming sharecroppers or tenant farmers. The latter owned a plow and mule and other equipment, rented land, and divided the crop with the landowner. The tenant farmers kept a larger share of their crop than the sharecroppers.

William Gregg in the 1840s had successfully founded the state's first textile mill in Graniteville, a few miles across the Savannah River from Augusta. A visionary, he saw a need and potential for manufacturing, but Calhoun and other political leaders opposed such activity as a threat to unity on the slave issue. Gregg responded in 1844, writing, "Shall we pass unnoticed the thousands of poor, ignorant, degraded white people among us, who, in this land of plenty, live in comparative nakedness and starvation?"[3]

Gregg saw the South's economic problem as a whole, recognizing that the preservation and development of natural and human resources were the only basis for permanent prosperity. Beginning in the 1880s the textile revolution in the upcountry created South Carolina's first nonagricultural industry and its first industrial working class.

The textile industry would remain the dominant manufacturing enterprise in the state for almost a century. The impetus came less from Gregg's vision than from the hydroelectric power from fast-running rivers on whose banks the early mills were built—and the opportunity that investors saw for profit. Existing finishing and manufacturing plants in New England provided a ready market for the yarn produced in the initial upcountry cotton mills.

In 1895 the city of Anderson adopted its nickname, the Electric City—a sobriquet it has retained—after engineer William C. Whitner, a native son, built near there on the Reedy River the South's first hydroelectric generating plant capable of transmitting electricity over long-distance lines. This development and improvements in long-distance transmission allowed textile mills to operate miles away from their power generating source. In 1897 Whitner developed a larger and more sophisticated system of transmission. Also, the world's first cotton gin powered by electricity was built in Anderson County.

A few years later North Carolina industrial magnate James B. "Buck" Duke moved into the electricity business with his Charlotte-based Duke Power Company. He developed more sophisticated hydroelectric generating plants and transmission systems, lowering the cost of producing electricity. Grasping the

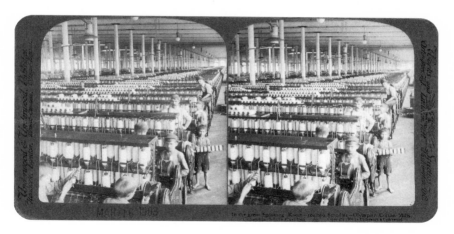

Columbia Mills spinning room, 1903. The textile revolution that began in the 1880s
had transformed South Carolina by this time. The stereoscope image shows the
spinning room of Columbia Mills, the structure that now houses the State Museum.
Courtesy South Caroliniana Library, University of South Carolina

potential for an expanded market for his electric power, he organized business
and professional men in towns throughout the Piedmont region of the Carolinas to pool funds and develop local textile mills that became customers for
his low-priced electricity. (Buck Duke's American Tobacco Company also
stimulated the spread of tobacco as a major cash crop in South Carolina's Pee
Dee region in the state's seven-county northeastern corner.)

Outside investors, some from Charleston and others from the North and
the upper South, also found the South Carolina upcountry an appealing place
for building textile mills. The raw material for the production of textiles was
abundant and near at hand.

Perhaps most important, mill owners found a cheap and willing white
labor source in the upcountry. The trials of tenant farming and sharecropping
had led many white South Carolinians to consider leaving agricultural work
for the first time. Working in the mills meant stable employment and something entirely new for most—a cash wage. The ex–tenant farmers were joined
by families who trekked down from Appalachian border counties.

Together, they lived in mill villages built and owned by the mill owners,
shopped in the company store, and listened on Sunday to company-paid
preachers in company-owned churches. They became a distinct social class as
families produced new generations of workers. The level of control and organization loosely resembled that of the plantation. In 1915 blacks became totally

excluded by law from all but the most menial jobs inside the textile mills, essentially a legal ratification of a system already in place. The textile industry formed the base on which the upstate rebuilt its economy after the end of Reconstruction.

Initially many locally formed companies opened cotton yarn mills with secondhand equipment from the textile centers of the Northeast. Northern-owned textile companies also opened branches in the South. Spinning and weaving plants would follow. After several decades, dyeing and printing plants began to be established, but most of the textile plants turned out coarse products until after World War II.

This second phase of economic development, which lasted from 1880 to 1940, was characterized by the limited scope of industrialization and the continued dependence of a decreasing but still large share of the population on a relatively unproductive agricultural system. The renewal of tobacco as a cash crop and the corresponding loss of rice to western competition highlighted agricultural changes.

SOON AFTER THE COLLAPSE of Reconstruction, whites had used their political and social power to begin disenfranchisement of black voters and the racial segregation of public life. The state's pioneering literacy tests for voters, begun in 1882 with the eight-box law, set the standard.

In the summer of 1895, C. A. Woods of Marion—an attorney, the president of the Bank of Marion, and a future judge of the U. S. Fourth Circuit Court of Appeals—wrote letters to lawyers and bankers throughout Mississippi asking how the "Suffrage Clause in your Constitution has worked." He got at least a dozen responses. All essentially agreed with Grenada Bank president J. W. Griffis, who wrote and underlined for emphasis that it "works admirably in every respect." Dem Price, a cashier at the Bank of Oxford spelled it out more plainly: "If a white man comes up to register who is believed to be willing to vote what they call 'right,' no questions are asked him."[4]

In 1895 Senator Tillman presided over the state constitutional convention he had called for as governor to enact what he would declare "the main purpose of our being here." That purpose was to deny African Americans the right to vote.[5] The new constitution borrowed heavily from the 1890 Mississippi state constitution's provisions for disenfranchising black voters, including a poll tax and a literacy provision designed to keep most blacks, but virtually no whites, from voting. A prospective voter unable to read a portion of the constitution had an "understand and explain option," which allowed him to register if he could "explain" a section of the constitution selected by the poll manager, who would always be white. This system worked to disenfranchise blacks while allowing illiterate whites to vote.

At the South Carolina Constitutional Convention, a handful of black delegates, including former congressmen Thomas E. Miller and Robert Smalls, argued forcefully against these provisions, knowing well that although they would lose, they were leaving a record for history. Smalls declared, "My race needs no special defense. . . . All they need is an equal chance in the battle of life."[6] The new constitution, however, left intact the provisions for a system of public education put into place by the Reconstruction government's constitution of 1868. When the white men "invoked the horrors of Reconstruction as the rationale for [blacks'] disfranchisement," Miller responded, "It was your love of power and your arrogance which brought Reconstruction to you."[7]

The new constitution also outlawed interracial marriage, but the convention took no action against the illegitimate sexual relationships of white men and black women. As the historian George B. Tindall has recounted, "Smalls sought to back the white delegates into a corner. He introduced an amendment that would bar from public office any white person guilty of cohabiting with a Negro and that 'any child of such a relationship should bear the name of its father and inherit property the same as if legitimate.'" Ben Tillman indicated that the Smalls proposal had some merit, proposing a substitute amendment to make miscegenation a crime "to protect negro women against the debauchery of white men degrading themselves to the level of black women." The convention rejected both amendments, but the issue of miscegenation brought up "the delicate question of defining 'Negro.'"[8]

The legislative committee recommended "one eighth or more" of "Negro blood" (at least one black great-grandparent). After one delegate proposed it be any black ancestry, Tillman's older brother George, a former congressman, pointed out he knew several families in his congressional district with a small degree of such ancestry. These families, he pointed out, provided soldiers who fought for the Confederacy. They were now accepted in white society, he pointed out, and should not be embarrassed.

The elder Tillman made what Tindall called the "astounding claim" that there existed on the convention floor "not one pure-blooded Caucasian," maintaining that all had at least one ancestor from another race. George Tillman proposed defining as Negro as anyone with at least one-fourth Negro ancestry. The convention kept the definition of one-eighth.[9]

One outcome of the convention was that Congressman Miller, a graduate of the University of South Carolina School of Law who wanted a state-supported black college with black governance and understood Tillman's commitment to racial segregation, worked out an agreement with Tillman to establish the Colored Normal, Industrial, Agricultural and Mechanical College of South Carolina in Orangeburg—today's South Carolina State University. Miller became its first president in 1896, serving fifteen years until forced out by Governor Coleman Blease.[10]

The big question after the new constitution was ratified in 1896 was whether the disenfranchising provisions would be found in violation of the U.S. Constitution. Two years later the U.S. Supreme Court gave its answer. In 1898 the high court gave its stamp of approval to black disenfranchisement in *Williams v. Mississippi*, a little-known case that upheld the principles incorporated into the South Carolina document. Because jurors were selected from lists of registered voters, disenfranchisement also meant a system of all-white juries. For African Americans disenfranchisement essentially introduced an era in which the law provided almost no protection for blacks.

The new constitution also severely limited the power of local government, and it centralized power in the legislature. Until the 1960s, county legislative delegations also controlled county governmental operations by writing the county budget, known as the supply bill, and any other local legislation.

The vote in 1896 to ratify the new constitution was close. Opposition came from those blacks still able to vote, anti-Tillman whites, and those concerned that the new literacy requirements would not fully protect illiterate whites, but they did not prevail.

WITH THE SUPREME COURT'S "separate but equal" doctrine established in 1896 in *Plessy v. Ferguson*, South Carolina moved on both the local and state levels toward the full adoption of legally imposed racial segregation, a process complete by the time of America's entrance into World War I. By 1904 public transportation had become almost totally segregated, although the *Charleston News and Courier* had editorialized against it. In 1915 the legislature passed a law that prevented black men from working in textile mills. The segregation of downtown stores and public facilities soon followed. "Whites only" and "colored only" signs gave visible expression to the color line.

The textile era and the system of racial superiority that made skin color a status symbol for poor whites combined to produce one of South Carolina's most fascinating and morally bankrupt politicians, Coleman Livingston Blease. He began his career as a state representative from Newberry County, a committed Tillmanite who, unlike his mentor, saw the electoral potential of South Carolina's new white working class of mill operatives. Elected twice to two-year terms, Blease became governor in 1911 and served until 1915.

His racist appeals worked. While presenting himself as their champion, Blease opposed every effort that could have improved lives of the mill workers, including child labor laws, a shorter workweek, and higher wages. Middle-class reformers might say they wanted child labor laws and better wages, but Blease warned darkly that what they really wanted was to see African American men working side by side with white wives and daughters in the sweaty spinning rooms. He posed no threat to mill owners.

When some reformers suggested that physicians might provide free medical care to young, poor women in the notoriously unhealthy mills, Blease promised to pardon any mill worker who shot the doctor who gave their daughter such an exam. Blease looked into the darkest depths of his supporters' hearts, their most primal fears and savage tendencies, and there found his political program.

Mill workers nevertheless loved the man they called "our Coley." While short on substance, Blease proved long on symbolism. He styled himself as the champion of the "lintheads," a term derived from the cotton lint that floated around in the textile mills and stuck to the hair of workers, and he mocked respectable townspeople just as the hardworking folk of the mill village had themselves been mocked. More significant, he rang all the chimes on the theme of white supremacy, reminding the South Carolina mill workers that their white skin made them socially superior to all black people. And he suggested that they could lose that status and their sense of independence if they failed to vote for Coley.

When some distressed South Carolinians asked the governor to investigate the dismemberment and lynching of a black man in Honea Path, he responded, "Whenever the Constitution comes between me and the virtue of the white women of the South, I say to hell with the Constitution."[11]

Although the inflammatory rhetoric of Tillman and Blease encouraged lynching, aristocratic planter Duncan Clinch Heyward expressed strong opposition to the practice during his two terms as governor from 1903 until 1907. In one case after an especially grisly group murder of a young black man who had sassed a member of the group, Heyward publicly said he was "utterly disgusted" with what happened. He used his own money to hire a Pinkerton detective to investigate. Six white men were subsequently arrested, a shock to local whites. A jury deliberated sixteen minutes before finding all six innocent.

The chagrined governor months later addressed an inflamed mob holding a black man accused of the attempted rape of a white woman in Greenwood County. As he stood on a platform urging the crowd to allow the legal process to proceed, Heyward realized his words had no effect. A horde of men subsequently tied the man to a pine tree. The mob shot him to pieces of bloody flesh during ten minutes of gunfire. People came for hours to look at what remained of the body, some taking souvenirs.

After a grisly lynching a week later in Dorchester County, where the sheriff without resistance allowed a mob to take a black prisoner from the jail a half hour after his arrest, hang him, and mutilate his body beyond recognition with gunfire, Heyward called a special term of the grand jury, who indicted the sheriff. Although a jury refused to convict, his successor as sheriff—a wealthy farmer whose performance as coroner at the inquest for the lynching victim had offended hundreds of blacks attendees—found himself the object of an organized boycott by black farmworkers. Shocked, he complained of receiving threats and losing thousands of dollars in unharvested cotton.

Although such protest by blacks was unusual, it demonstrated to whites that racial terrorism was not altogether safe, and it helped lay the foundation for future generations in their broader struggle for political and civil rights. Governor Heyward's actions also reinforced the efforts of white opponents of lynching.

After some lynchings blacks refused to bury the body of the victims, an attempt to force whites both to pay the burial expenses and to confront their actions. It also made a subtle claim on whites to recognize their humanity, which rabid white supremacists refused to do, citing the claims of Tillman and Blease that their victims were outside the law. (Altogether, 156 blacks and 4 whites were lynched in South Carolina between 1882 and 1947; in eight other southern states a higher number of lynchings occurred.)

Reform elements had been at work in the state since the early twentieth century, however, influenced by the national political movement known as Progressivism. Ethnic politicians, old-style aristocrats turned progressives, and middle-class white women all became involved in seeking to transform the state's political structure.

In reaction to the excesses of Blease, South Carolina elected Richard I. Manning to replace him as governor in 1916. Although connected by family and heritage to the old planter elite, Manning had adopted the progressive sentiments of Woodrow Wilson, the highly popular president who had lived in Columbia as a youth. Under Manning, reform became the order of the day in education, the tax structure, and agriculture. And he denounced lynching.

After four successive losses for statewide office, two for governor and two for the Senate, Blease revived his political career in 1924 by defeating Congressman James F. Byrnes in an election for the Senate. Blease's victory was widely credited to a rumor that Byrnes, an Episcopalian who grew up as a Roman Catholic in Charleston, had not really left that faith when he entered politics. With a revived Ku Klux Klan near the peak of its power, such an assertion in an overwhelmingly Protestant state ruined Byrnes's hopes that year. But in 1930 Byrnes ran again, this time defeating Blease and effectively ending his political career.

Even before they could vote, South Carolina's women played a role in the efforts at progressive reform, providing the bulk of support for prohibition drives and the improvement of schools. In the Columbia area they had shown a special interest in child labor laws, which resulted in the state's first progressive measure in May 1903, a law prohibiting the employment of children under the age of ten in the textile mills.

Other middle-class women in the Palmetto State organized early for women's suffrage. In 1892 Virginia Durant Young, a leader in the state Women's Christian Temperance Union, helped organize the South Carolina Equal Rights Association. By 1915, associations favoring the vote for women had emerged all over the state. Susan Pringle Frost of Charleston, who reflected both traditional and progressive values in initiating Charleston's movement for historic preservation, also favored the extension of the franchise.

The Pollitzer sisters of Charleston—Carrie, Mabel, and Anita—were active at the local, state, and national levels in the women's suffrage movement. Carrie, the oldest, also launched the petition drive that led to the admission of women at the College of Charleston in 1918. Mabel served as a state chairperson of the National Women's Party, and Anita served four years as national chair.

The South Carolina General Assembly, however, proved recalcitrant when Congress submitted the Nineteenth Amendment to the states for ratification in 1919. Although the necessary three-fourths of the states ratified the amendment granting women the right to vote, South Carolina's legislature did not ratify it formally until a symbolic vote in 1969.

Meanwhile a more populist politics of reform had emerged in Charleston. The politics of that city, unlike elsewhere in the state, showed similarities to the ward politics of the Northeast or other, more polyglot southern cities such as New Orleans. Concentrations of Irish Catholics, Jews, Italians, and German Lutherans lived in Wards 3, 5, 7, and 9, the Charleston neighborhoods north of Broad Street and east of King. They shared a lack of affection for the "South of Broad" elites who set the tone for Charleston society and dominated its municipal elections. These outsiders found their champion in John P. Grace, Charleston's first Irish-Catholic mayor.

He first became mayor in 1911, a time when Charleston retained but a shadow of its former glory. Two major natural disasters in the 1880s, a destructive hurricane in 1885 and a devastating earthquake in 1886 that destroyed or severely damaged roughly two thousand standing structures, had followed the devastation of the city during the Civil War.

By the early twentieth century, Charleston seemed more like a medieval city than a modern port. Hogs and dairy cows lived in the alleys and walked the streets, while buzzards provided a primary public sanitation service. The city had no professional fire department or police force.

In a city becoming known as "too poor to paint and too proud to whitewash," Charleston's elite had little interest in or vision of economic renewal. Most shops and even banks in the city opened in late morning, closed at midday to allow the proprietors to enjoy a long and leisurely three o'clock dinner, then reopened briefly before sundown. Charlestonians had the reputation of being lost in a dreamy contemplation of the past.

Grace was unwilling to let the city sleep. He instituted a series of reforms that began its modernization, such as raising taxes to pave roads and build sidewalks. Grace held office from 1911 to 1915 and again from 1919 to 1923. Seeing the city's potential for tourism, in his second term he saw to it that the city contributed to the building of the Francis Marion Hotel, which still stands on the corner of King and Calhoun streets across from Marion Square. The city finally developed professional police and fire protection and other services. Farm animals disappeared from the streets.

But the old elites of the city hated Grace. He lost in 1915 by a handful of votes to Tristram T. Hyde. Armed partisans for Grace and equally well-armed partisans for his opponent showed up at Democratic Party headquarters at the corner of George and King streets. A scuffle over ballots led to a wild shootout. Two ballot boxes were hurled into the street, a *Charleston News and Courier* reporter was shot and killed, and only intervention by police and local militia ended the violence.

Meanwhile, although African Americans lacked any meaningful vote in the early twentieth century, they did more than simply accept the marginal place whites attempted to assign them. Unable to challenge Jim Crow as a social system, they worked to improve their position within it. These efforts planted seeds of resistance that would come to fruition in the civil rights struggle.

The 1917 campaign by the Charleston County National Association for the Advancement of Colored People (NAACP) to have black teachers in black schools best illustrates these early efforts. Black students who attended segregated schools in the county were assigned white teachers, women and in some cases men who generally had little training and demonstrated little respect for or understanding of the intellectual abilities of their students. Black children learned from an early age the precepts of white supremacy.

The NAACP petitioned the county's legislative delegation to change this practice and to allow black teachers to teach in black schools. This assertion of autonomy, within the system of Jim Crow itself, involved some of the state's future civil rights leaders. Septima Clark is the best example. As a young neighborhood teacher she collected thousands of petition signatures in a burlap bag. She later taught in the public schools and became one of South Carolina's most important grassroots organizers in the early civil rights era.

Between 1910 and 1920 the NAACP became active on other fronts. In Columbia it successfully campaigned for a public library and a YMCA for blacks. Black women there raised funds to build a home for orphaned or abused children. Such seeds of activism would spring to life later in the twentieth century.

Meanwhile tens of thousands of black South Carolinians boarded northbound trains to seek greater freedom and a better life. A chain migration began when one or two blacks from a South Carolina town or city found jobs

This simple one-room schoolhouse on Coosaw Island was staffed by a graduate of the Penn School in the 1920s. *History of South Carolina Slide Collection*, I-13

in the North that produced a regular paycheck and sent word back to family and friends. From Lake City hundreds went north to Paterson, New Jersey. From Kingstree and surrounding Williamsburg County a steady stream moved to Rochester, New York. From Edgefield they formed a community in Coatesville, Pennsylvania, where Strom Thurmond's black daughter grew up. New York's Harlem became the favored destination for those leaving Charleston and Columbia. The South Carolina natives took with them and popularized their dances: the Charleston and the Big Apple, the latter from a Columbia nightclub by that name housed in a former synagogue, became cultural transfers. South Carolina lost between 10 and 30 percent of its black population in every decade in the first half of the twentieth century, a rate that continued until 1970. The state lost 10.7 percent of its black population between 1900 and 1910, 10.6 percent in 1910–1920, 29.5 percent in the Depression decade between 1930 and 1940, and 23.6 percent between 1940 and 1950. Between 1950 and 1970, 415,000 black South Carolinians migrated out of the state.[12]

6

WORLD WARS AND THE DEPRESSION

The entry of the United States into the First World War proved a watershed for the American South. Many South Carolinians benefited from the war. The price of cotton shot up to forty cents a pound, and mill wages grew in response to the demand for uniforms, tents, and other textiles by the United States armed forces.

Both black and white South Carolinians served in World War I, though in segregated units. Most white South Carolinians saw extensive action in the famed Thirtieth Division, called the "Old Hickory" division because it was made up of men from Andrew Jackson's old stomping grounds of South Carolina, North Carolina, and Tennessee. Black South Carolinians, fighting in the Ninety-third Regiment, also saw action across the Atlantic Ocean. Of seventy-nine Medals of Honor awarded during World War I, seven went to South Carolinians. One of them, Freddie Stowers from Sandy Springs in Anderson County, became the only African American to receive a Medal of Honor in either world war.

But South Carolina's economy suffered after the end of the war. By 1921 the price of cotton had dropped to ten cents a pound, below even prewar lows. The price for tobacco, a crop that had become important in the Pee Dee region in the 1890s, also dropped precipitously.

South Carolinians of both races faced a dark decade. As in much of the rest of the South, South Carolina's Great Depression began before 1929. Banks began to close, textile mills laid off, rehired, and then laid off workers. The rural population remained trapped in cycles of debt and tenancy, and the larger towns and cities languished.

The boll weevil, advancing eastward from Texas, hit South Carolina in the mid-1920s, devastating cotton crops and the already fragile economy while

Bootlegger still. This photograph was taken in Beaufort County in 1938. The making and running of moonshine occurred throughout rural South Carolina but was especially prevalent in the mountainous region of northern Greenville, Pickens, and Oconee counties, where it became common after World War I. *History of South Carolina Slide Collection*, D-127

disrupting lives throughout the state and region. Beginning several years before the stock market crash of 1929, the economic struggle and hardship South Carolina faced would last for more than a decade and a half.

Until World War II the lowcountry remained essentially agricultural, with cotton the dominant crop. In the early 1920s cotton farmers suffered devastating damage as the destructive boll weevil moved across the state, destroying their crop. Scientific methods would ultimately control this pest, whose presence moved some farmers into crop diversification. Although cotton survived with New Deal price supports and production controls, the major benefits went to the landowners. For most of its growers, however, the crop provided marginal income. From 1900 to 1940 more than 60 percent of the state's farmers, almost two-thirds of them black, rented their land as tenants or sharecroppers.

For six Pee Dee counties tobacco became the dominant income-producing crop and remained so for more than seven decades. In the 1930s President Franklin Roosevelt's New Deal Agricultural Adjustment Act (AAA) rescued tobacco farmers from the Depression through production controls and price supports.

IN 1934 SOUTH CAROLINA played a central role in one of the largest labor strikes in American history. There was growing resentment against the "speed-up" and the "stretch-out," crude new management techniques aimed at increasing productivity without increasing pay for workers. More than 150,000 textile workers throughout the South walked out in protest, inviting the United Textile Workers union for help in organizing. The strike spread from the South as far as Maine, though it was primarily centered in the southeastern Piedmont.

The speed-up increased the speed of the machines in the textile plants, where the inside temperature in the summer often exceeded ninety degrees with high humidity, and the stretch-out increased the number of machines assigned to workers. Workers become engaged in conflict with both the mill owners and often with state law enforcement officials. South Carolina governor Ibra Blackwood fully supported the mill owners, calling out the national guard on their behalf.

On September 4, the day after Labor Day, President Roosevelt sought advice from Jimmy Byrnes, calling him in South Carolina. Their relationship went back to 1928, when FDR was governor of New York. In a two-page letter sent the same day, Byrnes correctly analyzed the situation. He said the primary issue for workers was not the National Recovery Administration's order earlier that year cutting textile worker hours and pay. He cited two issues, the stretch-out system and discrimination against workers who joined the union.[1]

Two days after Byrnes mailed his letter, a crushing blow for the strikers came in the Anderson County town of Honea Path. That morning local union workers supported a "flying squadron" motorcade of unionists attempting the keep the plant from opening. Outside the main gate fistfights broke out between workers trying to come in for the morning shift and the strikers. The forewarned local plant superintendent, who also was town mayor, armed more than one hundred strikebreakers among his nonunion or "loyal" workforce.

Mack Duncan, a young nonunion worker handing out sawed-off broomsticks and other objects as clubs for loyal workers, recalled four decades later what happened next. "Then all of a sudden you heard shooting. For about five minutes it was just a din. . . . And when it was over there was a lot of people hurt lying on the ground. They'd been shot and beat. And seven people were killed." More than ten thousand attended the funerals.[2]

The strike led directly to the National Labor Relations Act, which provides protections for organized labor. Despite its provisions to protect workers seeking union representation, strike leaders were blackballed by the industry, and many were never rehired. The failure of the workers left many embittered about unions. In the 1990s an award-winning documentary, *The Uprising of '34*, provided graphic insight into and understanding of the strike from both the strikers' and mill owners' sides. South Carolina ETV, the state's public television network, initially declined to air the program but relented after publicized protests.

Although the strike failed, the mill workers found a new champion that year in Olin D. Johnston. A former textile worker himself who grew up in Anderson County near Honea Path, he completed a degree at Wofford College in Spartanburg after army duty in World War I and played tackle on the University of South Carolina football team while earning a law degree at the university.

He had received 49.8 percent of the vote in a Democratic runoff for governor in 1930 against the conservative Blackwood. In 1934 Johnston ran again for governor as a full supporter of Roosevelt's New Deal and won 56 percent of the vote against Blease, who was attempting a final comeback. Johnston fought for better education and health care for the working class. He gave full support to legislation Blackwood had signed in 1934 to create the South Carolina Public Service Authority (Santee Cooper).

In Washington, Byrnes had in his second term become a Senate floor leader for President Roosevelt and played a crucial role in getting White House support for federal funds to build the massive Santee Cooper project. Unlike Cotton Ed, Byrnes as a freshman senator threw his support behind Roosevelt in the White House and supported his New Deal of expanded power in Washington, with new programs and agencies aimed at restoring the economy and overcoming widespread economic fear. The New Deal created Social Security, farm subsidies, legal protection for organized labor, and new public works programs that provided jobs for huge numbers of the unemployed and for young people. Depression-era South Carolina embraced the New Deal in its early years, and Byrnes became a Congressional leader for its programs.

Four years of court battles followed to overcome opposition to Santee Cooper from private utility companies, private landowners who fought relocation of families, environmentalists disapproving of destruction of wildlife habitat and thousands of acres of virgin hardwood forest, and preservationists opposed to flooding of battlefields and historic sites. Leadership in building public support came from Governor Johnston and progressive mayor Burnet Maybank of Charleston, who became a protégé of Byrnes, succeeded Johnston as governor, and later served with him in the Senate.

Public works funding from Washington allowed construction of Santee Cooper to begin in 1939. At its peak nearly fifteen thousand workers used

South Carolina Public Service Authority. The Santee Cooper project would be the major accomplishment of South Carolina's New Deal Democrats. Senator James F. Byrnes played a key role in getting federal funds from the Roosevelt administration, and Charleston mayor Burnet Maybank led the campaign to organize political and public support in the state. Courtesy South Caroliniana Library, University of South Carolina, Santee Cooper Collection

handsaws and mule-drawn wagons to clear 160,000 acres, creating two major reservoirs, with 450 miles of shoreline. They would be named Lake Marion and Lake Moultrie.

A new power plant began generating electricity in 1942 and brought electric lights to rural areas lit before at night only by kerosene lamps. Santee Cooper, the popular name for the South Carolina Public Service Authority, in 2001 was providing almost all retail electricity for Berkeley and Horry counties and wholesale electricity to twenty cooperatives and two municipalities that served approximately six hundred thousand customers. Its two large man-made lakes provide boating, fishing, and sites for vacation cottages and long-term development for homes for younger families as well as for retirement communities. (In the 1990s the public utility created a regional water system that treated and transported water from Lake Moultrie to much of the lowcountry.)

IN 1938 JOHNSTON challenged Senator "Cotton Ed" Smith, whom Roosevelt had targeted because of his opposition to the New Deal. During the first part of his Senate career, Smith had espoused some progressive sentiments, such as a distrust of big business, banks, and Wall Street, that translated into votes for government regulation and investigations. He also had supported federal initiatives for better roads and a system to provide credit for farmers. With blacks unable to vote, he was a man who ran on cotton prices when times were good and racism when times were bad. But he became an irascible obstructionist to the New Deal. In his 1938 campaign Smith aroused rustic audiences when he told and retold his "Philadelphy" story.

Smith would first set the scene for his walking out of the 1936 Democratic National Convention after an African American minister was called upon to pray. Referring to him as a "blue-gummed Senegambian," Smith would quickly proceed, "He started praying and I started walking. And from his great platform in the sky, John C. Calhoun bent down and whispered in my ear, 'You done right, Ed.'"[3] He won reelection for his sixth term. Johnston, elected again as governor in 1942, two years later defeated Smith, then in failing health in his eightieth year.

Byrnes in his second term became a Senate floor leader for Roosevelt, who named him to the Supreme Court in 1941. After fifteen months as a Supreme Court justice, he resigned at Roosevelt's request in 1942 to assist in the war effort, first as director of economic stabilization in the White House. In 1944 he earned the unofficial title of "assistant president" as director of the Office of War Mobilization.

Those positions ensured that South Carolina got its full share of federal spending during World War II, including a revitalized shipyard in Charleston that in 1944 employed twenty-three thousand workers (almost a third of them black, concentrated in less skilled jobs) and a multitude of military bases around the state. The war effort employed and trained thousands of workers, many of them women, and moved the state forward economically. Although Roosevelt's New Deal spending programs had provided help and hope, the huge federal military spending in the state began turning South Carolina's economy around.

Byrnes's resignation from the Senate resulted in a political reshuffling in South Carolina. Governor Maybank, who as a popular and progressive mayor of Charleston had used New Deal programs to help revitalize the city, moved into the empty Senate seat in 1941.

Although an active contender for the vice presidential nomination in 1944, Byrnes was passed over in favor of Missouri senator Harry S. Truman. Byrnes served under Truman as secretary of state and helped shape postwar American foreign policy as the "father of atomic diplomacy" in what became the cold war with the Soviet Union.

When World War II ended, the pent-up national demand for new houses and for goods and services exploded. The GI Bill provided returning veterans with financial support to attend college, and in South Carolina many of them became the first in their family to enroll in higher education. Others returned from the war with new skills. Many returned with the experience of having known a larger world and with a different vision. Change and optimism were in the air, and the future in South Carolina was about to clash with its past.

7

CIVIL RIGHTS ERA

South Carolina played a unique role during the civil rights era. An established statewide network of strong black leaders ultimately coalesced with a succession of progressive governors to ease the transition to a multiracial society. It took the federal courts and federal law to force change and the courage of African American citizens to bring lawsuits. Although change did not come without resistance or without sacrifice, its path met far less confrontation and violence than in the Deep South states.

African Americans in South Carolina also exerted pivotal influence in events leading directly to *Brown v. Board of Education*. That seminal Supreme Court opinion in 1954 reversed the Court's late-nineteenth-century "separate but equal" doctrine that underlay the social fabric of the segregated South.

In addition a quest for stability among twentieth-century whites had emerged as a central theme in response to the felt memories of the Civil War's devastation and disruptive aftermath. This provided a climate for accommodation to change. Instead of confrontation, South Carolina fought to the end in the courts but obeyed the law when it mandated change.

Although the NAACP had established an urban presence in the state with branches chartered in twelve communities between 1917 and 1929, the organization had become almost defunct in Depression-era South Carolina. Only Columbia and Charleston maintained branches in 1930, and neither had active programs related to the cause of civil rights or equality.

Transformation of the NAACP's role in the state came from an unlikely source. Levi Byrd, an African American who had apprenticed and become the only skilled plumber in the Chesterfield County town of Cheraw, also had internalized a message he once saw scrawled inside a railroad car while unloading cargo as a laborer. At one end of the car was written, "What is your life?" At the other end it said, "Your life is what you make of it."

After a beating in 1933 by a group of white men, Byrd contacted the national NAACP. Despite limited formal education he maintained correspondence with the national body for years. After persistent effort he spurred the organization of a countywide NAACP branch in Cheraw. He then generated support to create in 1939 a statewide network of branches that transformed the organization.

Instead of a small, urban-based unit that primarily represented the interests of black professionals, the NAACP soon evolved into a broad-based, mass organization representing the diverse interests and aspirations of the full black community in the state. From fifteen branches in 1943, the number grew to forty-nine in 1946. Membership topped ten thousand. The number of branches reached eighty-four in 1955, but two years later fell by more than fifty in response to a white backlash after *Brown*. A new state law prohibited teachers from belonging to the organization. The state NAACP, however, soon fully regained its vitality.[1]

Meanwhile state NAACP president James M. Hinton of Columbia and black newspaper editor John H. McCray of the *Lighthouse and Informer*, a statewide weekly that provided a thoughtful voice and detailed reporting on civil rights issues, demonstrated strong leadership. They inspired a successful equal-pay lawsuit for teachers in 1944 and three years later led what became a successful effort in the courts to end the all-white Democratic primary. McCray also played a major role in organizing the Progressive Democratic Party, a pioneering political organization for blacks then excluded from participation in the state Democratic Party; its membership also was open to whites.

Beginning before and continuing throughout the civil rights era, Modjeska Monteith Simkins of Columbia served as an irascible and untiring champion of black civil rights and equality across the state. Serving as secretary in the early years of the state NAACP, she was the only woman officer. Simkins would earn the sobriquet of South Carolina's matriarch of the civil rights movement, and her portrait now hangs in a position of honor in the State House.

The strongest white leadership organization for racial change was from the South Carolina Council on Human Relations, an affiliate of the Atlanta-based Southern Regional Council. Director Alice Norwood Spearman, who grew up in a small-town South Carolina family with high social status, had traveled widely and possessed an indomitable spirit. She was once badly beaten in her

Columbia office by an angry young white man, and after recovery she returned with the same vigor as before.[2]

In 1944 U.S. District Court Judge J. Waties Waring, an eighth-generation Charlestonian of impeccable connections, demonstrated a firm commitment to the law on civil rights in the teacher pay equalization case. The state NAACP had brought in the top NAACP Legal Defense Fund lawyer, future Supreme Court justice Thurgood Marshall, to argue the case in Charleston, where black teachers received $360 their first year and $460 their third. Comparable pay for white teachers was $680 and $800.

Waring decided the case in fifteen minutes, after asking the school board attorney for dates of two previous equal pay cases from Virginia and Maryland that the U.S. Supreme Court had already decided, one in 1940. Waring, who cut Marshall off when he attempted to give the dates while the school board lawyer worked through his files, said, "What I was trying to determine was how long it has been since the School Board has known it must pay equal salaries to teachers." He added brusquely, "This is a simple case, and there isn't [any] need to take up the court's time."[3] The impact of his equal pay order rippled across the state.

Also in 1944 the Progressive Democrats ran Osceola McKaine of Sumter, who worked closely with Hinton and McCray, as a general election candidate for the Senate against Olin D. Johnston. They knew McKaine would not win, but McCray later wrote that McKaine's candidacy would lead many African Americans to register to vote for the first time.

McKaine had returned to his native Sumter in 1939 after twenty years in Europe. He had served there in World War I and returned to it from New York in anger and disgust after confronting the racial oppression and antiblack violence that swept America in 1919. In Ghent, Belgium, he opened a highly successful supper club, became fluent in four languages, and traveled widely in more tolerant Europe. That lifestyle ended abruptly when Hitler's German army invaded Belgium. McKaine bought a one-way ticket and departed.

Back home he found race relations more hopeful, led the revitalization of the Sumter NAACP, joined McCray's *Lighthouse and Informer* as executive editor, and extended his efforts beyond South Carolina as a highly skilled organizer and spokesman for the biracial Southern Conference on Human Welfare.[4] Meanwhile he provided inspiration for bright black youngsters, including Sumter native Jim Clyburn, who played on McKaine's youth baseball team.[5] (In 1992 Clyburn would become South Carolina's first post-Reconstruction black congressman.)

Osceola McKaine (third from left), with staff at the supper club he owned and managed in Ghent, Belgium, after service in World War I in Europe. When Hitler invaded Belgium in 1939, McKaine returned to his native Sumter, South Carolina, after twenty years abroad. He became an early leader and spokesman for civil rights in South Carolina as associate editor of the *Lighthouse and Informer*. One of the players on a youth baseball team he coached was James Clyburn, future majority House whip in the U.S. Congress. McKaine emerged as a nationally recognized leader and organizer for several civil rights organizations. Courtesy South Caroliniana Library, University of South Carolina

Meanwhile many black veterans returned to the state after World War II bitter, both over discriminatory treatment they had faced during the war and over the legally sanctioned segregation and denial of the vote they still experienced at home after fighting for freedom and democracy. Many white veterans also returned with a vision of a larger world outside the American South and a quiet recognition that change was in the air.

One of those black soldiers, army sergeant Isaac Woodward, returning in February 1946 to his wife in Winnsboro after his discharge, was arrested in Batesburg after exchanging harsh words with a bus driver in a dispute arising from Woodward's need to use a restroom. He was knocked unconscious with a nightstick and gouged in the eyes, leaving him permanently blinded.

After charges were brought by U.S. Attorney General Tom Clark, Judge Waring presided over the trial of the police chief who administered the beating. An all-white jury deliberated only thirty minutes before finding him not guilty. Waring biographer Tinsley E. Yarbrough attributes Judge Waring's fully developing sense of racial injustice to his experience in the Woodward case. The case also played a key role in President Truman's decision to appoint his President's Committee on Civil Rights.[6]

In February 1947, a year after Woodward's ordeal, a lynch mob of thirty-one taxi drivers from Greenville took twenty-four-year-old black laborer Willie Earle from the Pickens County jail after he had been charged with a Greenville cab driver's murder. They brutally beat him before taking his life with a shotgun blast to the face. Governor Strom Thurmond, a month after his inauguration, condemned the lynch mob murder and called for vigorous prosecution. He directed the state constabulary to work with the FBI in investigating the crime and brought in the state's top prosecutor.

In the end an all-white, all-male jury found all thirty-one defendants not guilty. State Circuit Judge J. Robert Martin, whose conduct of the trial earned state and national praise, responded by turning his back to the jury and dismissing them without thanks.

A *New York Times* editorial praised Thurmond and other officials (a number of whites, including clergymen in Pickens County, where the lynching occurred, spoke out publicly and vigorously against the crime) for doing "their utmost to bring Earle's slayers to justice." The May 23, 1947, editorial also noted that they received support from "a strong body of public opinion throughout South Carolina." It concluded, "There has been a victory for law, even though Willie Earle's slayers will not be punished for what they did. A precedent has been set. Members of lynching mobs may now know that they do not bask in universal approval, even in their own disgraced communities, and they may begin to fear that someday, on sufficient evidence and with sufficient courage, a Southern lynching case jury will convict."

Three years later NAACP Legal Defense Fund lawyers—with Harold Boulware of Columbia doing most of the legwork—found a provision in the 1895 state constitution that provided a degree of financial accountability for lynchings. In 1950 they won a three-thousand-dollar settlement (roughly twenty-five thousand dollars in 2005 dollars) from Greenville County for Willie Earle's family.

In 1950 Ernest F. "Fritz" Hollings, a twenty-eight-year-old state representative from Charleston, wrote a strong antilynching bill that the General Assembly passed and Governor Thurmond signed. This legislation set the death penalty as punishment for lynching and made mob violence not resulting in death a second-degree offense. The new law also provided for civil damages from local governments in whose jurisdictions the crime took place. No further lynchings occurred in South Carolina.

Meanwhile, in 1947 Judge Waring issued his ruling ending the all-white Democratic primary, the only election that mattered for electing local and state political officials. By now the transformed former segregationist believed that only federal intervention could alter the South's entrenched system of racial separation. Waring declared in *Elmore v. Rice*, "South Carolina is the only State which conducts a primary election solely for whites. . . . I cannot see where the skies will fall if South Carolina is put in the same class with these and other states."[7]

NAACP leaders and others began to organize voter registration drives that would have immediate impact. Across the state Burnet Maybank won 90 percent of the votes in the virtually all-black precincts in his 1948 bid for reelection to the U.S. Senate. He won a bare majority of the total votes in the five-way race in which his leading opponent had called for Judge Waring's impeachment. An estimated thirty-five thousand newly enfranchised blacks, just below 8 percent of the electorate, voted solidly for Maybank. This new patch of blackness in the political fabric allowed him to avoid a runoff election. White politicians took notice.

In response to a lawsuit—argued by Thurgood Marshall—to integrate the University of South Carolina School of Law, Waring, on the same day he struck down the white primary, accepted the state's assurance that it would create an "equal" law school at South Carolina State College in Orangeburg. Ironically, although the South Carolina State law school opened in 1947 to perpetuate segregation, several of its graduates used their legal training to help eliminate it. Two in particular stand out.

Matthew J. Perry, who as an undergraduate at South Carolina State traveled to Charleston to sit in Judge Waring's courtroom while Marshall argued the white primary case, became chief counsel for the NAACP in South Carolina. He played an important role in almost all major civil rights lawsuits in the state, including some argued in the U.S. Supreme Court. He litigated cases that desegregated public schools, the system of higher education, state parks, and other facilities in South Carolina. Other of his cases expanded constitutional protection for demonstrators in civil rights protest marches and other activities. One major case resulted in single-member districts in the legislature, which led to an increase of black legislators from an initial three in 1970 to thirteen two years later. Meanwhile the Voting Rights Act had removed barriers to black political participation. In response, Senator Thurmond moved to get Perry an appointment from President Gerald Ford to the U.S. Court of

Attorney Matthew Perry served as NAACP legal counsel in numerous successful civil rights cases in South Carolina, including Harvey Gantt's suit to be admitted to Clemson in 1963. In 1979 he became South Carolina's first black federal judge, and twenty-five years later a new federal courthouse in Columbia was named for him. In 2007 he received the Thurgood Marshall Award of the American Bar Association. *History of South Carolina Slide Collection*, C-112

Military Appeals, and President Jimmy Carter selected him as a federal district court judge. He became chief judge for the District of South Carolina. A new federal courthouse named for him was dedicated in Columbia in 2004.

Ernest J. Finney, who graduated from the South Carolina State School of Law in 1954, three years after Perry, successfully defended freedom riders, sit-in participants, and other civil rights demonstrators. Elected from Sumter County in 1972 to the S.C. House of Representatives as one of the new black legislators, he helped establish the Legislative Black Caucus and served as its first chairman. After election by the legislature as a circuit court judge in 1976, he advanced to associate justice of the S.C. Supreme Court in 1985 and in 1994 became the state's first African American chief justice.

THE MOST NOTABLE LEGAL ASSAULT on segregation took place earlier in Clarendon County, where blacks outnumbered whites two to one. African American farmer Levi Pearson believed his children should not have to walk nine miles every day to attend a segregated public school while white students received transportation by bus. Clergyman and school principal Joseph DeLaine, an active member of the NAACP who knew the state leaders, agreed. When Pearson and others petitioned the county school board, the board decided black students should continue to walk.

Thurgood Marshall returned to South Carolina, this time intending to tell Pearson and the other black parents that he would not take their case. The national NAACP already had decided to attack school segregation, but it was seeking an urban, high-profile setting in which to bring the case. However, the bravery and commitment of poor, rural, and vulnerable black people in Clarendon County so impressed Marshall, he later told associates, that he took their case.[8]

Harry Briggs, the first named of those who resisted pressure from whites and remained on the list of plaintiffs, lost his job as a service station attendant. The others also all experienced economic reprisals. DeLaine's church was burned to the ground, shots were fired into his home, and it was burned to the ground as well. Other reprisals forced him to leave the state.

Their case, *Briggs v. Elliott*, became the first of the four consolidated as *Brown v. Board of Education*, the U.S. Supreme Court's 1954 landmark case that reversed the "separate but equal" doctrine.[9] That case helped to launch what became the civil rights movement in the United States. Today the contributions of Joseph DeLaine and Levi Pearson are memorialized by an official state marker on an I-95 interchange in Clarendon County.

In his book *The Strange Career of Jim Crow*, the historian C. Vann Woodward wrote that after the decision in *Brown* in 1954 and the Supreme Court's implementation order a year later, "Something very much like a panic seized many parts of the South toward the beginning of 1956, a panic bred on insecurity and fear. Race relations deteriorated in many areas, and as both races recoiled, old lines of communication between them snapped or weakened. On the white side, resistance hardened up and down the line, and in places stiffened into bristling defiance."[10]

In South Carolina that resistance, in the form of citizens' councils, centered on Orangeburg County, whose population of almost seventy thousand was 60 percent black. The black population included faculty, staff, and students at historically black South Carolina State College and the adjoining United Methodist-affiliated Claflin College. A core of middle-class black leadership extended beyond the colleges.

The citizens' councils, composed essentially of middle-class whites and organized initially in the heavily black majority Mississippi Delta, had spread quickly. They reached South Carolina in August 1955 in immediate response to the local NAACP branch's petition demanding immediate integration of schools in Orangeburg. The organization spread quickly throughout Orangeburg County, with chartered councils in seven small incorporated towns in the county, everywhere receiving an initial strong endorsement from local whites. The Orangeburg group pledged to preserve a segregated school system and to "oppose the use of force by radicals and reactionaries" attempting to "disrupt the peace and good relations among the races." A council meeting in Orangeburg on August 9, 1955, attracted three thousand local whites. At that meeting state senator Marshall Williams encouraged "every white man in the area" to join the organization.

Council members opposed violence and sought to keep Ku Klux Klan members out of their organization. William Gordon, a professional black journalist then based in Atlanta, characterized Orangeburg's council members as "elite, church-going, club and business-minded folk who also claim to be God-fearing."[11]

Although autonomous citizens' council groups began forming elsewhere in South Carolina, leading to the creation of the Association of Citizens' Councils of South Carolina, its appeal in the state as a whole was quite limited. The leading historian of the citizens' council movement, Neil R. McMillen, characterized South Carolina as one of the "weak sisters of the Deep South."[12] The local groups focused primarily on political organization and lobbying.

In Orangeburg, however, the council's newspaper played on fears of miscegenation, attacked organized labor, and then launched a campaign of economic reprisal. They targeted the signers of the integration petition, whose names were published in Orangeburg's *Times and Democrat*, and members of the NAACP. Those employed by whites who refused to withdraw their names from the petition were fired. Many blacks lost their jobs, local banks called in loans, some retailers refused to sell to black customers, and milk firms stopped deliveries to homes of signers.

A black contractor lost most of his business. Jim Sulton, a successful black businessman with black and white clients, lost deliveries to his service station from Coke, as well as ice cream and bread vendors, and he retained his gasoline supply only through the intervention of Standard Oil Company with its local distributor. Although the economic squeeze went on for many months, in the end it backfired.

The state NAACP and others stepped in with economic help for those who suffered. Although hit hard financially, Sulton bought supplies from firms in Charleston. He organized a drive to raise money, clothing, food, and other necessities for victims of the council's campaign. In addition to providing supplies, the state NAACP in some cases paid rents, and it relocated several families.

The local NAACP then organized a counterboycott against local franchises of Coca-Cola, Sunbeam Bread, and other products not delivered to black merchants. The counterboycott, which preceded the Montgomery, Alabama, bus boycott by a few months, began at the two black colleges. Students refused to buy Cokes, and some began to make their own bread. After a meeting at Trinity Methodist Church in Orangeburg, NAACP state president Hinton said in a statement, "We are not angry with any one, but we are fully determined to spend our money with those who believe in FIRST CLASS CITIZENSHIP FOR EVERYONE, White or Black. I SAY AGAIN, 'ORANGEBURG TEACHES A LESSON,' one that it will do well for other communities to follow."

Less than three weeks after the counterboycott began, white-owned distributors and others denied any knowledge of economic retaliation against blacks and resumed deliveries to black-owned businesses. The collection of citizens' council dues fell off.

McCray reported that although blacks had suffered economically, the black reaction to the citizens' council campaign and the unity of the NAACP also brought economic hardship to many whites. A number of white businesses quietly sought to bring back African American customers. And several white lawyers quietly provided legal advice to local blacks. Meanwhile some white progressives in Orangeburg found the atmosphere oppressive and moved away.

With its defeat in Orangeburg, citizens' councils saw membership dwindle from a statewide peak of forty thousand in the summer of 1956 to less than a thousand by 1963.[13] The council activity in Orangeburg and elsewhere had served as a catharsis that absorbed the emotional fervor, and the state entered a temporary period of massive resistance that included repeal by the legislature of the state constitution's mandate for a system of public education. As the civil rights movement expanded throughout the South and exploded in violence in Alabama, Mississippi, and elsewhere, South Carolina received little national attention.

Editor McCray's influence, both as an aggressive journalist and as a political activist, made him a target for reprisals in 1950 that ultimately forced him to leave the state. His troubles began after reporting testimony that a black man and the white teenage girl he was accused of raping had actually engaged in consensual sex. Although the Associated Press also had reported the testimony, McCray alone was tried for criminal libel. After conviction in a politically charged atmosphere, he was sentenced to serve time on a chain gang,

Anti-Klan rally. In contemporary South Carolina Ku Klux Klan activities have drawn more protesters than supporters. Here a 1987 anti-Klan rally in Orangeburg, the site of so much past racial conflict, reflects significant change in the state's racial atmosphere. *History of South Carolina Slide Collection*, G-31

setting off a series of legal shenanigans that led to his forced departure and the subsequent demise of the *Lighthouse and Informer*. But before he left, he had prepared a new generation for what ultimately became the transforming civil rights movement.

The Reverend I. DeQuincey Newman, an ordained United Methodist minister who became a salaried NAACP field secretary in 1958 after serving as state president, emerged as the organization's chief strategist and a highly skilled political negotiator. The NAACP remained the dominant civil rights group in the state throughout the civil rights era.

Quietly determined Septima Clark stood out among the small group of black schoolteachers who lost their jobs for refusing to cancel their NAACP membership. She developed techniques she had learned from Wil Lou Gray, a white woman whose incessant lobbying of legislators got her state money to develop the South Carolina Opportunity School, a boarding facility that allows young people in difficult family circumstances to continue in school.

After losing her teaching job, Clark began teaching unschooled black men and women on Johns Island to read, to write, and about citizenship. They became registered voters. She subsequently moved to the staff of the Highlander Folk School in Tennessee, a biracial center that taught interracial cooperation and community leadership skills. Clark strongly believed that many untrained individuals possessed the potential for leadership, and she displayed an uncanny knack for spotting that quality in individuals and then developing it.

While teaching on Johns Island, a spacious area that today links Kiawah Island to the mainland, Clark was driven around in 1960 by folklorist and musician Guy Carawan and his wife, Candie, recently married white civil rights activists from California. At a "praise house" on Johns Island, Guy Carawan first heard the song "We Shall Overcome." An adaptation of a gospel song, it was sung in 1945 by unionized black workers on strike at a cigar plant in Charleston. Carawan left to become musical director at Highlander, taught the song there, and it soon became the anthem of the civil rights movement. Other movement songs he first heard on Johns Island included "Ain't You Got a Right to the Tree of Life" and "Eyes on the Prize."

On Johns Island the Carawans also met Esau Jenkins, a low-key organizer of civil rights activity on the South Carolina coast. He helped administer the praise house, where during all-night church meetings held on Christmas Eve and New Year's Eve, the congregation would take turns preaching, testifying, shouting, praying, and singing, as moved by the Holy Spirit. Jenkins, who became mentor to many activists, also attended retreats at Highlander.[14] Rosa Parks, who spent time at Highlander, later credited her exposure to Clark as giving her the resolve not to surrender her seat on the bus to a white person, the act that led directly in December 1955 to the Montgomery bus boycott, from which evolved the civil rights leadership of twenty-six-year-old minister Martin Luther King Jr.

Clark became a staff member of King's Southern Christian Leadership Conference, extending the reach of her freedom schools to some forty thousand black adults across the South. She joined King on his trip to Sweden to receive his Nobel Prize. And she served on the SCLC board and executive committee, where as a woman she found her presence often resented and her ideas usually given little attention or support.

Civil rights demonstrations, which under King served in part as a strategy in the Deep South to create sufficient tension so that white leaders became willing to negotiate, occurred less frequently in South Carolina.

Marching also allowed eager students to participate in what they saw as a struggle for freedom. On March 15, 1960, 389 students at South Carolina State, wearing their best clothes, marched through Orangeburg demanding equality of treatment. They were arrested, charged with breaking the peace, placed in a stockade, and doused with fire hoses. Among those shivering, wet students was James E. "Jim" Clyburn, who forty-five years later would serve in Congress in the third-highest position of the House Democratic Caucus. That night in the stockade classmate Emily England offered to share a cheeseburger with him, the start of what would become a long married life together. When Governor Hollings learned from Newman what had happened, he called Orangeburg officials, arranging for the arrested students to be moved inside overnight and making room in the main state prison in Columbia after the Orangeburg jail filled up.

Although the NAACP remained the dominant civil rights organization in the state, protests by college students in Orangeburg and Rock Hill led more aggressive civil rights organizations—the Congress of Racial Equality (CORE) and the emerging Student Nonviolent Coordinating Committee (SNCC)—to enter South Carolina in 1961.

After leading fellow students at Claflin College and South Carolina State in Orangeburg in sit-ins that directly challenged the entrenched system of segregation by sitting down at public lunch counters that by state law served only whites, Thomas Gaither became a CORE organizer and worked in Rock Hill with Friendship Junior College students. On January 31, 1961, the anniversary of the first sit-ins by students in Greensboro, North Carolina, he and nine Friendship students targeted McCrory's—a five-and-dime store, where blacks were welcome customers, except for sitting down and buying something to eat or drink.

Police were called in, arresting the group almost immediately on charges of trespassing. Attorney—and future chief justice of the South Carolina Supreme Court—Ernest Finney drove over from Sumter to defend them, but a local judge found them guilty. After being sentenced to thirty days of hard labor or a one-hundred-dollar fine, Gaither and eight others chose jail. Gaither later recalled, "We disarmed them by using the only weapon we had left—jail without bail. It was the only practical thing we could do. It upset them quiet a bit."[15] It also launched "jail, not bail" as a new tactic in the civil rights movement.

They had prepared for imprisonment, taking their toothbrushes along to the protest. Concerned parents and grandparents, some of whom had brought money to release their children, supported them after seeing their commitment. One student said, "If requesting first-class citizenship in the South is to be regarded as a crime, then I will gladly go back to jail again."[16] The treatment the nine faced was brutal. Several of the students were kept in solitary confinement for much of the time and subsisted on bread and water. Robert McCullough, the informal leader of the group, told the *New York Times* upon his release that the experience had "served to strengthen [his] conviction that human suffering can assist social change."[17]

(Almost forty years later an effort was made to commemorate the efforts of the Friendship Nine. A historical marker was placed in front of the building housing the McCrory's, which had closed in 1997. In February 2007 a new owner reopened it as the Old Town Bistro and made a special effort to preserve the civil rights history of the building, maintaining the original lunch counter and most of the original stools where the Friendship Nine had sat. These stools today are marked with small plaques bearing the names of the student activists.)

Meanwhile a group of young SNCC activists learned of the Rock Hill protest and sent four members, two men and two women, to join their student colleagues in jail. Three of them—Diane Nash, Ruby Doris Smith, and Charles Sherrod—would play significant roles in the movement. Although the sit-ins failed to ignite a large protest movement in Rock Hill, civil rights historians have written that they provided an important model of group identity. They also generated a feeling of anger among local whites.

On May 9, 1961, a CORE-sponsored interracial group testing a Supreme Court decision outlawing discrimination in interstate transportation boarded buses in Charlotte, North Carolina, heading for Rock Hill, twenty miles away. John Lewis—a seminary student from rural Alabama, a future SNCC president, and later a senior member of Congress—was first off the bus.

He walked toward the white waiting room, where a group of young white toughs waited. One, with ducktail haircut and clad in a leather jacket, pointed to a door with a "colored" sign and snarled, "Other side, nigger."

Lewis, unafraid and trained for nonviolent protest, calmly explained his right to be there because of the Supreme Court's *Boynton* case. "Shit on that," a white youth responded. As Lewis tried entering the waiting room, he would recall, "The next thing I knew, a fist smashed the right side of my head. Then another hit me square in the face. As I fell to the floor, I could feel feet kicking me hard in the sides. I could taste blood in my mouth."[18] A large white man in the freedom rider group, a Quaker and retired navy captain, lay down on top of Lewis to protect him and was kicked and beaten. A city policeman intervened only when a white female rider was knocked down.

A state police detachment the governor had sent in to supplant local police then appeared. The chief of the state police, J. P. (Pete) Strom, surprised the three riders by asking if they wanted to press charges. They declined.

Lewis later wrote, "We didn't see these young guys that attacked us that day as the problem. We saw them as victims. The problem was much bigger ... the sanctioned system of segregation in the entire South."[19]

The state police stayed in Rock Hill until after a second bus of Freedom Riders arrived with no violence. The riders got a warm reception at a mass evening meeting at Mt. Olivet AME Zion Church. The relatively minor confrontation in Rock Hill attracted little media attention.

But the next day at Winnsboro, an unscheduled stop after finding "closed" signs on the waiting rooms at the bus station in Chester, a local policeman arrested Henry Thomas for trespass as he entered the "white" area, as well as a white companion who tried to intervene. The police released him that night and delivered him to the bus station just before it closed, with carloads of hostile white men all around. Thomas, seeing them watching, walked to the white waiting room, entered, and calmly purchased a candy bar.

As he walked out, expecting to be killed, the Reverend C. A. Ivory, a Rock Hill minister and civil rights activist asked by CORE to keep an eye on things, drove up. Thomas jumped in the car, ducked down at Ivory's command, and they sped away to meet others in the group at Sumter.

Two white companions, a man and a woman, had been left behind and quickly found themselves unwelcome. Finney and James McCain drove from Sumter, bailed the man out of jail, and all hastened back to Sumter, spending several days at rallies and meetings before moving on to confront violence in Alabama that made their South Carolina experience seem tame.

John Lewis returned to Rock Hill in January 2008, this time as a member of Congress. He spoke to a mixed black and white audience of seven hundred at the city's fifth annual Martin Luther King Jr. Interfaith Prayer Breakfast. Mayor Doug Echols introduced him—and apologized for what happened earlier. Lewis, unprepared for the apology, told a reporter afterwards that he fought an urge to cry. "It's a step toward reconciliation," he said.[20]

ALTHOUGH FRITZ HOLLINGS made strong segregationist speeches in his early political campaigns, once inaugurated as governor at age thirty-seven in January 1958, he quickly became fully acquainted with Reverend Newman, and both realized that each could work with the other. They met almost weekly. Hollings recalled, "He was always complaining, but came to understand that I was trying to protect the safety of everybody. People don't understand that these officers of the law thought they were doing their duty in arresting people who were demonstrating and marching without a permit. Over four years, DeQuincey Newman and I got to respect each other and became good friends. Once he understood, permits for planned demonstrations and marches were asked for and given. Newman was the leader."[21]

If Newman was the yin of the NAACP, lawyer Matthew Perry was the yang. He helped get the South Carolina State students released on bail the next day, but then a state judge delayed their trial for more than a year.

Perry meanwhile defended a case of hundreds of protesting young blacks arrested in 1961, while marching around the State House in Columbia with protest signs, and charged with breach of the peace. After convictions by trial judges were upheld by the S.C. Supreme Court, Perry appealed directly to the U.S. Supreme Court. There he argued and won *Edwards v. South Carolina,* which today is included in a list of historic decisions by the Supreme Court. The nation's highest court, after noting that "there was no violence or threat of violence" by the students, who sang patriotic and religious songs, held that South Carolina "infringed upon their rights of free speech, free assembly, and freedom to petition for redress of grievances," as guaranteed by the First Amendment.[22] The case represented a significant extension of First Amendment protections that later allowed civil rights marches throughout the South. It also provided the basis for Perry to get the delayed state convictions of the 389 South Carolina State students overturned by the U.S. Supreme Court.

Although South Carolina fought integration to the end through the courts, when at last a date was set in January 1963 for Harvey Gantt to break the color line and enter Clemson under court order, Hollings set the direction the state would follow in his final speech to legislature. It came four months after riots at the University of Mississippi left two dead and scores injured when James Meredith enrolled there as Governor Ross Barnett advocated defiance.

In his speech Hollings told the 170 assembled legislators: "As we meet, South Carolina is running out of courts. If and when every legal remedy has been exhausted, this General Assembly must make clear South Carolina's choice, a government of laws rather than a government of men. As determined as we are, we of today must realize the lesson of one hundred years ago, and move on for the good of South Carolina and our United States. This should be done with dignity. It must be done with law and order."[23]

Four decades later at a conference on civil rights history in South Carolina, John West—a state senator at the time Hollings spoke and who followed him as governor eight years later—called those words "the gutsiest speech I ever heard." He explained that South Carolina "could have gone either way, and Fritz provided the leadership that people followed."[24]

When the Fourth Circuit Court of Appeals ordered Gantt's admission a few weeks before the speech by Hollings, Senator Thurmond said the court order "substituted fiction for fact, and expedience for law." During the litigation process Gantt had said, "It's time we stepped out to claim some of our rights. It's not that we want to take these things to the courts, but that seems to be the only way to get anything done." He was enrolled at Iowa State University as an architectural student at the time, having gone there in 1961 because Clemson would not voluntarily admit him.[25]

A week after Hollings spoke, former University of South Carolina president Donald S. Russell set a tone at his inaugural as governor by hosting an outdoor barbecue on the grounds of the governor's mansion to which all the people of South Carolina were invited. Days later Gantt—a first-rate student with an outgoing personality—enrolled at Clemson. Despite some threats that state police intercepted and treated seriously, there was no federal intervention and no violence. He initially faced hostility on the campus, but it gradually faded. The *Saturday Evening Post*, then a major national magazine, published an article about Gantt at Clemson titled "Integration with Dignity."

8

POLITICS OF TRANSITION

In preparing the state for the breaking of the color line, Hollings set a new direction for South Carolina, a clear break with the past. An important period of political transition, however, had preceded him, beginning with Lieutenant Colonel James Strom Thurmond returning home from World War II focused on a single goal: running for governor in the 1946 Democratic primary, the only election that then mattered.

It was still the one-party, Democratic "solid South" that had emerged from the Compromise of 1877. The Republican Party remained essentially a paper organization in the state, sending delegates to the party's national convention and distributing patronage during Republican administrations. Thurmond, who on D day had gone in behind German lines aboard a glider that crash-landed beyond the beaches of Normandy, projected the image of a vigorous war hero. A former state senator and circuit court judge, he was elected as a forty-three-year-old progressive Democratic New Dealer. In his campaign he displayed the relentless, focused energy and combative political instinct that would make him twentieth-century America's most enduring political figure.

His inaugural speech, written by erudite Charleston lawyer and Thurmond confidante Robert Figg, outlined an expansive program aimed at a progressive future. It called for industrial development, repeal of the poll tax, and improved education for blacks and whites. Thurmond broke tradition by appointing a black physician to a state advisory board and calling for an end to the poll tax. John Gunther, in his 1947 book *Inside U.S.A.*, referred to Thurmond as "the liberal governor" of South Carolina.

As a radio panelist in Kentucky in early October 1947, Thurmond had asserted, "We who believe in a liberal political philosophy, in the importance of human rights as well as property rights, in the preservation and strengthening of the economic and social gains brought about by the efforts of the Democratic Party . . . will vote for the election of Harry Truman and the restoration of Congress to the control of the Democratic Party, and I believe we will win."[1]

Before the end of that month, the President's Committee on Civil Rights issued its report, *To Secure These Rights*. It called for legislation against lynching, for ending discrimination in employment, and for strengthening the civil rights division in the Justice Department. Historically and politically, its recommendations amounted to undoing the Compromise of 1877.

In his classic study *Southern Politics in State and Nation* (1949), political scientist V. O. Key Jr. subtitled his chapter on South Carolina "The Politics of Color." He wrote, "South Carolina's preoccupation with the Negro stifles political conflict. Over offices there is conflict a plenty, but the race question muffles conflict over issues latent in the economy of South Carolina. Mill worker and plantation owner alike want to keep the Negro in his place. In part issues are deliberately repressed, for, at least in the long run, concern with genuine issues would bring an end to the consensus by which the Negro is kept out of politics. One crowd or another would be tempted to seek his vote."[2]

Even as Key was writing, however, a new politics for the state already was being ordained by the confluence of U.S. District Judge J. Waties Waring's decree ending the white primary and by Governor Thurmond's 1948 Dixiecrat campaign, a psychological body blow in dislodging the state's seven-decade allegiance to the Democratic Party.

Civil rights became the central issue in 1948. President Harry S. Truman made proposals in the spring, which the Democratic platform reinforced that summer with an expansive plank on civil rights that urged an end to discrimination in employment and voting. Motivated politically—his eye was on 1950 and the Senate seat held by Olin D. Johnston—and also by what he, as a racial paternalist, saw as a challenge to southern honor, Thurmond responded to the civil rights initiatives of the national party by reversing course politically and accepting the Dixiecrat nomination for president.

In his acceptance speech in Birmingham, Alabama, Thurmond breathed defiance. Building on language he had used in a May speech in Jackson, Mississippi, he jabbed his right index finger at the crowd to emphasize each point and declared, "I want to tell you, ladies and gentlemen, that there's not enough troops in the army to force the Southern people to break down segregation and admit the Nigra' race into our theaters, into our swimming pools, into our homes, and into our churches."[3] As the cheering crowd whooped it up, a group of student delegates from the University of Mississippi paraded with large

States' Rights Democrats. J. Strom Thurmond led the 1948 States' Rights Democratic ticket in response to President Truman's civil rights initiatives. Here he and his running mate, Fielding L. Wright of Mississippi, appear as the standard bearers for what became known as the Dixiecrats. *History of South Carolina Slide Collection*, B-187

Confederate battle flags. Nevertheless, Thurmond forever denied running a racist campaign.

He carried the four states that listed him on the ballot as the official candidate of the Democratic Party: Alabama, Louisiana, Mississippi, and South Carolina. Those states gave him thirty-eight electoral votes, and he picked up a thirty-ninth from an elector in Tennessee.

The impact of the Dixiecrat campaign was that it aroused white emotions about race and broke loose the psychological moorings that tied the Deep South to the national Democratic Party. As Thurmond said, the South was "no longer in the bag."

In becoming the region's champion in defending segregation, Thurmond had anticipated a political momentum that would carry him into the U.S. Senate. But in the 1950 "campaign of the century," Senator Johnston turned back Thurmond's attempt to unseat him. The emerging, newly enfranchised black electorate voted solidly against Thurmond and provided Johnston's margin of victory. For example, Johnston carried the almost all-black Ward 9 in Columbia, 1,249 votes to 72. As Modjeska Simkins put it, "Strom vilified Negroes in 1948 . . . and we swore vengeance."[4] They accepted New Dealer Johnston's need

Modjeska Monteith Simkins. One of South Carolina's most important civil rights figures, Simkins worked as an outspoken activist in Columbia for more than sixty years. Her portrait hangs in the State House. *History of South Carolina Slide Collection*, C-134

to hold the support of working-class whites with racial rhetoric that fully matched Thurmond's segregationist image.

Thurmond would return four years later, however, to win an unprecedented write-in campaign for the Senate to fill a seat vacated by the unexpected death of Senator Maybank. Technically under state law the state Democratic Executive Committee appointed an alternate candidate if a party nominee died, and the deadline for certifying the party candidate was 5 P.M. on the day of Maybank's funeral in Charleston. The executive committee picked state senator and Democratic National Committee member Edgar A. Brown of Barnwell, the legislature's most powerful figure as Finance Committee chairman and twice before an unsuccessful candidate for the Senate.

In this case the vacancy to be filled was no minor office but, because of the Democratic Party's dominance, a full term in the U.S. Senate without a vote by the people. Thurmond received important support for his write-in candidacy from Governor James F. Byrnes, the state's most influential national political figure since John C. Calhoun, and he pledged to resign after two years so the people could vote. Thurmond won the write-in election and received 90 percent of the vote in the election two years later.

The three most dominant political figures of twentieth-century South Carolina, James F. Byrnes (with his wife, Maude), Lt. Gov. Ernest F. "Fritz" Hollings, and U.S. Sen. J. Strom Thurmond, 1955. Courtesy of Ernest Hollings's personal collection

Byrnes had returned to South Carolina after resigning as secretary of state in January 1947 following a period of growing tension between him and President Truman. The president named General George Marshall as Byrnes's successor. Byrnes and his wife, Maude, returned to Spartanburg, living in semiretirement while he returned as needed to Washington as the well-paid associate of a prominent law firm and represented Hollywood film studios in the appellate courts.

In response to Truman's Fair Deal proposals for national health insurance, expanded unemployment benefits, increased deficit spending, and larger public subsidies, the fiscally conservative Byrnes made a public break in 1949 with the president. Byrnes had become embittered with both Truman and the national Democratic Party and soon moved to develop opposition support in the South. In a speech that fall at the Southern Governors Conference in Biloxi, Mississippi, he attacked Truman's policies and urged the region's governors to "perform a great public service" by "standing together and fighting" for a greater role in spending federal tax dollars.[5]

The politically sophisticated Byrnes saw the possibility of the South wielding the balance of power between the two political parties. He saw himself as a leader who could make real Calhoun's complex theory of the concurrent majority, with the South counterbalancing the New Deal liberals. If Byrnes planted the seed, however, in the end it would be Thurmond who played the key role in transforming the party of Lincoln and in making the South a region of Republican dominance at the end of the twentieth century.

Much as Calhoun had deferred to a society devoted to the dying institution of slavery after returning to the state when his national ambitions failed, Byrnes too sought to protect the racial status quo after his return. With his prestige, international exposure, and Washington experience at the highest echelons of all three branches of the national government, one scholar of the twentieth-century American South says, "No one was better placed to lead South Carolina into a realistic acceptance of racial change." Instead he took the lead "in masterminding the region's resistance to racial change."[6]

Encouraged by South Carolina House Speaker Solomon Blatt and others to run for governor in 1950, Byrnes won in a campaign that was more coronation than contest, riding around the state in a chauffeured car while Thurmond and Johnston slugged it out at stump meetings in every county. Byrnes was the only person ever to serve in both houses of Congress, a presidential cabinet, the Supreme Court, and as governor. A statue dedicated to him on the State House grounds in May 1972, shortly after his death, includes an inscription, "The most distinguished South Carolinian of his time."

In his inaugural address as governor in 1951, Byrnes urged a 3 percent sales tax "to provide for the races substantial equality in school facilities. We should do it because it is right. For me, that is sufficient reason." He added, "If any person wants an additional reason, I say it is wise."[7]

Byrnes clearly had in mind the legal questions already being raised from Clarendon County. *Briggs v. Elliott* was tried in December 1950 before a special three-judge federal district court in Charleston. With his school equalization program, Byrnes sought to provide a regional model to protect the system of racial segregation under the "separate but equal" doctrine the Supreme Court had set forth in 1898 in *Plessy v. Ferguson*.

In the Clarendon County case, Chief Judge John J. Parker of the Fourth Circuit Court of Appeals and District Judge George Bell Timmerman Sr. accepted the Byrnes equalization program as meeting the requirements of the Constitution. But Judge Waring dissented, calling segregated schools per se unconstitutional.

Waring soon retired from the bench and moved to New York with his second wife, a divorced "Yankee" woman who had publicly disparaged southern segregationists. She showed her disdain for contemporary white southern social mores by entertaining blacks in her home on lower Meeting Street. The Warings were scorned by people in white Charleston, especially after Elizabeth Waring spoke at the black YWCA and described southern whites as "sick, confused, and decadent people."[8] When lightning struck a house next door to the judge's beach cottage on Sullivan's Island, the owner put up a sign that read "Dear God, he lives next door."[9] Less decorous forms of local appreciation for the Warings included hurling rocks through their front window, burning a cross in their yard, and subjecting them to threatening mail and phone calls.

In the 1952 presidential campaign, Byrnes shocked the state's Democratic establishment by inviting Republican candidate and World War II hero Dwight D. Eisenhower and introducing him at a huge State House rally. Byrnes showed the state's expanding white middle class that it was now all right to vote for a Republican. Eisenhower received 49 percent of the vote, barely losing South Carolina to Democrat Adlai Stevenson.

Stevenson carried South Carolina again in 1956, but with only a plurality after Byrnes, disappointed with Eisenhower's selection of Chief Justice Earl Warren and the outcome of *Brown v. Board of Education*, helped organize a group that got conservative Virginia senator Harry F. Byrd Sr. on the ballot as a petition candidate. He split the anti-Democratic vote with Eisenhower. Stevenson received 136,372 votes, less than the combined vote of 88,509 for Byrd and 75,500 for Eisenhower under the Republican label.

Byrnes, in his final year as governor, was disappointed with the Supreme Court's decision in *Brown. v. Board of Education*. But warnings by him and others that immediate school integration would result in violence, all contributed to the 1955 implementation order (known as *Brown II*) to proceed with "all deliberate speed." Political leaders in the South considered it a victory.

Byrnes met and corresponded behind the scenes with other southern governors to develop a strategy to thwart the implementation of *Brown*. That strategy included challenging its implementation in local courts and setting up church-sponsored schools for students encouraged to withdraw from public schools, part of a larger program across the South of "massive resistance."[10]

After the Supreme Court sent *Briggs v. Elliott* back down to South Carolina, Chief Judge Parker of the Fourth Circuit Court of Appeals, a North Carolinian who had accepted South Carolina's school equalization program earlier, now wrote in 1955 that the Constitution "does not require integration.

It merely forbids segregation."[11] A decade later the Clarendon County school district remained totally segregated. In Parker's North Carolina the state passed a "pupil placement" act and a "freedom of choice" school attendance option that resulted in a handful of top-performing black students enrolling in previously all-white schools while all-black schools in the state remained totally segregated.

The Supreme Court, however, held firm in the 1957 Little Rock school integration crisis, where President Eisenhower sent in federal troops to enforce a federal court order. (Ultimately the Supreme Court accepted rulings in the late 1960s by Eisenhower-appointed federal judges on the Fifth Circuit Court of Appeals, then stretching across six former Confederate states from Georgia to Texas, that overturned Judge Parker's "*Briggs* dictum." Determining at last that the time for deliberate speed had ended, the Supreme Court in 1970 issued an order leading to massive and immediate school desegregation in the South.[12])

After Byrnes, colorless two-term lieutenant governor George Bell Timmerman Jr. was elected governor in 1954, and South Carolina moved toward massive resistance after the *Brown* decision. A quiet and committed segregationist, Timmerman joined with state senator L. Marion Gressette, who chaired a fifteen-member committee charged with defending segregation, in passing a legislative package that included deleting the constitutional mandate for a public school system in the state and repealing the state's compulsory school attendance law. Another provision, cast in deliberately race-neutral language, called for an end to state funding both for any state-supported college to which a student was admitted under federal court order and for all-black South Carolina State College. Gantt's admission to Clemson, however, effectively marked the end of South Carolina's period of massive resistance.

9

A NEW ERA EVOLVES

Few political figures anywhere could match the depth and quickness of mind, tartness of tongue, and innovative outlook that made Fritz Hollings a transitional figure for South Carolina. In preparing the state for the breaking of the color line, Hollings set a new direction, a clean break with the past. He already had moved the state on a new path of economic development.

Elected lieutenant governor at the age of thirty-two, he won election as governor four years later in 1958 in a brutal campaign against Donald S. Russell, a political novice and Byrnes's protégé who in many ways had served as a dynamic president of the University of South Carolina. Hollings believed political necessity forced him, as it had Olin Johnston in his race against Thurmond eight years earlier, to engage in racial rhetoric as a defender of segregation (he had declared the NAACP "both subversive and illegal.")

By the time Harvey Gantt enrolled at Clemson as the Hollings administration ended, however, the youthful governor had served as a creative leader in moving the state forward on an innovative two-pronged path of industrial development that continues into the twenty-first century. In preparing the way for Gantt at Clemson, Hollings fully understood that acceptance of social change without violence played an essential role in luring outside capital to invest in the state. He also never forgot an incident in his World War II military experience, seeing black American soldiers going to the rear of a restaurant in the South to get food from a window while German prisoners of war sat inside eating at a table and thinking to himself, "That ain't right."[1]

To understand fully the significance of the crucial, final speech Hollings made to the legislature calling for acceptance of the federal court order to integrate Clemson, understand that it occurred the same month that Alabama's newly elected governor, George C. Wallace, established himself as the South's new champion of segregation. In his inaugural address that January, Wallace declared to the people of his state, "I draw the line in the dust and toss the gauntlet before the feet of tyranny, and I say . . . segregation now . . . segregation tomorrow . . . segregation forever."[2]

IN SEEKING ECONOMIC DEVELOPMENT Hollings became the first southern governor to go abroad and personally court overseas corporations to invest in the American South. And he got results, setting an example many other southern governors would begin to follow. Hollings moved at the same time to create and develop a broad system of post–high school technical and vocational education. One component involved the state picking up expenses— even if it meant paying salaries for the new company's training staff—to provide a trained workforce ready to start work when a new plant opened. A willing, inexpensive, and trained workforce, in combination with cheap land and cooperative state and local government officials, proved attractive to new industries.

Hollings picked progressive legislative leaders such as future governors Robert E. McNair and John C. West to look at pioneering new programs in North Carolina and to propose a more innovative plan for South Carolina. The legislative group reported the state's 50 percent school dropout rate and low percentage of college graduates—they represented fewer than 5 percent of their first-grade classes. A greatly expanded technical-vocational training program, however, would soon provide South Carolina workers more marketable skills that would attract new industry.[3]

Hollings understood from experience in the legislature that the institutional weakness of the office of governor left him with little more than the power of persuasion. He made the most of that power. To get state funds and launch the technical education program for the state, for example, Hollings visited Edgar Brown in his Columbia hotel room one evening early in the 1961 legislative session. The governor delivered a fifth of bourbon.

After coaxing, cajoling, and pleading his case with the kingpin of the powerful S.C. Senate, a man shaped by the experience of the Depression and committed to protecting the state's money as if it were his own, the evening ended with an empty bottle and an agreement for a one-paragraph insertion to the state appropriations bill that would go to the printer the next morning. Perhaps because of the bourbon, the two men failed to include terms of service for members of the board that would direct the new agency. The initial appointees served permanently for more than a decade until the agency was merged into a new administrative body.

With the state paying all costs for recruiting and training a workforce, it meant then and it still means that new manufacturing plants could open with virtually no "start-up loss time." Hollings hired North Carolina's technical education director, Wade Martin, by promising him authority to decide on objective appraisal of need in terms of the locations of technical education centers throughout the state—without political interference. Today the technical education centers double as a junior college system that provides core academic courses for college credit, as well as training students as nurses, dental technicians, and data processors and for other vocational careers.

Hollings also lured Walter Harper, a skilled and experienced industrial recruiter, from North Carolina. The governor then moved his office out of the State House and next door to Harper's in a nearby state office building. The youthful governor also found, two blocks away at the University of South Carolina, School of Business dean James A. Morris, an articulate and sophisticated Harvard-trained economist who would enhance Hollings's understanding of the concept of overhead socialization of capital. Hollings quickly grasped the direct relationship between state expenditures for public education at all levels and economic growth and development. And he possessed the political skill to transform ideas into reality.

In addition he intuitively grasped the quest for stability that had emerged as a central theme in his native state in reaction to the internalized memory of the disastrous path that had flowed a century earlier from the impulsive action that had led first to secession and then to ruin. In the summer of 1962, weeks before riots exploded at the University of Mississippi when its first black student enrolled, South Carolinians demonstrated in choosing Donald Russell as their next governor that they had learned the lesson that acts of defiance have consequences.

In the Democratic primary (Republicans that year for the last time fielded no opposition for statewide office), state representative A. W. "Red" Bethea, hoping to create a runoff that would empower him as a broker, voiced rhetoric for defiance that paralleled Wallace's in Alabama. But Bethea, already twice a competitive statewide candidate for commissioner of agriculture, received only 7 percent of the vote. Russell, a man of first-rate intellect who later became a federal appeals court judge, gave lip service to segregation, saying the state should select the best legal mind to deal with the problem. Voters elected him with a 62 percent landslide, twice the votes received by the outgoing lieutenant governor, Burnet Maybank Jr.

In that same primary Senator Olin Johnston turned back a challenge from Hollings, who had antagonized much of the state's white electorate by campaigning actively and decisively in the state for liberal Democrat John F. Kennedy in his 1960 presidential election. When Lyndon Johnson was elected to a full term as president in 1964, Olin Johnston actively supported his Great Society programs.

Russell, who presided over Gantt's actual admission to Clemson a few days after Hollings's speech to the legislature, made the central social event of his inaugural a barbecue on the grounds of the governor's mansion, then located on the edge of a low-income black neighborhood in Columbia. "All of the people of South Carolina" were invited. Some eight thousand people turned out, ranging from black maids clad in housedresses to society matrons in furs. Russell understood that the South's complex racial etiquette at that time allowed people of both races to stand and eat together comfortably, but a sitting meal would have been a violation. The event's symbolism spoke loudly.

In 1964, after ten years as a rambunctious and reactionary Democrat following his write-in campaign, Senator Strom Thurmond (he had dropped the J.) moved his Dixiecrat followers into the mainstream of the Republican Party. He dramatically switched his party affiliation to endorse and support conservative Arizona senator Barry Goldwater for president.

Three years earlier, before a group of southern Republican leaders meeting in Atlanta, Goldwater asserted, "We're not going to get the Negro vote as a bloc in 1964 or 1968, so we ought to go hunting where the ducks are." He then spelled it out, saying that school integration "was the responsibility of the states. I would not like to see my party assume it is the role of the federal government to enforce integration in the schools."[4]

With that preface Goldwater's campaign and Thurmond's subsequent switch launched the race-based Republican "southern strategy," which in more muted form would continue to influence the GOP image into the twenty-first century in South Carolina. Thurmond's switch came after Goldwater voted against the landmark 1964 Civil Rights Act, which Thurmond called "the worst, most unreasonable and unconstitutional legislation that has ever been considered by the Congress."[5] (He expressed similar opposition the next year to the Voting Rights Act, which removed the barriers to full black participation as voters.)

Congressman Albert Watson, unopposed as a Democrat in his congressional race in 1964, joined Thurmond in campaigning for Goldwater. Watson turned Republican early in 1965 after Democrats stripped him of his two years of seniority. He boldly resigned from Congress and then won back his seat in a special election with 70 percent of the vote against a credible opponent.

Aside from his native Arizona, Goldwater won only in the four states Thurmond carried as a Dixiecrat and in Georgia, attracting the most racially conscious white southerners. He won with 59 percent of the vote in South Carolina (in Mississippi, where statewide black voter registration remained less than twenty thousand, Goldwater received 87 percent). Goldwater's appeal went beyond race, however, to include a smaller role for the federal government and emphatic support for a strong military as well as outspoken opposition to Communism in the midst of the cold war—all positions that Thurmond also shared.

The state's political landscape at the national level soon consolidated. When Senator Johnston died in 1965, Russell resigned, partly at the instigation of President Johnson, to become senator. Lieutenant Governor McNair took the formal oath to succeed Russell as governor and then immediately appointed Russell to the Senate vacancy. With "self-appointment" an issue in a special election in 1966 for the remaining two years of the Johnston term, Hollings defeated Russell in the Democratic primary, but in November narrowly survived a challenge from state senator Marshall Parker as the Republican nominee, a signal of the GOP's emerging strength in state politics.

Hollings overwhelmingly won reelection in 1968, and for the remainder of the twentieth century he and Thurmond accumulated seniority and power in Washington. They represented opposite sides of the coin of political change, with someone always able to bring home the bacon to South Carolina regardless of which party occupied the White House.

During these years of swirling change in the South, new forces were transforming politics in South Carolina. They left dead or dying the three dominant characteristics that had prevailed since Reconstruction: one-party politics designed to unify the white man against the black; the policy and practice of excluding blacks from effective political participation; and a reaction to the perceived waste, graft, and mismanagement of Reconstruction that had manifested itself as a reaction against social legislation. From Wade Hampton onward, it had been accepted as an article of faith among South Carolina political leaders that the least expensive government was the best government.

The 1964 Civil Rights Act and 1965 Voting Rights Act transformed life in the American South. The Civil Rights Act outlawed discrimination in employment and public accommodations, and it provided the framework for genuine school desegregation. Profound change followed in South Carolina with a minimum of turmoil, reflecting the power of the rule of law. As behavior changed, a change in attitudes followed. Racism by no means disappeared, but it significantly diminished as new forms of understanding developed. Although a significantly expanded black middle class emerged, widespread black poverty remained, but became less visible.

The forces of progress, however, generated a counterforce of reaction that manifested itself with the rise of the Republican Party (see chapter 11). As McNair took office as governor in April 1965, change was in the air. He had spent fifteen years as legislator and lieutenant governor, showed keen political instincts as a results-oriented pragmatist, and moved along the path that Hollings and Russell had set. A poll during his 1966 campaign for governor showed voters more concerned about race than any other issue, but with whites and blacks both basically moderate. Forty-two percent of the whites and 49 percent of the blacks considered the pace of integration in South Carolina "about right," but 57 percent of the whites believed it too fast and 48 percent of the blacks too slow. Whites essentially wanted to go no farther but were realistic enough to know they could not turn back.

A series of events reflected the turmoil of the time. In dealing with five major racial confrontations, McNair demonstrated strong, responsible, and effective leadership and communications skills in all but one: the tragic Orangeburg Massacre.

At 10:33 P.M. on February 8, 1968, an eight- to ten-second fusillade of gunfire by state highway patrolmen—who had been issued deadly buckshot for a crowd control situation on the campus of the historically black South Carolina State College campus—left three students dying and at least twenty-eight others with gunshot wounds. This tragedy, the first of its kind on any American college campus, preceded by more than two years the killing of four students by Ohio National Guardsmen at Kent State University.

Unlike Kent State, national media barely covered what happened at Orangeburg. The shooting occurred at night with no vivid TV images, the students were black, and press attention had shifted to growing protests against the war in Vietnam and from civil rights to urban riots outside the South. Harvard University social psychologist Thomas F. Pettigrew interpreted the civil rights riots, frightening to white America as a whole, as a reaction to the twin forces of rising expectations and relative deprivation.[6]

Less than a year earlier McNair had responded to a student protest and class boycott at South Carolina State by getting information from numerous sources. He met with student leaders, listened to their grievances, and appointed a blue-ribbon committee that investigated and made recommendations for reform. McNair led in implementing almost all of them.

In 1968, however, during a week of escalating racial tension over efforts led by State students to desegregate Orangeburg's only bowling alley, McNair communicated almost exclusively in Orangeburg with police at the scene, primarily Chief J. P. "Pete" Strom of the South Carolina State Law Enforcement Division (SLED). The governor also urged the U.S. Department of Justice to get an expeditious ruling in federal court as to whether the bowling alley was covered under the Civil Rights Act of 1964, which widely outlawed discrimination in public accommodations.

The mood of the nation had changed in response to the urban riots. McNair, whose father had been a deputy sheriff as well as a farmer in Berkeley County, had attended national conferences regarding such violence. He returned determined that any such outbreaks in South Carolina would be met with force.

The shooting climaxed the third night of turmoil that began when violence erupted between students and police wielding riot batons in a shopping center parking lot outside the bowling alley. A police officer and nine clubbed students, including two females, were hospitalized. The two young women were each held by one patrolman while beaten by another. Other injured students remained overnight in the college infirmary.

The beating of the young women especially enraged others students, who returned to the campus, breaking store windows and damaging automobiles along the five-block route. Total damage, based on insurance claims, was less than five thousand dollars. Although bowling never stopped inside the bowling alley that night, the state responded as if to a major urban riot.

McNair received state police reports based on input from the FBI and army intelligence that led him to believe the turmoil was part of a national Black Power movement masterminded by Cleveland Sellers. A soft-spoken veteran civil rights activist in Mississippi and Alabama and a national officer in the fading Student Nonviolent Coordinating Committee (SNCC), he had returned to his native South Carolina with a specific mission. He actively opposed the Vietnam War, and in Orangeburg he sought to develop "Black Awareness" among students. That effort was part of his pioneering effort to develop programs in African American studies in higher education. The FBI kept him under close surveillance.

Sellers had never focused on the local issue of the bowling alley, whose refusal to admit black bowlers had been a sore point in Orangeburg for years in the black community. He learned of the confrontation while visiting an antiwar coffeehouse in Columbia, forty-five miles away, and returned immediately to Orangeburg to observe what was happening. Jack Bass and Jack

Nelson's *The Orangeburg Massacre* (1970) details the limited role of Sellers, who received a gunshot wound, and the injustice of his subsequent conviction and imprisonment for riot.

Unlike the year before, McNair never met with students or even conferred during the crisis with the college's acting president, M. Maceo Nance. Two nights after the violent fracas outside the bowling alley, the jittery small city was armed to the teeth, with rumors flying that it would be burned. For a second night angry and frustrated students threw rocks and bottles at passing cars and taunted police from near the edge of the campus. They lit a bonfire on an adjacent street, feeding it with banister rails and window shutters from an unoccupied house. A fire truck was ordered to the scene.

Sixty-six highway patrolmen and some city police were ordered to move up to protect the firemen. Students retreated to the campus interior. As police advanced onto the edge of the campus, behind an embankment, one was struck in the face by a retreating student's tossed wooden banister rail and knocked to the ground, bleeding. Some thought he had been shot.

As students who had retreated to the campus interior moved forward to watch the dousing of the bonfire, some shouted epithets and a few threw objects. Some patrolmen shouldered their weapons as tension built. As the students grew near, one officer fired his carbine two or three times in the air, intending them as warning shots.[7] Others, hearing gunfire, began firing riot guns (short-barrel shotguns defined as weapons to disperse a crowd or mob and not intended to maim or kill) loaded with lethal buckshot. Each double-ought shotgun shell contained nine to twelve pellets the size of a .38 caliber pistol slug. One patrolman fired six shots from his .38 Colt police special. Of the more than thirty students shot, at least twenty-eight received bullet wounds from the side or rear, some in the soles of their feet while diving for cover. Despite an initial Associated Press report of an exchange of gunfire, no evidence of gunfire from the students at the time of the police gunfire ever surfaced. No order to shoot was given.

The morning after the shooting, McNair held a press conference where he expressed concern about the state's image. He called it "one of the saddest days in the history of South Carolina. The years of work and understanding have been shattered by this unfortunate incident at Orangeburg." He reported incorrectly at a press conference that the shooting occurred off the campus and included three other factual inaccuracies. His information apparently came from state police. He blamed the shootings on "black power advocates."[8]

The tragedy at Orangeburg created a wave of bitterness among black South Carolinians, reminding them of earlier violence their race had suffered.

Reverend Newman, the great conciliator in civil rights, observed in an unguarded moment, "The fact that such a thing could happen and did happen is an indication that despite all that might be considered progress in terms of interracial cooperation, beneath the surface South Carolina is just about in the same boat as Alabama and Mississippi."[9]

At the raucous Democratic National Convention in Chicago in 1968, McNair, as chairman of both the Southern Governors Conference and the National Democratic Governors Conference, was considered a finalist to become Vice President Hubert Humphrey's running mate. He maneuvered to include six black delegates with a half vote each and an equal number of black alternates, the first integrated South Carolina delegation to a national Democratic convention. It was the only Deep South delegation that went unchallenged. At the state convention, blacks already were approaching proportional representation.

An incident at the 1968 convention illustrates the change in South Carolina Democratic Party politics. One afternoon there was an unscheduled delay as the South Carolina delegation was waiting for a visit from Humphrey. He was running more than an hour behind schedule.

In a spontaneous move Newman arose slowly and suggested that the state's national committeeman, eighty-year-old state senator Edgar A. Brown, say a few words. Brown had attended every national convention since 1924, and the suggestion drew hearty applause.

Rev. I. DeQuincey Newman (right) was one of South Carolina's most important civil rights figures as South Carolina field secretary for the National Association for the Advancement of Colored People (NAACP) from 1958 to 1970. He played a key role in ending South Carolina's Jim Crow laws. He later became the first black state senator since Reconstruction. *History of South Carolina Slide Collection*, B-212

For Newman, the veteran South Carolina NAACP leader, this convention was his first as a delegate since 1956—and it was the Republican National Convention he had attended that year. "I've perhaps known Senator Brown longer than most of you," Newman said in his soft voice. "I remember shining his shoes at a barber shop in Kingstree the first time he ran for the United States Senate." That was in 1926. Now they were fellow delegates. It was quite a change. Newman smiled slightly, then recalled how as a thirteen-year-old he had followed Brown around Kingstree and how Brown had purchased a gray fedora in a local store. "The purchase probably was intended to win favor from voters in Kingstree," Newman deadpanned, "but it didn't help much."

Brown chuckled heartily and then entertained delegates with memories of the 1924 convention, where his fistfight with a Pennsylvania delegate in the platform committee was broken up by William Jennings Bryan. After awhile Brown looked over at Newman, couldn't decide how to address him, and finally blurted out, "I. D., do they call you preacher or reverend?"

Newman replied gently, "Well, Senator, in polite company, I couldn't say what . . ."

Laughter filled the room and cut him off, and a smiling Brown nodded his head and declared, "Yes, I've been called some of that, too."

The smuggest smile in the room came from a state official who knew that one afternoon a few years earlier Edgar Brown had to be physically restrained in his law office in Barnwell from going out with his cane into the street after Newman, who was leading a voter registration drive and street demonstration against registration procedures in Barnwell County.[10]

Humphrey arrived, made a standard campaign pitch, and rushed to his next meeting. He had visited South Carolina the year before and came away impressed with McNair and the state's progress in race relations and economic development.

Before his departure for Chicago, McNair staffers in Columbia had packed several cartons of brochures to distribute if he became Humphrey's vice presidential running mate.[11] But after Humphrey's nomination, one of his aides asked the state NAACP president, the Reverend A. W. Holman, if he could actively campaign for McNair. He replied, "No. . . . Were it not for Orangeburg, I would have supported him. Afterwards, I could not in good conscience ask other Negroes to do so." He said later, "I'm positive it was the death blow to his chances to get the nomination."[12]

Nine patrolmen were tried the next year by the Department of Justice on charges of imposing summary punishment without due process of law, a civil rights violation. All were acquitted.

At the same time, Cleveland Sellers, who was among those shot by patrol gunfire, was convicted in 1970 of rioting and imprisoned for seven months. At his trial, after ten prosecution witnesses all failed to link Sellers with the events of February 8 in any way except for being shot that night, Judge John Grimball directed a verdict of acquittal on the charges of conspiracy to riot and incitement to riot. "Nobody here has ever put the defendant into the area of rioting on Wednesday or Thursday [the night of the shooting] with the exception that he was wounded and that to my mind means very little," Grimball said.[13]

He let stand the charge of riot for activity on Tuesday night in front of the bowling alley after former Orangeburg police chief Roger Poston testified he saw Sellers "move from group to group" in front of the bowling alley and that the groups became more agitated after he moved away. Poston added, however, that he heard nothing that Sellers said and saw him commit no illegal or disorderly acts.[14] When asked on cross-examination if Sellers was not in fact peaceful and orderly, Poston replied, "As far I could tell."

Sellers later explained that he would go from group to group to ask what was going on, that they quieted down to tell him, and then became vocal again when he moved away. He was sentenced to a year in prison, was released five months early for good behavior, and upon his release was referred to as a political prisoner by the director of the state Department of Corrections.

In 1993, after having returned to South Carolina with a master's degree from Harvard and Ph.D. from the University of North Carolina at Greensboro, he received a pardon from the state Probation, Parole and Pardon Board and soon joined the faculty of the University of South Carolina. He became director there of the African American Studies Program. Forty years after the shooting, Sellers became the president of historically black Voorhees College, an Episcopal-affiliated school in Denmark, South Carolina. In 2006 his younger son, Bakari, was elected to the South Carolina House of Representatives.

McNair rarely spoke about Orangeburg, but tense racial events in the final years of his administration indicated he had learned from it.

In Charleston in 1969, striking hospital workers seeking union representation linked organized labor and civil rights in a one-hundred-day strike that attracted national attention. A year after the assassination of Martin Luther King Jr., the Charleston crisis marked the last major victory for his Southern Christian Leadership Conference. At one point his widow, Coretta Scott King, and his top aide, Andrew Young, led a downtown march that fourteen thousand people joined. The city's police chief walked at the front of the group as a symbol against violence.

McNair became actively engaged. Late in the strike negotiations, Charleston banker Hugh Lane set up meetings between McNair and William "Bill" Saunders, an aggressive black leader groomed by Esau Jenkins. Saunders had helped organize the workers and was the one man that local black militants trusted. Lane had served with Saunders on the biracial Charleston Community Relations Council. McNair met with him twice. (Saunders, who grew up in deep poverty on Johns Island near Charleston and at fifteen served in the U.S. Army in the Korean War, later founded the Committee on Better Racial Assurance [COBRA]. He also served as Charleston County Democratic Party chairman and became a member of the state Public Service Commission.)

Saunders had been critical of McNair as insensitive to black people's demands for justice and dignity because of McNair's initial, hard-line anti-union position and had also viewed him as the perpetrator of the Orangeburg Massacre. By the end of the strike, however, Saunders said, "I found out he's not the biggest son of a bitch after all; he's about as fair as you can expect from anyone in that kind of business."[15]

The turmoil resulted in nine hundred arrests, the mobilization of five thousand National Guardsmen, support for the strikers from the AFL-CIO, and the ultimate threat of closing the Port of Charleston by the state's most powerful labor union, the longshoremen, along with the unstated threat of closing other ports on the East Coast.

In the end a crucial call came to the governor's office from White House aide Harry Dent, former top staffer for Senator Thurmond. His message amounted to an ultimatum from the White House: get the strike settled. The strike ended with the Medical University of South Carolina reluctantly backing down. The three hundred or so black workers, almost all women, considered it a victory.

The final settlement occurred on the hundredth day, after behind-the-scenes negotiations between the SCLC's Young and the just-arrived vice president of MUSC, James Colbert. (Colbert's son Stephen made the disclosure in January 2008 with Young on his Comedy Central program, *The Colbert Report*.) Rosetta Simmons, who chaired a negotiating committee at the Charleston County Hospital, said at a meeting three weeks later at which settlement terms were announced to end the strike there, "It has accomplished a lot for the poor people of the city. . . . We are returning to work with a relation of mutual respect and dignity."[16]

Another notable aspect of the strike was the quiet role played by Jim Clyburn, a young schoolteacher who had become director of the South Carolina Commission of Farm Workers, in negotiating the final settlement. At a commemoration of the strike thirty-eight years later, at which Clyburn—then serving as Democratic majority whip in the U.S. House—presided, he said his role in the hospital strike started his political career. Also attending that reunion of participants in 2007 was veteran state senator Robert Ford, who as a twenty-one-year-old organizer for SCLC had been called in to work in the strike, his first visit to Charleston.

Twenty-two-year-old Edrena Johnson had written in her diary while in jail on April 25, 1969, one of roughly a hundred people arrested that day with Dr. King's colleague, the Reverend Ralph David Abernathy, "We, the black people of South Carolina, will no longer sit back and be counted. We're going to stand up for what is right because we're soul from our hearts and soul power is where it's at." After returning to classes as a job trainee, she added, "Well, our nights in jail are over and I don't want to see the inside of a jail again, but if need be I shall go if this is what has to be a part in getting what we want. A little advice from one so young: share what little you have and the greatest joy shall be your victory."[17]

Three days after final ending of the strike, the *Charleston Evening Post* told its predominantly white readers, "Important lessons have been learned this summer. The most important is that of the growing power of elements of the community who have hitherto been relatively voiceless. That not everyone approves of the manner in which the power has been used is beside the point. What is to be borne in mind is that a new spirit is abroad, which has the power to disturb the equilibrium of institutions and customs which have remained on dead center so long that most people have come to take them for granted in that position."[18]

People there soon noticed that "new spirit." A year later, as part of the state's tricentennial celebration, the 1930s Broadway musical hit *Porgy and Bess* was performed in Charleston—the setting for the story—for the first time. An all-black local cast was celebrated by white patrons—a massive symbolic breakthrough in interracial social relations.

In January 1970, when Greenville County schools—the state's largest school district—prepared for a massive midyear court-ordered integration plan that involved busing to provide racial balance in every school, McNair finally demonstrated bold leadership. In sharp contrast to fellow southern governors in Louisiana and Florida, who were espousing defiance, McNair flew to Greenville and told a local television audience that South Carolina had "run out of courts, run out of time, and must adjust to new circumstances."[19] His stance made the front page the next day in the *New York Times*, the *Washington Post*, the *Los Angeles Times*, and the *Charlotte Observer*.

Because of aroused local feelings, the *Greenville News* ran the story on the back page.

The governor's office received scores of letter from Greenville County residents, some castigating him for surrendering, but more thanking him for leadership that provided them with direction. The integration plan there, designed by the school board and its attorney (the father of state senator, future governor, and U.S. secretary of education Richard W. Riley), recognized that desegregation involved a burden that should be shared by all. It provided the model for the busing plan in Charlotte, approved a year later by the Supreme Court in *Swann v. Charlotte-Mecklenburg Board of Education.*

Shortly thereafter, Darlington County adopted a midyear integration plan that in the small town of Lamar created attendance zones in which the overwhelming majority of whites would attend one majority-white school, grades 1–12. Another with grades 1–12 would be almost 90 percent black, with the rest of the students virtually all from poor white families.

On opening day a mob of angry and frustrated whites attacked school buses carrying black children. They also attacked highway patrolmen sent by McNair to maintain order. U.S. Attorney General John Mitchell refused to send any federal representatives, not even the state's lone U.S. marshal, to join with the state police in enforcing a federal court order.

Nine days earlier Republican congressman Albert Watson, warming up to run for governor, had addressed a massive "freedom of choice" protest rally at Lamar. McNair and Lieutenant Governor West, who would run for governor as a Democrat, both spurned invitations to appear. In a widely publicized appearance, Watson told the rally that *"every section* of this state is in for it unless you stand up and use *every* means at your disposal to defend [against] what I consider an illegal order of the Circuit Court of the United States." Watson, whose congressional district did not include Lamar, had drawn applause when he opened his remarks by declaring, "There are some people who said, 'Congressman, why are *you* coming over here this afternoon to speak to some of those hard core rednecks over there?' You know my response to them? 'Those citizens are interested in their children, and I'll stand with them.'"[20]

The state prosecuted members of the mob that attacked the school buses and highway patrolmen. An all-white jury in Darlington County found them guilty.

The violence at Lamar, although never mentioned directly by West in the campaign for governor in 1970, was a crucial issue that hurt Watson with many whites who had voted for Richard Nixon in 1968. West's campaign slogan, placed on billboards throughout the state, was "Elect a Good Man Governor."

In May 1970, however, in response to a student uprising at the University of South Carolina in Columbia in protest of the Vietnam War and the deaths of the students that month at Kent State in Ohio, McNair had responded in a manner parallel to Orangeburg. The governor sent the highway patrol onto the University of South Carolina campus with shotguns loaded with buckshot and commanded by one of the patrolman acquitted at the federal trial. The disruption on campus began with a student takeover of the school's administration building that housed the office of the president, with a student undercover agent for SLED playing a significant leadership role in that event. After two tense nights, with some firing by police of tear-gas canisters, the situation ended with no gunfire.

In his final address to the legislature eight months later, McNair referred to Orangeburg and Lamar as names that "remain scars on our state's conscience, and symbols of the human problems we have faced."[21]

ON THE CAMPUS of South Carolina State University today, a granite maker is dedicated to the three students—Henry Smith, Delano Middleton, and Samuel Hammond—who were killed. The names of twenty-seven others were added at the annual memorial service in 2000, during which Governor Jim Hodges spoke, expressing deep regret for "a great tragedy for our state." Three years later, Governor Mark Sanford issued a formal statement of apology.

Not until his biography, *South Carolina at the Brink: Robert McNair and the Politics of Civil Rights, 1965–1971*, was published in 2006 did McNair publicly talk about the most tragic event in his career. As governor at the time he now accepted responsibility for what happened at Orangeburg. He appeared still convinced, however, that what happened in 1968 had flowed from the Black Power movement rather than student frustration fed by the indignity of being denied the right to bowl because of skin color four years after passage of the 1964 Civil Rights Act. As of 2008 the state had yet to make a formal study and report of what happened. The book *The Orangeburg Massacre* had been placed in every public high school and middle school library, where it was soon joined by the new McNair biography.

A LOOK AT 1970 POLITICS in South Carolina reveals the initial extent and effect of these changes that occurred in the 1960s. Watson, Senator Thurmond's handpicked candidate for governor, lost to West, a racial and political moderate, by twenty-eight votes. In addition to the election of West, three blacks were elected to the all-white legislature. West hired the first black staffers, Jim Clyburn and George Hamilton.

Clyburn, who had run for the S.C. House of Representatives from Charleston, had heard about 2 A.M. that he had been elected by roughly five hundred votes, went to bed, and learned before 9 A.M. that there had been a miscount. Someone miscarried a one, he was told, and it meant he lost by five hundred votes. A top political reporter called from the *Charleston News and Courier* a few minutes later and asked his reaction. He recalls replying, "Maybe I should have gotten enough votes to insulate against that."[22]

West was impressed when he read Clyburn's response and called him. When he met with West to discuss the job offer, Clyburn said he would not accept it because he was quite outspoken and did not want to create any embarrassment for the governor. Clyburn recalled West responding, "If I were black with as much on the ball as you, I'd be much more strident than you are." Hearing that, Clyburn accepted.[23]

Five years after passage of the 1965 Voting Rights Act, 220,000 blacks—24.5 percent of the state's registered voters—had registered. Except for almost 4,000 votes for thirty-five-year-old lawyer Thomas Broadwater, a write-in candidate for the new, black protest United Citizens Party, West received virtually all the remaining votes from African Americans. In 1970 West got his winning margin by pulling support from both Nixon and Wallace voters to add to solid African American support. For example, in the upper-middle-class, suburban Arcadia precinct near Columbia, Nixon in 1968 had received 667 votes, compared with 132 for Humphrey and 69 for Wallace, but West narrowly lost to Watson, 433–410. In Anderson County, which Wallace carried with a majority of 6,419, compared with a combined total of 5,043 for Nixon and Humphrey, West defeated Watson almost two to one, 10,532 to 5,362. In Columbia's Ward 9, where all but 24 of the 1,904 registered voters were black, the vote was West 1,006 and Watson 19.

These examples illustrate clearly that West got support from Nixon voters reacting to Watson's redneck appeal and from Wallace voters, many of them traditional Democrats reacting against the Nixon administration's economic and school policies. Thurmond had promised in 1968 there would be freedom of choice under Nixon, and in 1970 Democrats literally played his words back in the campaign on television and radio under the label "broken promises." The schools had been integrated and freedom of choice was dead, already struck down by the Supreme Court even as Thurmond had uttered his promises. Meanwhile textile mills were tightening their belts; workers were going on "short time," and some were being laid off.

The significant point was that Albert Watson, a strong personality with popular mass appeal and the full support of Thurmond, could not win as a segregationist in a state that twenty years earlier was known nationally for its traditional domination by the politics of color.

Two-party politics marked the end of white solidarity in South Carolina. Initially the black voters in many counties could not elect one of their own, but they could and did decide which white candidate won. Some of the old-time segregationist leaders in the State House saw what was happening and made adjustments. Others were voted out of office.

There developed a new breed of Democratic white political candidates, men and women whose racial views in the past would have meant sure defeat. In at-large elections in Richland County (Columbia) in 1970, no Democratic candidate for state representative received more than 45 percent of the white vote, but Democrats (including two blacks) won all ten House seats. The black candidates received 30 percent of the white vote.

To understand South Carolina politics and the state's overall record of accommodation rather than confrontation during the civil rights era, an understanding of racial attitudes in the state is necessary. For almost three centuries an aristocratic racism had dominated the white South Carolina social and political structure—a racism in which blacks were looked upon as children rather than a lower class of being and in which lower-class whites also were looked down upon. In contrast Calhoun's theory of democratic racism—in which slavery provided the basis for a white democracy, with skin color a badge of equality among all whites—prevailed in the Deep South.

The tens of thousands of upcountry South Carolina farmers who settled the raw frontiers of the Deep South after Eli Whitney's cotton gin provided the means of separating the lint from the seeds took with them Calhoun's theories of race and planted them with the short-staple cotton. A corollary of Calhoun's theory was that blacks were a little less than human and therefore subject to treatment that could be brutal.

Degrees of the two varieties of southern racism were found in all southern states, but the system of aristocratic racism, which gave more value to stability and an orderly society, prevailed in South Carolina, an Old South state. Although Calhoun married a Charlestonian, the cavalier men of influence there never took his theories on race seriously. The wealthy men of commerce there and the lowcountry planters of the colonial period had attempted to develop an aristocratic society. They cultivated a sense of noblesse oblige that in race relations developed as paternalism. Planters preferred to be thought kind rather than cruel. (Captured runaways or slaves who committed specific offenses, however, might be sent to the official Charleston "workhouse" for punishment, including whipping. Specific provisions of law designated the number of stripes for different offenses.)

Race was the dominant force behind political and social decisions, but with aristocratic racism there ultimately developed a value system in which stability was valued almost as much as segregation. The devastation following secession and the Civil War taught South Carolinians a lesson. Thus, with a percentage of black population second only to Mississippi, South Carolina's resistance to the 1954 desegregation decision of the Supreme Court generally eschewed violence.

THE STATE, the largest daily newspaper in South Carolina and one with an aristocratic tradition dating back to its being founded in 1891 to oppose Tillman, endorsed West in 1970. The editor of the newspaper, William D. Workman Jr., had run for the U.S. Senate in 1962 as a Republican. He and West shared a bond: both graduated from the Citadel in the early 1940s.

At the 1970 state Democratic convention, L. Marion Gressette, second in seniority in the S.C. Senate and the state's official voice of resistance on segregation in the late 1950s and early 1960s as chairman of the official School Segregation Committee, sat with the integrated Calhoun County delegation. (A few years later, after I. DeQuincey Newman was elected as the first black state senator since Reconstruction, Gressette asked him to sit for a photograph of the two of them together, which Gressette framed and displayed in his office.)

The Democratic Party in South Carolina had special cause to emphasize unity and to treat blacks respectfully in 1970. State government, controlled by Democrats, had done little to open job opportunities for blacks. Other causes of discontent led to formation of the United Citizens Party. Although its charter came too late to get Broadwater and other candidates on the ballot, his candidacy reflected a discontent among younger blacks with the performance of the South Carolina Democratic Party. Election of the three black legislators, however, refuted the contention of militants that black Democrats could not get elected to the State House.

THROUGHOUT THIS PERIOD of change, ordinary and not-so-ordinary black people in communities small and large throughout South Carolina provided extraordinary courage and leadership. Two such persons representative of them all were Victoria DeLee from rural Dorchester County and Thomas "Tom" McCain in Edgefield County.

DeLee, a tall, stocky, and physically intimidating daughter of a sharecropper in Dorchester County, possessed a quick wit and sharp tongue. Despite limited education, she was motivated by a desire "to vent the anger she felt about racial oppressions." She refused to be intimidated. Despite being shot at and having her home burned, she litigated, demonstrated, and advocated for more than two decades for voting rights and school desegregation. She received support from the meager resources of the American Friends Service Committee's one-person office in the state.

In 1969, with press reports that the Nixon administration was on the verge of revising guidelines for enforcing the 1964 Civil Rights Act's provisions for school integration, AFSC staffer M. Hayes Mizell in Columbia organized a bus trip in which a group of almost thirty poor blacks from around the South who had fought to make school integration real would confront Attorney General Mitchell.

In the Great Hall of the Department of Justice, they sat for hours—a few on chairs and others on desks and the floor—awaiting Mitchell's return from an appearance before Congress. At one point Jerris Leonard, assistant attorney general for civil rights, came in and called such activity "intemperate." A law school graduate from Marquette University who had served twelve years in the Wisconsin legislature and run as the Republican nominee for the U.S. Senate, he soon found himself in a face-to-face confrontation with DeLee.

Mizell recalled, "He was clearly in over his head." Leonard, clearly frustrated, suddenly turned and walked out of the room, with DeLee trailing him, wagging her forefinger at the back of his head. She finished her response by shouting, "and you're as phony as baloney!"[24]

On the bus trip to Washington, the African American parents had sung the spiritual "Leaning on the Everlasting Arms," with its message that no matter what, God is always with you. On the way back home, they sang:

> Tell ol' Nixon, time is windin' up,
> Tell ol' Nixon, time is windin' up.
> Destruction is in this land;
> God's gonna move His hand;
> Time is windin' up.

A photo of DeLee subsequently facing Mitchell in his office, after the departure of Leonard, ran the next week in *Newsweek*. Mizell later recalled, "We had done everything this government had asked of us in order to make Title VI of the 1964 Civil Right Act work."[25] Attorney General Mitchell observed about civil rights, "Watch not what we say, but what we do." Unless forced by the Supreme Court, they did little.

In 2007 DeLee at eighty-two, after recovering from a long illness, was walking three or four miles every day with friends, living alone, and enjoying her garden and chickens while keeping up with her children, grandchildren, and great-grandchildren. And she was still doing missionary work for her church, visiting the sick and telling them that they could make it. She had seen her share of troubles, but said, "I don't regret nothin' I ever done."[26]

McCain, neither of whose parents got beyond the sixth grade, remembers his father repeatedly quoting to his children from the book of Ecclesiastes, "Remember thy creator in the days of your youth." His father never missed church on Sunday, and he believed in the social gospel. The combination of social justice and making use of the strength of one's youth proved powerfully motivating.

The oldest of eight children, seven of whom attended college, Tom earned a doctorate, as did his sister Emma. He demonstrated for civil rights while a student at historically black Payne College in nearby Augusta. As one of the few black graduate students when he enrolled in 1965 at the University of Georgia, McCain was assigned a single-cot dormitory room converted from a small study for a previous black student. McCain marched back to the assignment desk and told the attendant he wanted a room just like everyone else's. In a few minutes he moved into a full room with a bath, two beds, windows, and a study desk.

Looking back at it all in 2007, he said, "It was an era I came through that I really don't know that I could have done differently because it was a time when things needed to get done, and I was led by some force to do it." He spoke of his own children, "who have no idea of what it was like walking to school while white students rode the bus, going to a one-room school with eight grades and one teacher." As a Head Start administrator, he added, "Poverty remains the big issue in low income communities."

Rather than forcing change through militant confrontation, he got the support of the southern regional office of the American Civil Liberties Union. There he found South Carolina native Laughlin McDonald—who was, like Hayes Mizell, a young white southerner who fought for racial justice.

With McCain as the lead plaintiff, McDonald won lawsuits that ended segregated chain gangs in Edgefield County and the practice of separating the names of white and black voter registration lists that had been manipulated by local officials to ensure predominantly white juries. Another lawsuit ended the playing of "Dixie" and flying of the Confederate battle flag—powerful white symbols linked to the Confederacy—at majority black Strom Thurmond High School. The most important case took ten years of litigation before the

U.S. Supreme Court ruled that the Edgefield County Council would be elected by single-member districts.

The initial single-member district election for county council resulted in a three-to-two black majority. The council elected McCain county administrator, a position he held for ten years.

Unlike DeLee, through it all McCain remembers never receiving any physical threats. He did become the target of a lawsuit by the school board, however, which sought $245,000 in damages from him. McDonald, together with white ACLU lawyers Herb Buhl and Armand Derfner in South Carolina, won the case.[27]

THE BEGINNING OF THE END of one-party politics in South Carolina dates back to the 1948 Dixiecrat campaign. Thurmond's receiving 74 percent of the presidential vote in his home state, he said more than two decades later, showed the people of the South that the sky would not fall if they failed to support the national Democratic Party.[28]

Before it began to crack in 1948, the traditional Democratic solid South had come in South Carolina to mean white political unity against blacks, which submerged economic issues in which poor whites had a stake. Franklin D. Roosevelt, who while recuperating in Georgia from polio gained a clear grasp of the poverty that gripped the South, received tremendous support from South Carolina voters in his early New Deal years for programs of economic recovery.

When Congress passed legislation in 1935 to create the New Deal's landmark program of Social Security, however, powerful southern Democratic congressmen insisted on excluding farm and domestic workers from coverage. Those two categories employed well over half the black workforce in the South.[29] Eleanor Roosevelt's publicized concern about the plight of blacks and the Democratic Party's concern in the 1940s with rights of blacks and organized labor created the beginning of disenchantment among southern whites that in the decades ahead would expand.

In the 1950s retired industrialist David Dows, then living in Aiken, and others began quietly to build a strong modern Republican Party in the state. The state's industrial development was bringing in managers who had been active Republicans, and they were one source of new leadership.

New party leaders sensed their future lay not in a biracial coalition. Reverend Newman, who in 1956 attended the Republican National Convention as a delegate, quit the party after its 1958 state convention, after blacks no longer held any leadership roles. "They made it clear that blacks were no longer welcome in the Republican Party," he said later.[30]

In 1960 it had been considered an upset when John F. Kennedy—fully supported by Governor Hollings—won in South Carolina, defeating Richard Nixon by less than ten thousand votes. Beginning with the election of Columbia businessman Charles Boineau to the S.C. House in 1961 as the first Republican legislator of the twentieth century, the 1960s served as a decade of ferment in which the real development of the modern GOP in South Carolina took root. Direction came from state chairman J. Drake Edens of Columbia, a disciplined economic conservative and heir to a supermarket fortune who traveled all over the state in building a grassroots party organization.

To some extent the new Republican Party in South Carolina descended from the old Bourbon class in the state, but it was more than that. There were the new South Carolinians who had moved into the state from outside the South, where many had been active in the national Republican party. There was also a small reform element that viewed with a sense of despair the generally reactionary one-party Democratic rule in the state.

The new suburbanites, many of them college-educated economic conservatives, in-migrants to the state, or upwardly mobile couples from small towns or farms, provided core strength in building a modern Republican Party in the 1960s. This suburban middle class was protesting both the social and economic liberalism of the national Democratic Party and finding in the Republican Party a measure of social respectability. The Democratic label began losing status for these whites as blacks flocked to the party of John F. Kennedy and Lyndon B. Johnson, whose New Frontier and Great Society programs promised new economic opportunity and dignity.

In 1962 journalist William D. Workman Jr., longtime Columbia correspondent for the *News and Courier* in Charleston and other newspapers and a popular veteran state capital political reporter, ran for the U.S. Senate as a Republican against Olin Johnston. Workman's winning 43 percent of the vote made politicians take notice. Also that year state representative Floyd Spence switched to the Republican Party, narrowly losing a race for Congress from the Second District, which included Columbia. The Democrat who defeated him was Albert Watson. Eight years later Spence won the congressional seat as a Republican. He held it until his death in 2001.

But it was the 1964 Barry Goldwater campaign that brought the Republican Party to full bloom in South Carolina and fully launched the race-based Republican southern strategy, which in more muted form would continue to influence the GOP image in South Carolina. Although overwhelmed nationally, Goldwater swept South Carolina, with 59 percent of the vote, reflecting a confluence of both Thurmond's Dixiecrat followers and the strong grassroots organization built by Edens.

In 1966, with Thurmond heading the ticket, Republicans ran competitive challengers for governor and all congressional seats. They recruited scores of candidates for the legislature, winning twenty-five seats, seventeen in the S.C. House and eight in the Senate.

State senator Marshall Parker's coming within eleven thousand votes of defeating Hollings in a U.S. Senate race stunned the state Democratic Party, which for years was little more than a loose organization that conducted primary elections every two years. Forced into action, Democrats for the first time began to develop a permanent staff organization at the state level and political organization at the local level.

In 1968 Thurmond made a lasting impact on American political history in moving the Republican Party—and ultimately the Supreme Court—to the right. Thurmond played a decisive role that summer in blocking confirmation of the liberal associate justice Abe Fortas as chief justice, keeping that opening for the next president. (Nixon would appoint Warren Burger.) Thurmond simultaneously became the dominant figure at the Republican National Convention in Miami, where conservative southern delegates were strongly attracted to Governor Ronald Reagan of California. Thurmond played a central role in swaying and holding two-thirds of the southern delegates for Richard Nixon, which was decisive in his getting the nomination.

Thurmond, a retired Army Reserve major general, was attracted by Nixon's strong position on national defense policy and assurances that Nixon understood and was sympathetic to the South on school desegregation, and especially by personal assurances from the candidate that he would appoint "strict constructionists" to the Supreme Court. And he believed Nixon could win. At Miami Beach Thurmond was a one-man fire brigade.

A few minutes after Reagan had gotten a rousing reception—but no votes for the first ballot—in a talk to the South Carolina delegates, Thurmond was approached in the lobby of the Versailles Hotel by a young delegate from Georgia who sought his advice. The senator put an arm around the young man's shoulder and explained quietly: "It boils down between Nixon and Rockefeller. If Nixon gets it on the first ballot, it will avoid complications." To other southerners Thurmond declared, "Vote with your heads, not your hearts." In a one-on-one meeting with Reagan, Thurmond told him, "I'll be for you next time."

Thurmond campaigned nonstop across the South that fall, blunting George Wallace's third-party effort and helping Nixon carry South Carolina and three other southern states—North Carolina, Tennessee, and Florida—in which Wallace previously held plurality leads. "Strom just killed us," a top Wallace campaign aide said later.[31] That election led to four Supreme Court selections by Nixon, including Chief Justice Warren Burger and future chief justice William Rehnquist. Nixon also gave national impetus to the southern strategy.

Thurmond, the man who led Deep South Democrats in a bolt from their party in 1948, led southern Republicans fully into the GOP mainstream twenty years later. He had traveled a long, circuitous route.

With Thurmond leading the way, the South Carolina Republican Party in 1968 devoted its efforts to the presidential election. The state's revitalized Democrats, without McNair or a fellow southerner on the ticket, ignored the presidential race and went all out for state and local Democratic candidates.

Both strategies worked. The Republicans carried South Carolina for Nixon, whose 38 percent of the vote was a winning plurality against Democrat Hubert Humphrey and independent Wallace. The Republicans, however, lost seventeen of their twenty-five seats in the legislature and made no gains in congressional races. Meanwhile Democratic senator Fritz Hollings this time defeated Parker by 150,000 votes.

IN 1970 THE SURGE of Republican strength appeared to slow down. The GOP increased its membership in the 124-seat S.C. House of Representatives from 5 to 11, but that was still less than the 17 held four years earlier.

The decade of the seventies opened with the South Carolina Democratic Party firmly in control of state government. The components of this dominance included the influence of local courthouse Democrats; the voting strength of blacks; a residue of loyalty among traditionally Democratic textile workers in the upcountry; and backing by business and commercial interests seeking continued fiscal restraint, racial quiet, and economic growth.

IN HIS INAUGURAL address in January 1971, Governor West declared, "The politics of race and divisiveness have been soundly repudiated in South Carolina." The inaugural symbolized the beginning of South Carolina's fourth century, and West noted the historic setting:

> It is appropriate on this occasion marking the beginning of the new century in South Carolina that we set for ourselves certain goals, goals whose urgency and priority at this moment in our history cannot be questioned.
>
> The time has arrived when South Carolina for all time must break loose and break free of the vicious cycle of ignorance, illiteracy, and poverty which has retarded us throughout our history.

The new governor went on to outline a program aimed at broad social progress. The presence of the three black legislators (James Felder and I. S. Levy Johnson of Columbia and Herbert Fielding of Charleston) in the General Assembly at the time reinforced the image of change. By 2007 their number had grown to thirty-five—twenty-seven in the House and eight in the Senate—and Jim Clyburn had just become Democratic whip in the U.S. House of Representatives, ranking only behind the Speaker and majority leader. Before his 1992 election to Congress, Clyburn had served eighteen years as commissioner of the Human Affairs Commission, an agency that West established in response to the Orangeburg Massacre and Charleston hospital workers' strike to identify and defuse racial conflicts before they escalated.

SOON AFTER WEST'S inauguration in 1971, Senator Thurmond added a black staff member—the first member of the state's congressional delegation to do so—and a new image for Thurmond began to emerge. His new staffer, state Voter Education Project director Thomas Moss, helped him fully extend to blacks his unsurpassed record of constituent service and guided him as he reached out to the state's black community. In a statement for *Ebony* magazine, Thurmond said, "I am confident that we have more in common as Southerners than we have reason to oppose each other because of race. . . . equality of opportunity for all is a goal upon which blacks and Southern whites can agree."[32]

Three decades earlier another native of South Carolina, W. J. Cash, concluded in his 1941 classic, *The Mind of the South*, "Proud, brave, honorable by its lights, courteous, signally effective, sometimes terrible, in its action—such was the South at its best . . . violence, intolerance, aversion and suspicion toward new ideas, an incapacity for analysis, an inclination to act from feeling rather than from thought, an exaggerated individualism and a too narrow concept of social responsibility, attachment to fictions and false values, above all too great attachment to racial values and a tendency to justify cruelty and injustice in the name of those values, sentimentality and a lack of realism—these have been its characteristic vices in the past. . . . In the coming days, and probably soon, it is likely to have to prove its capacity for adjustment far beyond what has been true in the past."[33]

Rapid change and adjustment to change came as Cash predicted. For Thurmond the change reflected an understanding of the state's new political math. He later voted for the Martin Luther King birthday holiday and a twenty-five-year extension of the Voting Rights Act in 1982. Tom McCain voted that fall for Thurmond. "When he changed his philosophy, I figured he deserved my vote," McCain said.[34] Thurmond lived to age one hundred, setting records as the longest-serving and oldest U.S. senator.

His legacy comes from his significant role in changing the culture of the Republican Party and, through his decisive role in the 1968 election of Richard Nixon, changing the direction of the U.S. Supreme Court. His unmatched record of constituent service won the hearts (and votes) of hundreds of thousands of his constituents who needed help, such as getting a son or daughter home from the military during a family crisis.

At his funeral on July 1, 2003, which Thurmond himself planned, liberal Democratic senator Joseph Biden of Delaware eulogized him in Columbia's First Baptist Church—the site where South Carolina delegates initially met to consider the Ordinance of Secession. Although Biden spoke bluntly of his disdain for Thurmond when first elected, at age twenty-nine, to the U.S. Senate in 1972, he moved on to speak of change. "The brave man chooses while the coward stands aside," Biden said. "Strom knew . . . that the time had come to change himself. Only a special man like Strom would have the courage to accept it, the grace to acknowledge it and the humility, in face of enmity and mistrust, to pursue it to the end." Little more than a year later, the name of Thurmond's black daughter, Essie Mae Washington-Williams, was added to those of his other children on the base of the seventeen-foot-tall statue of him on the State House grounds.

Unlike Thurmond, Hollings remained consistent as a progressive voice. Before retiring in January 2005, he influenced and initiated major legislation in the Senate, such as creating the National Oceanic and Atmospheric Administration (NOAA), saving the federal food stamp program, and sponsoring innovative legislation for preserving and protecting coastal marshes and lowlands. After a series of "hunger tours" in 1969, Hollings forcefully presented his findings. Congress responded by expanding the food stamp program and added the Special Supplemental Nutrition Program for Women, Infants, and Children (WIC). For South Carolina he initiated a plan for conservation easements in the ACE Basin (named for the Ashepoo, Combahee, and Edisto rivers) south of Charleston. The plan protects some 135,000 acres of tidal marshes and connecting lowlands, restricting development, preserving natural beauty, protecting endangered species, and retaining nature's capacity for storm protection.

As they accumulated eighty-six years of seniority between them (Thurmond forty-eight and Hollings thirty-eight), they succeeded in securing hundreds of millions of federal dollars for projects in South Carolina.

THE GREATEST STIMULUS for change came from the 1964 Civil Rights Act and the 1965 Voting Rights Act, both of which Thurmond and the great majority of other southern members of Congress vigorously opposed. The public accommodations section (Title II) of the Civil Rights Act created a legal mandate that eased the way for lunch counter, restaurant, motel, and hotel owners who already were beginning to drop racial bars under pressure from the civil rights sit-in movement. For those unwilling to move voluntarily, the new law forced change. But the thrust of change came most directly from Title IV, which mandated that schools and other public institutions such as hospitals must desegregate, and Title VII, which outlawed discrimination in employment. The new law forced a change in behavior that led to changes in attitude and social relationships.

It was no longer a matter of protesting against the Supreme Court and questioning its authority. The mandate of Congress now fell directly on the shoulders of school boards and superintendents. The difficult task of developing a unitary school system began in earnest under the prodding and direction of the executive branch. By the 1980s, however, the Supreme Court had begun backing away from remedies to maximize racial integration in public schools.

Once blacks were allowed to register to vote regardless of literacy, the legislature initially appropriated money for statewide adult education programs to attack problems of illiteracy. It became politically safe to reinstate the compulsory school attendance law.

Title VII directly assaulted a caste system in which blacks had been excluded from manufacturing and many other jobs. In gaining new economic opportunities that paid better wages, the state's black population also provided an expanded market for goods and services. The expanded freedom and economic opportunity ended net out-migration among blacks in the state. The interaction between social, economic, and political transformation opened a modern new era in the state that continues to evolve.

Race still mattered. But after three hundred years in which concern about race had dominated politics, stifled creative thought, and held back economic and educational development, South Carolina in 1970 opened its fourth century in the midst of developing new human relationships and a mood of cautious optimism.

10

POPULAR CULTURE

Even amid all the conflict over race, there existed in South Carolina and throughout the South an ongoing and deep cultural exchange that included food, music, religion, and even the taboo arena of sex. White southerners enjoying the taste of succulent boiled peanuts in the summer, sweet potatoes in the fall and winter, and rice year round seldom recognized that these and other foods had come with the slave population from Africa.

Country and bluegrass music fans rarely recognized that the banjo, whose music they took for granted, was originally an African instrument that blacks working for the railroad took to the mountain regions of the South. (Bluegrass musicians themselves generally are proudly aware of their borrowed instrument's source.)

Many of the gospel songs sung in church, especially in small towns and the countryside, were the same in both white and black churches. Thomas Dorsey, who wrote popular gospel hymns such as "Peace in the Valley" that were sung in many white churches, was an African American who started out as a blues musician.

Although a distant second to New Orleans, Charleston, with its Jenkins Orphanage Band that toured Europe, produced some first-rate jazz musicians. Jazz itself was never recognized by the New York and Boston gatekeepers of what constituted art until after jazz musicians won recognition and acclaim in Paris and elsewhere in Europe and the music crossed back over the Atlantic.

And in mid-twentieth-century South Carolina, as elsewhere in the South, both black and white church attendance was higher than in the country as a whole. For whites it meant a religion that taught brotherhood in a culture that taught separation. Blacks absorbed in church the prophetic demand for justice and also a message of forgiveness. For all, the church projected an underlying

Southern 500. The Darlington International Raceway was built in 1950. The 1.36-mile track hosted the Southern 500 every Labor Day. The final Southern 500 was held in 2004 as NASCAR's fan base and national headquarters moved outside its native region. *History of South Carolina Slide Collection,* F-60

The Jenkins Orphanage Band is shown in this picture from 1900 in their discarded Citadel cadet uniforms. The band raised money for the black orphanage by performing throughout the United States and Europe. *History of South Carolina Slide Collection,* G-33

message of love. In the years ahead the moral message received by the overwhelmingly Protestant population in South Carolina would ease the transition into a biracial society that continues to evolve.

By far the most sensitive issue of all involved sexual relations and racial identity, as demonstrated in defining who was white and who was black at the 1895 state constitutional convention. Arguing against defining anyone with one-sixteenth or more black blood as nonwhite—on the grounds it would disqualify too many people identified as whites—George Tillman prevailed over his younger brother Ben.

Many of these underlying cultural elements would come into play in 1950 at Charlie's Place, a nightclub in Myrtle Beach owned and operated by Charlie Fitzgerald, a husky, six-foot-three black man whose skin color denoted some white ancestry. The story of what happened at Charlie's Place at midcentury remains little recognized, yet it reflects a defining part of South Carolina's cultural heritage. The whole story was uncovered through oral history interviews by New York writer Frank Beacham, a native of Honea Path, South Carolina, whose grandfather had been mayor and plant superintendent there during the 1934 textile strike.

Many of the nation's top musicians—Ray Charles, Duke Ellington, Lena Horne, Count Basie, Billy Eckstine, Billie Holiday, and other names among the "race music" artists of the 1940s and 1950s—made stops at Charlie's Place. Music that mixed jazz and blues with black gospel, with a provocative beat and sometimes raunchy lyrics, was taboo on radio stations in the state, one of which proclaimed with pride that it played no "jungle" music.

Unknown to their parents, however, many music-loving white teenagers listened late at night, sometimes to a radio tucked under a pillow, to Nashville's 50,000-watt WLAC, which played the "devil's music" under its new name, rhythm and blues. On trips to Myrtle Beach, some of the more daring learned about and ventured into Charlie's Place. They wanted to learn the dance steps that they watched there.

They saw a slowed-down version of the popular jitterbug—a new dance that was called the shag. The earlier "dirty shag" was more erotic with greater body contact, but the shag was a slower, eight-step dance introduced at Charlie's Place by Cynthia Harrol, a young black woman from the Orangeburg County town of Elloree. She waited tables and worked behind the bar. The black clientele gave her the nickname "Shag."

Harry Driver, one of those youthful white dancers at Charlie's Place who would become an early member of the Shag Hall of Fame, told Beacham a half century later:

It was the beat—the way they moved. They had a history of African tribal dance. What we learned from the blacks was their rhythm and tempo— the moves. You watch a white person do a syncopated walk and then watch a black do it. The blacks put more into it than you can imagine. We emulated what they did. Everybody claims to have started the shag. Nobody started it. It evolved from one dance to another in a big melting pot.

We were totally integrated because the blacks and whites had nothing in our minds that made us think we were different. We loved music, we loved dancing, and that was the common bond between us.[1]

Another of those early dancers told Beacham that white boys and girls danced with black partners; it was the dance that mattered to them, not race.

In 1950 racial feelings intensified, especially among poor whites for whom skin color provided their only source of social status, in response to the rulings of Judge Waring and that year's raucous and racially charged U.S. Senate race between Olin D. Johnston and outgoing governor J. Strom Thurmond. The Ku Klux Klan made one of its periodic revivals, and Klan activity spread in Horry County across the Intracoastal Waterway from Myrtle Beach.

Word got to the state "grand dragon," Leesville grocer Thomas Hamilton, about the black nightclub that attracted white teenagers. On a Saturday night in late August, a Klan motorcade with scores of robed Klansmen cruised into Myrtle Beach. They slowly drove past Charlie's Place, and Fitzgerald called the police, warning there would be bloodshed if the Klan returned. Instead of providing protection for the club, the police passed Fitzgerald's message on to the Klansmen, who apparently took it as a dare.

Roughly sixty Klansmen returned just before midnight. They overwhelmed and disarmed the fifty-nine-year-old Fitzgerald, who regularly wore shouldered pistol holsters, and threw him into the trunk of one of their cars. Then they attacked the club. They smashed windows and fired hundreds of rounds of gunfire into the building, while patrons scrambled beneath overturned tables and chairs. Repeated gunfire silenced the hated jukebox with its rhythm and blues recordings—what today would be known as beach music. The dancer and waitress named Shag suffered a back injury from being beaten, and a Klansman smashed her fingers by slamming a cash register drawer shut on them as she tried to protect the club's money.

The Klansmen left behind one of their members in Klan regalia, bleeding from a gunshot wound in the back that some law enforcement officers later believed came from the Klan gunfire. Doctors who removed the dying man's bloodied bed-sheet robe saw he was wearing a police uniform from the county seat town of Conway.

Meanwhile Klansman viciously beat and whipped Fitzgerald on a deserted road, one of them taking a knife and slicing off a piece of each ear, and left him there to die. Fitzgerald managed to stagger to Highway 17, where a motorist picked him up. He survived and reopened the club, but died five years later from cancer.

The sheriff arrested Hamilton and nine other Klansmen. A grand jury refused to indict any of them. Hamilton returned to Horry County in November, wearing his grand dragon's bright green robe, and spoke to a crowd of more than five thousand from the back of a truck in a tobacco field. He denied the slain policeman had been shot by a fellow Klan member, and he verbally attacked the sheriff, who two years later was voted out of office.

Hamilton later returned to Horry County and joined other Klansmen in taking some of their targeted victims across the North Carolina state line before inflicting punishment. That act prompted federal prosecution and a conviction, with Hamilton serving a term in federal prison. State officials in South Carolina moved quickly to clamp down on Klan activity, and in the years ahead State Law Enforcement Division (SLED) agents placed informants in the Klan, recorded speeches at their rallies, and cracked down on violence. The Klan never again became a political force in the state.

The shag and beach music survived and thrived, but only among whites. Maurice Williams, a black musician from the 1950s who with his Zodiacs recorded the beach classic "Stay" and still played for shaggers into the twenty-first century, told Beacham: "The beginning of beach music was predominantly rhythm and blues, but today if you say to a young black man, 'Come on, let's go and listen to a beach music show,' he'll say, 'I ain't going to that white music.' The average black kid in his twenties or thirties doesn't know what this is all about. They see a beach music festival, and it's all white music. It's strange. They haven't studied the history of their music and the guys who recorded it enough to know what beach music is all about. They just don't know any better."[2]

More than three decades after the Klan assault on Charlie's Place, the legislature formally designated the shag as South Carolina's official state dance.

THOSE NATIONALLY KNOWN black musicians and singers who performed for "their own" at Charlie's Place and in Atlantic Beach clubs did so only after a night of performing at the Ocean Forest Hotel, which paid their regular performance fee. Until demolished in 1974 to make way for new development, the Ocean Forest had served over four decades as a premier setting for white society.

In the 1930s a black owner of a self-service laundry purchased an ocean-front section north of Myrtle Beach and named it Atlantic Beach, where it remains an independent municipality. In the decades that followed, its nightlife attracted many of the Ocean Forest performers who had shown up at Charlie's Place. Eventually purchased by a consortium of black professionals, Atlantic Beach became known as "the Black Pearl of South Carolina."

Coastal Horry County had begun as a getaway spot in the late 1890s, when a small, family-owned railway line made it possible for people in the nearby Pee Dee region to visit the beach for fishing, picnicking, and camping overnight near the sand dunes. In 1912, when only a handful of permanent residents lived in what is now Myrtle Beach, major property owner Franklin G. Burroughs provided the land and wealthy midwestern industrialist Simeon Chapin the capital that would develop Myrtle Beach into a major tourist destination.

In 1934 Myrtle Beach State Park, a project of the New Deal, opened as a new attraction. It remains as a little-publicized beachfront retreat for visitors. The dredging of the Intracoastal Waterway in the 1930s physically separated Myrtle Beach from the rest of Horry County.

Following World War II and the nation's general economic recovery, paved highway US 501 opened in 1948, linking Myrtle Beach to the Horry County seat, Conway, connecting there to paved roads throughout the Carolinas. Also in 1948 a new facility that was known to generations of tourists as the Pavilion reopened on Ocean Boulevard from the burned ruins of the original. It featured a Ferris wheel and some children's rides, expanding over time into eleven crowded acres that featured a 1912 carousel; one of America's few remaining wooden roller coasters, the Hurricane; and for half a century an organ, built in 1900 by German craftsmen, that filled the gaudy nights with sound.

In 1954 Hurricane Hazel, a monstrous, category 4 storm, struck the region, washing away miles of beaches and destroying more than a thousand homes. Local response, however, fueled economic growth. New motel and hotel construction replaced many family homes and neighborhoods. In 1957 the South Carolina legislature raised the region's profile, officially designating the sixty-mile stretch of beach, from the Waccamaw River at Georgetown to the North Carolina border, as the "Grand Strand." The modern era of prosperity for Myrtle Beach had begun.

In 1984 the shag became the official state dance of South Carolina, and by then the term *beach music,* a name given by its mass of followers to the beat of rhythm and blues, had achieved currency. The more daring white teenagers throughout the Pee Dee region had begun some two decades earlier to sneak away on weekend nights to participate on the dance floor at black clubs in Bennettsville and Timmonsville that sometimes brought in name performers to provide the music. Beach music had begun to expand as a feature on radio stations scattered throughout the Carolinas. The shag and beach music evolved into icons of popular culture in South Carolina, with shag clubs located as far away as New York City.

ALTHOUGH THE BEACH remained the lure of the Grand Strand, Myrtle Beach had become much more than an oceanfront getaway. The building of a massive convention center and construction of scores of golf courses attracted businessmen, and a ten-month season drew golfers from all over the nation wanting to sample the nineteenth-hole bars and relax at the nightclubs. Amusements such as wax museums, miniature golf, and shooting galleries attracted families with small children; and teenagers followed the footsteps of parents in flocking to Myrtle Beach for fun and nightlife frolic. The relaxed days meant time soothingly soaking up the sun's rays on the beach and splashing in the surf.

This postcard picture features the old Folly Beach fishing pier in 1942. Pier fishing at Folly remains a popular pastime. *History of South Carolina Slide Collection,* D-151

In 1989, after Hurricane Hugo decimated the Carolina coast, massive investment, rebuilding, and another round of expensive beach renourishment brought the tourist economy back in full. Sprawl spilled over into North Myrtle as rebuilt beachwear and T-shirt outlets became bigger and gaudier than ever and outlet stores lined up along highways 17 and 501. Summer road traffic became congested, and the area's permanent population grew rapidly.

The 2006 closing of the Pavilion, a landmark symbol of what Myrtle Beach had been, marked a watershed in the history of the Grand Strand. The opening two years later of a sprawling $400 million, fifty-five-acre Hard Rock Park, with a planned three thousand workers, concerts involving name entertainers, and rides for all, boosted hopes for an expanded tourism. The new park also extended the gaudy sprawl westward on Highway 501. Compared to the Pavilion, however, it was far from the beach, prices were more expensive, and nostalgia was absent. With a failing economy and soaring gas prices, the Hard Rock Park filed for bankruptcy after its first season. Planned development of I-73 to provide a direct interstate connection to Myrtle Beach promises future growth, as well as the prospect of greater traffic woes and related problems of uncoordinated and barely regulated growth. Still, the closing of the Pavilion saddened many baby boomers, and indeed their children, who retained powerful and nostalgic memories of Myrtle Beach and its youthful initiation rites and mating rituals.

The brightest lights of the twenty-first century's downtown tend toward the glitter of neon as Myrtle Beach and its environs proclaim themselves the "Golf Capital of the World." For the Myrtle Beach region, the new century's developments, including high-rise beachfront developments, combine with tens of thousands of retirees who helped boost the Grand Strand's year-round population to more than two hundred thousand.

Will Moredock, a journalist and sharp critic of the contemporary development, finds there still exists a sense of sentimental attachment for millions to whom Myrtle Beach "is the memory of a warm summer night, full of stars and youth and hope."[3] The romance of the beach, the ocean, and nostalgic memories remain, but the ultimate test will come in confronting the twenty-first century's first major hurricane.

11

THE REPUBLICAN RISE

Although Democrats seemed to have retained their dominance in 1970, the 1974 Democratic primary for governor reflected submerged party tensions that would push open the door for Republican growth. A reform element in the party sought progressive change, both in addressing long-ignored issues of public policy and in opening the process to new ideas.

Two of the legislative "young Turks" were Senator Richard W. Riley Jr. of Greenville and Representative Joseph P. Riley Jr. of Charleston. Although unrelated, they shared a common vision, and both would achieve prominence as political leaders. Dick Riley would become a progressive two-term governor whose leadership as a reformer in public education attracted national acclaim. Joe Riley, elected in 2007 to his ninth four-year term as mayor of Charleston, transformed his beloved city into an internationally recognized urban oasis that combined restoration and architectural preservation of a historic past with a panoply of modern cultural attractions ranging from high art to fine food. He narrowly lost the Democratic nomination for governor in 1994.

In 1974, however, the Democratic Party imploded in a battle between traditional and reform elements. That election's long-term impact fueled Republican growth.

Reform newcomer Charles D. "Pug" Ravenel became a catalyst for change. After growing up in Charleston, he led the Harvard football team as quarterback, became successful on Wall Street, and returned home to challenge the Democratic establishment. In winning the party nomination as a reform-minded newcomer in a bruising campaign against the Democratic "good ol' boys" in his first political race, however, Ravenel once referred to the S.C. Senate "as a den of thieves."[1] The legislature in South Carolina elects all judges, and former legislators held almost all top-level judgeships at that time.

In a lawsuit challenging Ravenel's eligibility because of the state constitution's five-year residency requirement for a governor, Circuit Judge Julius B. "Bubba" Ness (a former state senator and future S.C. Supreme Court chief justice) ruled Ravenel ineligible. The South Carolina Supreme Court upheld that ruling. The U.S. Supreme Court declined to hear an appeal.

Meanwhile native South Carolinian William Westmoreland, a four-star general who commanded American forces in Vietnam, sought the Republican nomination after being courted by both parties. He demonstrated surprising ineptness as a political candidate, however, losing decisively in the Republican primary to party activist James B. Edwards. An oral surgeon and state senator from Charleston, he shared the conservative philosophy of Barry Goldwater and rising icon Ronald Reagan. Edwards entered the primary—the first in which voters rather than the state GOP convention would nominate their candidate—in part to increase the turnout and thereby help build the Republican Party. But Edwards, by then an established party activist, also believed he could win.

In the turmoil that followed, Democrats reopened their state convention and nominated veteran congressman William Jennings Bryan Dorn, who had lost the primary runoff election to Ravenel. Dorn narrowly defeated Dick Riley, the choice of Ravenel supporters. Ravenel announced he would vote for Dorn but would not endorse him, which angered and embittered many loyal Democrats, who saw it as a rebuff to the party. In contrast Riley remained a party loyalist, endorsing Dorn as a symbol of party unity and chairing an issues committee for him. (Dorn's subsequent endorsement of Riley, four years later, would play a decisive role in Riley's 1978 election as governor.)

Despite his Old Guard, ultraconservative image, Dorn's voting record in Congress showed a progressive streak. He had supported President Lyndon Johnson's antipoverty programs and stood alone among southerners in the House in opposing antibusing legislation.

Near the end of the campaign, in response to a hostile questioner at a forum in Greenville, Dorn made one of the most forthright statements on race heard from an American politician in the 1970s, although the press barely noticed it:

Do you think we're going back to the days when the bus went around and picked up the black children and took them to school and came back and picked up the white children? Those days are gone forever. My children ride the bus 10 miles each way to school, and they go to a good consolidated high school, and it's part of a child's education these days to go to school with children of different races and different colors and learn it's one small world we live in and that we've got to get along with Chinese and Japanese and people from all countries. My father used to be school superintendent in Greenwood, and I remember when he consolidated the schools and it ended classism in Greenwood County. And busing might end another kind of "ism."[2]

Edwards, meanwhile, proclaimed himself the candidate of change and, despite a late surge by Dorn, won the fall election with 51.6 percent of the vote. As governor Edwards sharpened his political skills and moderated his views as he confronted state issues as chief executive. His election and four-year term made him a major figure in the story of Republican growth in the state. He elevated the Republican Party's political status, which made it easier to build party organization and recruit candidates. His appointments to state boards and commissions placed party activists in positions of influence. He helped keep alive the political life of his party's defeated candidate for lieutenant governor, former state senator Carroll Campbell, by appointing him to a position of visibility on the governor's staff. Campbell would become a pivotal figure in the development of the state Republican Party.

In January 1975 James B. Edwards (center) became South Carolina's first Republican governor since Reconstruction. Here he is shown at his inauguration on the State House steps with the outgoing governor, John C. West. *History of South Carolina Slide Collection*, B-207

In 1978 Riley's primary runoff victory, with support from Dorn, unified the Democrats, and Riley won election as governor. He battled for and won a change that allowed a governor to serve two successive terms, which strengthened the office of governor. Riley built widespread citizen support for his educational reforms in his first term, then won a second term easily, demonstrating to the legislature that the public would support statewide tax increases for public education. As a reform-minded legislative leader and as governor, Riley focused on issues of governance, including judicial reform, and initiated programs with long-term impact for education and health care. As governor, he led efforts that won congressional approval for the first time of a national policy for low-level nuclear waste in 1980 and high-level waste in 1982. His administration emphasized citizen involvement, with the heavy use of grassroots organizational support and unprecedented numbers of blacks and women on his staff.

His signature achievement, the comprehensive Education Improvement Act in his second term, won South Carolina national recognition for leadership in education reform. The education reform package, including higher taxes to pay for it, provided for merit pay and pay raises for teachers, comprehensive testing to determine individual pupil deficiencies, remedial education, cash bonuses to schools that improved, and a building program. It passed because Riley convinced business leaders and voters that continued economic growth required investment by the state to provide a better-educated workforce. The number of jobs in the state increased by roughly a fourth during his two terms. He later served eight years as U.S. secretary of education under President Bill Clinton. There his goals included reducing class sizes in grades 1–3, helping students develop computer skills, and expanding after-school programs.

The election of President Ronald Reagan in 1980 allowed white southerners to defend their historic opposition to federal authority—the source for implementing civil rights initiatives in the 1960s. Political scientists Earl and Merle Black, in their authoritative 2003 book *The Rise of Southern Republicans*, observed, "As more and more white men and women became accustomed to voting Republican in presidential elections, and as a large majority of white conservatives and a significant minority of white moderates came to identify themselves as Republicans, a base of solid GOP grassroots support emerged."[3]

Reagan also built on the Republican southern strategy that Barry Goldwater had used in 1964. The opening of his 1980 presidential campaign in Neshoba County, Mississippi, where three civil rights workers had been murdered sixteen years earlier, symbolized that the strategy remained alive and well. Two of its leading tacticians were South Carolinians: Harry Dent, a former aide to Thurmond who became a top White House political aide to Richard Nixon, and Lee Atwater, who moved into the Reagan White House and later ran the successful 1988 campaign of President George H. W. Bush. Dent had further strengthened southern Republicanism by bringing many South Carolinians and other southerners to Washington as part of the Nixon administration.

Atwater and Campbell, who was elected to Congress in 1978, together directed Reagan's 1980 campaign in the South. Unlike the pugnacious style of segregationist governor George Wallace, Reagan's low-key style was more refined and coded. In a candid 1981 interview about the southern strategy, Atwater told political scientist Alexander Lamis:

> You start out by saying "Nigger, nigger, nigger." By 1968 you can't say "nigger"—that hurts you. Backfires. So you say stuff like forced busing, states' rights, and all that stuff. You're getting so abstract now [that] you're talking about cutting taxes, and all these things you're talking about are totally economic things and a by-product of them is [that] blacks get hurt worse than whites. And subconsciously maybe that is part of it. I'm not saying that. But I'm saying that if it is getting that abstract, and that coded, that we are doing away with the racial problem one way or the other. You follow me—because obviously sitting around saying, "we want to cut this," is much more abstract than even the busing thing *and* a hell of a lot more abstract than "Nigger, nigger."[4]

The National Election Survey in 1996 showed that conservative white Republicans, a core element of GOP support throughout the South, still strongly believed that the federal government is not responsible for assuring that blacks received fair treatment in employment. Ninety-four percent of conservative Republicans in the South opposed policies designed specifically to "help" blacks.

Reagan's appeal to white southerners, however, went beyond race. His optimism, his anti-Communism, and his capacity to project an image that resonated with their sense of religious and family-based moral values undercut most of what had remained of traditional Democratic loyalty.

With the election of Campbell as governor in 1986, Republican growth surged in South Carolina. By the end of Campbell's second term, the Christian Coalition had become an active part of the Republican base, moving the party to adopt wedge social issues such as opposition to legalized abortion, which many conservative Christians opposed as an assault on life. Their support expanded the Republican base beyond white metropolitan and suburban economic conservatives, who themselves were expanding in number. Republicans also were gaining numbers from the upscale retirees, professionals, and managers moving into South Carolina. Conflict over social issues led many of them to identify as Republican-leaning political independents.

Campbell took office after eight years of congressional experience and well-established Washington contacts. He also had earned a master's degree in political science from American University, which deepened his understanding of government. Campbell reinforced Riley's emphasis on improving educational opportunities and economic development, projecting an aggressive image as a reformer.

His major achievement came in offering a giant package of tax and other incentives to BMW, which resulted in the German automaker building a highly automated auto assembly plant with well-paid workers near Spartanburg, which attracted many other new companies to the state to supply components. BMW officials considered Campbell's combined leadership role, flexibility in confronting issues, and his engaging personality during intense negotiations as playing the critical role in the company's decision to locate in South Carolina (see chapter 13).[5]

Unlike Riley, who saw his role as less partisan and who paid little attention to building the Democratic Party, Campbell gave major attention to building the Republican Party. He strengthened the party structure with professional staff, beefed up fund-raising, and helped recruit candidates.

Under Campbell, Atwater protégé Warren Tompkins moved from executive director of the state Republican Party to serve as Campbell's first chief of staff in the governor's office. In personal, one-on-one meetings, Tompkins later explained, Campbell persuaded more than a dozen Democratic legislators to switch parties, at least ten of whom remained in office more than fifteen years later. They became a critical element in the GOP's winning control of both houses of the legislature.

"He told them the Republicans would welcome them and provide financial and other support for their campaigns," Tompkins said. He also made it clear that Republicans would recruit candidates to run against them if they remained Democrats.[6] Those who switched during Campbell's eight-year tenure provided the margin in 1994 for a Republican majority in the House that widened in the next decade. Campbell also effected substantial consolidation of state government, giving the governor more authority in appointing agency officials. For the first time a cabinet of officials appointed by the governor directed a significant number of state agencies.

Meanwhile "Operation Lost Trust," a highly publicized federal sting operation that began in 1989 under a Republican administration in Washington and continued for more than five years, exposed legislative corruption and resulted in convictions of legislators for taking bribes for votes on specific legislation. The convicted included both Democrats and Republicans, but there was a disproportionately high percentage of black Democrats.

In 1997, however, U.S. District Judge Falcon B. Hawkins, the trial judge, found widespread prosecutorial misconduct in appeals brought by five legislators, three of them black. He detailed unsupervised abuses by a former Republican legislator, who had been arrested on drug and other charges and then was hired and paid up to four thousand dollars a month to offer bribes. The government "lost control" of this "star witness," Judge Hawkins asserted, allowing him to solicit which legislators he wished to attempt to bribe, "specifically . . . members of the Black Caucus."

The case had taken on the character of a show trial, and Judge Hawkins found it inappropriate that U.S. Attorney Bart Daniel called a press conference in a courtroom in the federal courthouse to announce the initial indictments. The judge said it created "an atmosphere of public expectation from which the government could not retreat."

"The breadth and scope of the government's misconduct . . . was and is shocking to this court," Hawkins said in his forty-one-page order, citing extensive failures to provide evidence helpful to the defendants as required by law. It found the government engaged in "repetitious, flagrant, and long-standing misconduct."[7] Although the Fourth Circuit Court of Appeals overruled his dismissal of the indictments and noted that exchange of money for votes had been recorded, the only black defendant subsequently tried, was ultimately acquitted.

The legislature in 1997 asked the Department of Justice to make a full investigation. Four years later the department's Office of Inspector General "did not find prosecutorial misconduct" in the matter, but the OIG was critical of the government's management of its discovery obligations, including failures by the FBI. Despite the reformist image that the Republican Party had cultivated, political analysts Glen T. Broach and Lee Bandy wrote in the South Carolina chapter of *Southern Politics in the 1990s* that it had "coexisted with a less explicit, more retrograde racial appeal rooted in the state's darker past of oppression and segregation."[8]

CAMPBELL'S COMBINATION of articulate charm, successful record as governor and party builder, and reputation as a skilled and aggressive campaigner appeared to make him a contender as a vice presidential running mate for Republican Robert Dole in his 1996 presidential campaign. Under close scrutiny, however, early acts in Campbell's political career damaged his prospects, and he was not a finalist. He clearly had demonstrated considerable personal and political growth. His initial political act as a young businessman, however, involved his leading a caravan of cars from Greenville to Columbia at the end of 1969 to parade in front of the governor's mansion in protest against Governor McNair's support of compliance with the court-ordered Greenville school desegregation plan.

A more damaging issue evolved from Campbell's successful campaign for Congress in 1978 against Greenville mayor Max Heller, who as an eighteen-year-old Jewish youth in Austria managed to escape the Nazi occupation by immigrating to the United States. He settled in Greenville after reaching out to someone he had met who had been touring Europe. Heller moved over time from a floor sweeper to owner of a small manufacturing plant, became active in civic affairs, and served two terms as a progressive and popular mayor before running as the Democratic candidate for Congress against Campbell. In 1978 Heller had spearheaded the beginning of upscale development in a badly deteriorated downtown Greenville, an effort reflected in today's vibrant Main Street shops and eateries and the outstanding twenty-first-century Upcountry History Museum.

Campbell's campaign polled voters, asking if they would vote "for a candidate who was a Jew," "for a foreign-born Jew," and, a reported third question, "for a foreign-born Jew who didn't believe in the Lord Jesus Christ." Late in the campaign and after a meeting with Campbell's campaign manager, garage owner Don Sprouse got on the ballot as a petition candidate. He asserted on television that Heller, who had been leading in the polls, should not be elected to Congress because he was not a Christian and did not "believe Jesus Christ has come yet." Sprouse received 1,700 of the roughly 100,000 votes. Campbell defeated Heller by almost 6,000 votes.

During Campbell's 1986 campaign for governor, *New York Times* reporter Phil Gailey wrote an extensive article in which Campbell vigorously denied any involvement with the Sprouse campaign. Campbell said he had only recently learned of the contact in 1978 with the third-party candidate by his campaign manager, who, Gailey wrote, "had assured him that neither Heller nor his religion had been discussed." Campbell said the questions in the poll represented legitimate demographic polling. He denounced the raising of the anti-Semitism issue from 1978 in his 1986 campaign as a "vicious smear campaign" against him.[9]

The story of political anti-Semitism in the 1978 congressional race first broke into print in 1983 in a newsletter, "The Baron Report," published by Democratic campaign consultant Alan Baron. He reported hearing of the three questions from Arthur Finkelstein, Campbell's pollster, during a dinner conversation. Both men were Jewish. After that report appeared, Campbell wrote Baron that his account was "inaccurate" and "outrageously wrong." Campbell said he was assured by his pollster that questions related to Heller's religion were legitimate because Heller himself often spoke of his experience as a Jewish immigrant from Austria who fled the Nazis and built a new life in America. The initial *Times* story quoted Heller as saying, "You don't put anything in a poll unless you're interested in using it. It at least gives some indication of what their thinking was in the campaign."[10]

A few weeks later Gailey reported in the *Times* that Lee Atwater had accused Columbia civic leader and Democratic fund-raiser Samuel Tenenbaum of using "Gestapo tactics" in trying to link him and Campbell to the 1978 anti-Semitic controversy. He compared Tenenbaum's allegations to "Hitler's big-lie theory." Atwater, by then already a strategist for Vice President George H. W. Bush and also to the Campbell gubernatorial campaign, apologized two weeks later in a meeting with Tenenbaum. It was arranged by Gordon Zachs, an Ohio businessman who served as Bush's political liaison with Jews. That, too, was reported in the *Times*.[11]

Although Atwater in 1978 had been heavily involved in Strom Thurmond's reelection campaign against a challenge by Pug Ravenel, he also was working with the Campbell campaign. Years later Ravenel's 1974 campaign manager, Marvin Chernoff, ran into Atwater at a restaurant in Columbia, where they ate lunch together and swapped political war stories. There, according to Chernoff, Atwater told him about the polling data about Heller: "He told me, 'We wanted to get it out.' He planted the seed with the third candidate, telling him they wanted to say it, and he did." After telling the story to Gailey, who printed it, Chernoff was called a liar by Atwater. Later, when Atwater was dying of a brain tumor, Chernoff said he received an apology from him. Chernoff added, "He never told me Campbell was cognizant of it."[12] Governor Campbell's second chief of staff, Robert "Bob" McAlister, said Campbell privately had blamed Atwater for pursuing the issue during the 1978 campaign.[13]

For Tenenbaum the issue went beyond political anti-Semitism to the principle embedded in the United States Constitution that there shall be no religious test for public office, the provision for which South Carolina delegate Charles Pinckney played the principal role at the Constitutional Convention. Tenenbaum said he personally told Campbell after he became governor, "If you apologize to Max Heller and the people of South Carolina, it's closed." He added, "But he never did that."[14]

When Campbell emerged as a contender to become Dole's running mate in 1996, Tenenbaum contacted a cousin who worked in the law firm that was vetting Campbell, asserting that the vetting lawyers needed to contact him. Tenenbaum also brought the 1978 campaign controversy to the attention of national Jewish organizations. He suggested to the lawyers that they should call the Anti-Defamation League (ADL), an organization headquartered in New York and created after the 1915 lynching in Georgia of Jewish businessman Leo Frank.

When the lawyers discussed the situation with ADL officials, asking if the background of Campbell's 1978 campaign would be a problem, Tenenbaum said they were told, "Yes, because he never apologized for it." Dole selected as his running mate former congressman and pro football quarterback Jack Kemp.

IN THEIR SUBSEQUENT DEVELOPMENT, Republicans also benefited from underlying tensions within the biracial Democratic coalition. The NAACP joined Republicans in challenging in federal court a House reapportionment plan following the 1990 census that Democrats had designed with an emphasis on protecting Democratic incumbents. The NAACP/Republican plan, supported by black representatives, created more majority-black districts, but also removed black Democratic voters from districts that elected progressive white Democrats, many of whom either retired or lost reelection bids.

The result led to a Republican majority in the S.C. House after the 1994 elections. Although the number of blacks increased from eighteen to twenty-four, there were nine fewer white Democrats. Two others switched after the election to shift majority control to the Republicans. As a result blacks lost influence because they no longer were part of a majority Democratic coalition.

In the S.C. Senate, where blacks opted instead to protect white Democrats, Republicans gained control only after the 2002 election, when veteran senator Verne Smith of Greenville County switched parties in 2003. Republicans meanwhile had widened their majority in the House. With control of both houses of the legislature, Republicans soon began meeting in closed House and Senate caucuses to decide on a party position on most major legislation. Individuals weren't bound by the caucus vote, but it was understood that if you bucked the party position too often, you would face opposition in the next primary. Such secrecy hinders the legislative process because it limits the feedback legislators get from informed voters on emerging issues.

Meanwhile, in 1994 born-again Christian David Beasley, a Democrat in the House who switched parties, narrowly won the gubernatorial election. His support for removing the divisive Confederate battle flag from atop the State House dome cost him sufficient support four years later that Democrats regained the governor's office with House Democratic minority leader Jim Hodges in 1998.

Hodges worked effectively to strengthen public education, expanding early childhood programs and winning public support for a statewide lottery to support education improvement, but his reelection campaign failed to energize his supporters. He lost in 2002 to Republican Mark Sanford, who had established a reputation during six years in Congress as a maverick with a libertarian outlook.

Even with his party in control of both the S.C. House and Senate, however, few of Sanford's initiatives received legislative approval. The Republican Party's platform of reform had been replaced by a focus on cutting taxes and reducing state services, with Sanford unsuccessfully seeking public funds for parents enrolling children in private schools or homeschooling them.

Democrats showed some signs of resurgence in 2004, with a record turnout in February for a Democratic presidential primary that attracted more voters than a six-candidate field in June for the Republican nomination to the U.S. Senate vacated by the retirement of Fritz Hollings. Democrats gained a S.C. House seat in 2004 and another two years later, but they barely held on to the office of state superintendent of education in 2006 and lost that of state treasurer, the last seat held by a Democrat on the powerful state Budget and Control Board. Sanford won reelection with 55 percent of the vote.

The retirements of Thurmond in January 2003 and Hollings in January 2005 marked the end of an era in which the state enjoyed the benefits of extensive bipartisan seniority in Washington. Thurmond's debilitation at the end of his record U.S. Senate career helped persuade Hollings to retire two years later on January 2, 2005, a day after turning eighty-three. Congressmen Lindsey Graham's victory in 2002 to succeed Thurmond and Jim DeMint's in 2004 to succeed Hollings gave Republicans control of both seats for the first time since Reconstruction and strengthened the GOP's hold on the state. For South Carolina it meant going in two years from senators, one from each party, with a combined eighty-four years of seniority to two Republicans with a combined two years of seniority.

Although acknowledging his support of segregation as a political necessity when he got elected as governor at age thirty-seven, Hollings reminisced about serving on the state's legal team to help argue the state's case for school segregation before the Supreme Court in 1952 at an early stage of *Brown v. Board of Education*. He heard an opposing lawyer say, "How in the world can you ask them to serve in the front lines in Europe and when they come home, ask them to sit in the back of the bus."

Hollings said, "As a veteran, that struck me. I realized that just ain't right."[15]

Graham and Sanford, who had served together in Congress, both sought to distance the Republican Party in the state from the racial southern strategy. Sanford officially issued an apology for the Orangeburg Massacre, and he agreed to meet in Augusta, Georgia, with the state NAACP during his 2006 reelection campaign, which his Democratic challenger, state senator Tommy Moore, declined to do. The organization had refused to hold its annual meeting in the state as part of its boycott against continued display of the Confederate battle flag on the State House grounds.

The loss by Governor Hodges in his 2002 reelection campaign, victory by DeMint in the U.S. Senate race in 2004, and reelection of Governor Sanford in 2006 placed the Republican Party in a position of unsurpassed dominance in the state. The return of Democratic control in the U.S. Congress that year, however, resulted in two South Carolina Democrats emerging in major leadership roles nationally. Fifth District representative John Spratt became chairman of the House Budget Committee, and Sixth District representative Jim Clyburn became Democratic whip, the third-ranking party leader in the U.S. House of Representatives.

Democrat Jim Rex's victory for state superintendent of education, combined with three other statewide candidates getting 47 to 49.9 percent of the two-party vote, indicated that Democrats remained competitive and that Republican-leaning independents held the balance of political power in the state.

The state's Republicans remained dominant in the 2008 fall elections, but Democrats made gains over their 2004 totals in the percentage of votes they received in forty-four of forty-six counties. Republican John McCain won 54 percent of the presidential vote in 2008, but Barack Obama's 45 percent put him four points ahead of John Kerry's vote four years earlier.

The party split in the S.C. Senate remained unchanged, but Democrats gained two seats in the House—despite not contesting Republicans for fifty seats—and the GOP elected its first black legislator in the modern era. Obama did not campaign in South Carolina in the fall, no doubt hurting two Democratic congressional challengers who ran competitive races. Republican incumbents Henry Brown (60 percent in 2006) defeated Linda Ketner 52–48 in the First District, and Joe Wilson (63 percent in 2006) defeated Iraqi-war veteran Rob Miller 54–46 in the Second District. The Republican grip on the state had loosened.

12

BEYOND THE BOZART

In his biting 1917 essay "The Sahara of the Bozart," Baltimore satirist H. L. Mencken opened with a couplet from Richland County's J. Gordon Coogler, whose extensive body of work combined high ambition with limited talent: "Alas for the South; her books have grown fewer. / She never was much given to literature." Mencken, hardly able to contain his satirical wit, used Coogler's poetry as an example of what he called the South's "torpor and doltishness." He said of the South that "in all that gargantuan paradise of the fourth rate there is not a single picture gallery worth going into, or a single orchestra capable of playing the entire nine symphonies of Beethoven, or a single opera house, or a single theater devoted to decent plays or a single prose writer that can actually write." He added that no decent scientists or historians bothered to live in the region either.[1]

Mencken's hyperbolic attack on the culture of the South drew numerous responses. The Fugitive poets, a group that included Robert Penn Warren, John Crowe Ransom, and other early-twentieth-century literary figures, wrote their manifesto, *I'll Take My Stand*, in 1930 in part as a response to Mencken.

Charleston had responded earlier. In a 1921 essay that appeared in the first yearbook of the Poetry Society of South Carolina, Hervey Allen challenged Mencken's estimation of the "Bozart South." Allen, and through him other important society members such as Josephine Pinckney and DuBose Heyward, argued that, in fact, the cultural life of the nation would be reborn in southern regionalist writing.

This controversy over the South's artistic failings, despite the hearty defense from the Poetry Society and the Fugitives, does point to a serious lag in the region's cultural production. In antebellum South Carolina, artistic activity came primarily from the aristocratic classes. The art they produced reflected their values. The sectional controversy had pushed William Gilmore Simms, by far South Carolina's most important antebellum author, into becoming less an author and more an amateur historian, his novels and nonfiction works defending the significance of the Palmetto State in American history.

Charleston native Henry Timrod provides another example. Although he contributed a significant amount of verse to the *Southern Literary Messenger* and produced in 1860 a small chapbook of his poems, he received almost no attention outside his region. The poetry he produced during the Civil War, verse like "Ethnogenesis," "A Call to Arms," and "Carolina," poems that praised the origin of the Confederacy in almost mystical or religious terms, did garner a great deal of regional attention. He died in poverty, and a posthumous collection of his poems received some critical attention. Alfred Lord Tennyson called Timrod "the poet laureate of the Confederacy." Whether Tennyson intended it as a compliment remains unclear.

Following southern defeat in the Civil War, the poverty-stricken region became even more culturally barren. Economic hard times forced the formerly leisured classes to focus on growing corn and sweet potatoes rather than producing poetry. The few literary journals that had flourished in the antebellum era lost their subscribers. While New Orleans and Richmond produced several important writers in the immediate postbellum period, South Carolina became a cultural wasteland for virtually half a century.

The dearth of new ideas caused by the influence of slavery before the Civil War was replaced afterward by the numbing effect of the state's catastrophic defeat. In *A Study of History* Arnold Toynbee uses South Carolina in the period after the war as an example of "the nemesis of creativity." He theorized that the memory of catastrophe caused the people to act as if living under a spell.[2]

The state's cultural rebirth occurred in early-twentieth-century Charleston. By 1915 tourism already was becoming the new economic engine for the city, which became a model for the historic tourism movement. Entire areas began undergoing renovation and transformation, and new historic districts were created.

Many of Charleston's older families took the lead in the city's historic preservation movement. Susan Pringle Frost, who had become a successful real estate agent, became the driving force behind the renovation of the Joseph Manigault House and the transformation of large swaths of Tradd and Church streets, which had been filled with tenement dwellings and African American alleyway housing such as found on Catfish Row in the opera *Porgy and Bess*. The 1917 publication of *The Dwelling Houses of Charleston, South Carolina,* by

Charleston natives Alice Ravenel Huger Smith and Daniel Elliott Huger Smith, further strengthened the feeling of Charleston elites for their architectural past.

Perhaps architecture is the area of art—and often unrecognized as such—in which South Carolina has most retained a sustaining interest. In Charleston especially, but scattered throughout the state, are many churches, homes, and public buildings two centuries old or older that represent architectural treasures.

In the lowcountry several still-functioning county courthouses were designed by Robert Mills, whose design for the Washington Monument is his most notable achievement. A native of Charleston, Mills lived for a time at Monticello with Thomas Jefferson, who early recognized his talent. Mills, who practiced in Philadelphia for more than a decade before returning to Charleston in 1820, moved permanently to Washington in 1830.

Restoration and preservation of old buildings is an especially serious pursuit in Charleston, where the Historic Charleston Foundation and the Preservation Society of Charleston have long been engaged in protecting buildings, sites, and structures of historical or aesthetic significance, many dating to the colonial period. Such efforts made Charleston the early national leader in strict city ordinances for historic preservation. The Historic Charleston Foundation received national recognition for reclaiming entire sections of the old city through its purchase of dilapidated, once-fine homes and resale of them to private owners for restoration.

REVITALIZATION MEANT more to the city than tourist dollars. Throughout the 1920s, Charleston lived on the edge of the larger and emerging Southern Renaissance, a regional artistic and literary movement that would include the work of fellow southerners William Faulkner, Thomas Wolfe, Eudora Welty, Robert Penn Warren, and other internationally acclaimed literary figures. The movement belonged to the larger American literary phenomenon of regionalism. Regionalism celebrated national identity while focusing on the more exotic aspects of local life.

Although South Carolina's role in the Southern Renaissance centered on Charleston, it also found expression elsewhere in the state. Upcountry writer Ben Robertson's *Red Hills and Cotton* in 1942, for example, exuded the regionalist spirit of the era. He praised his native region as a place at once full of regional peculiarity while also being deeply and inherently American. A war correspondent for the *New York Herald-Tribune,* he took a two-month break from reporting to write his lyrical, insightful, and affectionate book. He died in a plane crash the year after *Red Hills and Cotton* was published.

Among the native South Carolina writers, none wrote with more eloquence and poetic insight than James McBride Dabbs. Although a first-rate "Dabbs Reader" remains to be published, an article in the *Christian Century* shortly after his peaceful death in 1970 called him "one of the truly religious intellectuals of southern history; and his greatness was founded on the fact that where other Southerners saw dualism he saw relationships."[3] In addition to numerous articles and essays in national publications, he wrote *The Southern Heritage, Who Speaks for the South?* and *Haunted by God.*

Other writers outside of Charleston contributed further to this period of cultural effervescence. Julia Peterkin, writing and living on her ancestral plantation at Fort Motte in Calhoun County, used her sympathetic understanding of African American rural life in the writing of critically acclaimed works such as *Green Thursday, Black April,* and her 1929 Pulitzer Prize–winning *Scarlet Sister Mary.* Peterkin received a significant degree of criticism from her native region for her willingness to challenge the white South's shibboleths of racial identity. Like other South Carolina writers of the era, however, her achievements were soon overshadowed by the work of literary giants from other parts of the South, such as Faulkner, Wolfe, Welty, and Warren.

South Carolina's traditional emphasis on manners, suggesting that being overly truthful is impolite, may account for the state's never producing a major novelist. Good manners also reduced the level of brutal meanness that has characterized much of the Deep South, provoking there a quiet sense of outrage that stimulated literary creativity.

IN CHARLESTON DURING October 1920, a weekly gathering of poets and writers evolved into the Poetry Society of South Carolina. The Poetry Society became the nexus for a variety of cultural endeavors, including the Charleston Museum, the Charleston Etcher's Club, and the Society for the Preservation of Old Dwellings. The organization provided crucial early support for Charleston's artistic community.

The Charleston Museum developed as another important cultural institution in the life of the city. Laura Bragg, director of the museum for two decades, came from New England in 1909 after an apprenticeship at Boston's Isabella Stewart Gardner Museum. She became the official director of the Charleston Museum in 1920, formalizing her role as a volunteer for most of the previous decade. A founder of the Poetry Society, she became one of many Charleston newcomers who contributed much to the city's cultural flowering. Despite her unconventional lifestyle and refusal to adopt the cultural traits of the southern belle, Bragg played a key role in the development of the Charleston Renaissance.

Charleston also became home to the state's only significant movement in pictorial arts. Alfred Hutty, one of the most important American etchers of the twentieth century, visited the city in 1919 and immediately wrote his wife that he had "found heaven." Hutty became known for both his representation of Gullah life in Charleston and his romantic and haunting representations of the lowcountry's natural beauty.

Charleston native Elizabeth O'Neill Verner also used her talents in painting and etching to portray the beauty of Charleston and its environs. Verner lovingly depicted scenes of her native city, seeking, like Hutty, to strengthen the image of Charleston as a place with a rich cultural and historic legacy. Born to a working-class, Irish Catholic family on Legare Street, Verner remained outside most of Charleston's traditional circles of social power. Nevertheless her artistic achievements put her in close contact with traditional elites through her involvement with the Poetry Society and the Preservation Society.

But it was DuBose Heyward who became the national face of the Charleston Renaissance with the publication of his 1925 novel, *Porgy*. It became the basis for his collaboration with George Gershwin on the opera *Porgy and*

Alfred Hutty's etching of "Maum Anne," an elderly African American woman of Charleston, represents the Charleston Renaissance's effort to represent all aspects of Charleston life. *History of South Carolina Slide Collection, G-79*

Bess, a musical production that a decade later would bring Heyward's affectionate vision of Charleston's African American community to an international audience.

Porgy illustrates many of the themes of the Charleston Renaissance, as does the life of the author himself. Heyward, scion of a South Carolina family that traced its lineage to a signer of the Declaration of Independence, grew up literally only a few steps away from urban Gullah communities that thrived in the spacious "rows" hidden off Church and Tradd streets. These small communities, unique in some ways to Charleston's urban environment, became the basis for *Porgy*.

Heyward also learned from his mother, Janie Screven Heyward, a profound appreciation for Gullah culture. Mrs. Heyward, due to her own fascination with African American life, collected stories, folklore, and songs of the black community and often performed them, in dialect, for women's social events. Janie Heyward also privately published verse and so-called plantation stories in the mold of Joel Chandler Harris's tales of Uncle Remus.

In his early life Heyward also accumulated a significant amount of personal experience with the city's African American life. His first job, necessary to support his genteel but cash-poor family, was as an insurance collector in Charleston's black neighborhoods. Between 1900 and 1903 he had also spent his summers on the rice plantation of a relative, working as a field supervisor. In 1905 he worked as a cotton checker on the Charleston docks. Here he came in contact not only with Gullah life, but also with Charleston's exotic underworld. Brothels and bars flourished along the Cooper River docks, and black dockworkers and sailors mixed freely, and sometimes violently, in this world little known to genteel Charlestonians.

Heyward's appreciation, understanding, and affection for African American life, as well as his fascination with the darker side of his beloved city, all found expression in his novel. Borrowing heavily from both his observer's familiarity with "row culture" and the underworld of the docks, Heyward tells the story of a doomed affair between the crippled beggar Porgy and the former prostitute Bess. Bess is the "property" of the black stevedore Crown. The affair between Porgy and Bess only becomes possible when Crown flees Charleston to escape a murder charge. When he returns to claim Bess, Porgy kills him. Though the police do not suspect Porgy for the crime, he ends up in jail for contempt after refusing to talk to the police. The novel ends with Bess leaving Charleston to seek a new life in Savannah.

Porgy quickly received critical acclaim. Critics praised the Charleston aristocrat's ability to portray black life sympathetically and indeed to design an entire tragic drama in which black community life became a central character. So well received was the novel that a little-remembered stage version was quickly produced in New York in 1927. Seeking authenticity, the New York Theatre Guild brought in Charleston's Jenkins Orphanage Band to provide atmospheric music. The orphanage, woefully underfunded since its inception, had been created by the city to care for dependent African American children. The amazingly talented band, however, brought in ten thousand dollars a year from touring with such jazz greats as Ferdinand "Jelly Roll" Morton and William "Count" Basie and performing in Europe.

White elites, as well as African American orphans, provided music for the play. The Society for the Preservation of Negro Spirituals, an organization of young, aristocratic whites who collected the words heard on plantations and in African American churches, also traveled to New York to perform in the play. Both in Charleston and in other venues in New York, they performed these pieces for white audiences.

George Gershwin's far more renowned opera *Porgy and Bess* opened in 1935 on Broadway and became a smash hit. The opera never played in the city in which it is set until 1970, when it sparkled as the celebrated high point in the state's tricentennial celebration. On opening night its black, all-local cast mixed afterward at a champagne reception with mostly white—but some black—patrons. The production not only drew sellout audiences for the full run, but there was both knowing laughter by white patrons and smug smiles by black performers during some choice lines that captured human relationships that for generations had existed between whites and blacks in the city. As a cooperative venture between whites and blacks, the celebratory production marked not only a breakthrough of Charleston social barriers, but also a healing of the trauma incurred during the city's 1969 hospital workers' strike.

Earlier, during the 1930s, the initiatives of the New Deal had reinvigorated the dramatic arts in Charleston. Mayor Burnet Maybank successfully used Works Progress Administration (WPA) funding to restore a seedy hotel on the corner of Queen and Church streets back to its original use as the Dock Street Theatre. The original theater, the first building in America built specifically for dramatic performances, had opened on February 12, 1736. The street name changed from Dock to Queen a month later, but the theater kept its name. The new Dock Street Theatre opened in November 1937 with its front on Church Street, where it now faces the only active Huguenot church in the United States.

When Governor Robert E. McNair convened a Governor's Conference on the Arts in 1966—which led to the creation of the South Carolina Arts

Commission—he told the group "that by enhancing the arts we are enhancing our state in the eyes of those looking for good places to live, to visit, and to do business."[4] The governor acted after the National Endowment for the Arts, part of President Lyndon Johnson's Great Society program, made instant money available. It marked the beginning of a lively period of ferment in South Carolina, including the establishment of a permanent South Carolina art collection.

The state's tricentennial celebration in 1970 sparked a forward-looking cultural renaissance in the state that has continued. As in all other aspects of life in South Carolina, racial traditions had played a major role in shaping the state's cultural patterns. State senator Eugene N. "Nick" Zeigler of Florence, an English major and a Harvard-educated lawyer who spearheaded the effort to enhance the state's cultural life, addressed that reality in 1970 as the legislature created the South Carolina Arts Commission:

> Slavery and the Negro undoubtedly had a pervading influence on the cultural development of South Carolina which should be noted. . . . First the taboo against a discussion of slavery led to a closed society in which new ideas inviting change in human society were suppressed or unarticulated. This sorely inhibited the development of the professional artist. Second, the potential audience, already inadequate, was further reduced because of the mass of illiterate slaves in the State. The law which outlawed teaching Negro slaves to read and write was, in effect, a cultural and intellectual poison for which there seemed no antidote. Third, the seeming insolubility of the slavery question caused intellectual patterns of thought which were divorced from the reality. Tremendous social problems and the movement of social history had to be ignored or rationalized so that creative effort tended to become stylized, artificial, and sterile.[5]

Zeigler also pointed out that the presence of African Americans provided both new talent and a rich cultural subsoil that inspired much of the significant art that the state produced after the Civil War.

A concern for culture and the arts is evident outside of Charleston, especially in Columbia and Greenville, but elsewhere as well. The South Carolina Arts Commission provided much of the impetus. The economic growth of the upstate, and perhaps the old desire to "keep up with Charleston," helped motivate this trend. Greenville in particular has moved to create a new downtown image to reflect the developing prosperity of the upstate, despite the region's class divisions.

The beginnings of concern for the visual arts there dates to 1935 and the formation of the Greenville Fine Arts League. The league, which received a

New Deal–era grant that funded small local exhibitions, made some efforts in the direction of art education. Beginning in 1958 public and private efforts joined in the wake of rapid economic development to secure funding for an art museum. In 1974 county funds and private donations financed an impressive Greenville County Museum of Art on the city's Heritage Green. By the late twentieth century the museum's standing allowed it to compete successfully for major exhibitions.

The museum gained little attention, even locally, until the 1979 loan of a major collection of more than two hundred works of Andrew Wyeth. A decade later owners Holly and Arthur Magill removed the collection and sold it. The Greenville Museum, however, in 1998 began acquiring its own Wyeths and now has thirty-three paintings surveying his career from 1937 to 2001. The museum also has a nationally recognized southern collection.

In addition the museum holds an extensive collection of world-renowned South Carolina native Jasper Johns's paintings. Johns, born in 1930, spent his early years in Allendale. His work has been described as Neo-Dadaist for its combination of dreamlike abstraction and powerful symbolism. He is also known for incorporating everyday objects into both his sculpture and paintings, including images from pop culture such as flags, numbers, targets, and maps. The catalog for the New York Museum of Modern Art's 1996 *Jasper Johns: A Retrospective* asserted that the artist was present "at or near the origin point of virtually every generative idea of importance in avant-garde painting and sculpture in America for four decades."[6] In an interesting example of his cultural weight and wide appeal, an animated Jasper Johns once made an appearance on the television cartoon *The Simpsons*. The Metropolitan Museum of Art paid twenty million dollars in 1998 for his painting *White Flag*.

Equally as notable as the Greenville Museum, given the size, value, and significance of its collection, is the Bob Jones University Museum and Gallery. This collection, filled with late medieval, Renaissance, and baroque masterpieces, was assembled, beginning in 1948, over a thirty-year period by Dr. Bob Jones Jr. Baroque art had fallen out of favor with art collectors during the 1950s, allowing Jones to acquire valuable works at near bottom prices. The small fundamentalist school became one of America's most important repositories for these materials.

Today the collection contains about four hundred works in its Old Masters Collection, including painting by Peter Paul Rubens, Sir Anthony Van Dyck, and Tintoretto. The large gallery also contains collections of Russian icons and Israeli artifacts. The latter are known as the Bible Lands Collection. Visitors often are fascinated both by the breadth of the collection, advertised by the university as "Greenville's Best Kept Secret," and by the irony of the fundamentalist school preserving so many of the masterpieces of Counter-Reformation Catholic Europe.

Visitors to the Gibbes Museum of Art in Charleston come face to face with the city's art history. The Gibbes is recognized nationally for its fine collections of historic portraits and miniature portraits, especially those by Charles Fraser (1782–1860). Its collection of more than five hundred paintings features Charleston landscape views, portraits of notable South Carolinians, and paintings, prints, and drawings from the eighteenth century, and it includes a strong component of American art that relates to Charleston from the eighteenth century to the present.

The Gibbes was developed by the Carolina Arts Association, founded in 1858. In 1905 the gift of a significant endowment from local merchant James Shoolbred Gibbes allowed the building of an impressive Beaux Arts exhibition hall on Meeting Street. The overall collection includes more than ten thousand objects.

From a small museum, planetarium, and natural history collection at the corner of Senate and Bull streets in Columbia, the city in the 1990s developed the new Columbia Museum of Art on Main Street. The city's commercial interests fully supported a sixteen-million-dollar capital campaign. The new facility, with twenty thousand feet of exhibition space, serves as an anchor for the city's downtown revitalization efforts. The museum has earned a reputation for strong educational programs and community outreach.

Although its collection is relatively small, its most prominent holding consists of 77 high-quality works from the Samuel H. Kress collection of 3,100 works of European Old Master paintings, sculpture, and decorative arts. Eighteen hundred were donated to the National Gallery of Art in Washington, D.C. The remaining 1,300 pieces were distributed across the United States to communities where Kress five-and-ten-cent stores served the public. The Columbia Museum's Kress Collection includes "The Nativity," a large and rare fresco transferred to canvas circa 1475–80 by Sandro Botticelli, a preeminent Florentine Renaissance artist.

Often overlooked as a South Carolinian of significance is Samuel F. B. Morse, inventor of the Morse code and the telegraph, those now-obsolete forms of communication that in the nineteenth century were the first form of instant electrical communication. The telegraph marked the end of the Pony Express, and Morse developed it after leaving the state. Born in 1791 at Charlestown, Massachusetts, he moved in 1813 to Charleston, where a first cousin became the tenth president of the College of Charleston.

Neither scientist nor engineer, Morse was an artist whose paintings are prominently displayed throughout South Carolina. One hangs in the governor's mansion in Columbia and another in Charleston's City Hall. The same creativity led him to convert the letters of the alphabet into a system of dots and dashes that could be transmitted via electricity for instant long-distance communication.

COMPARED TO OTHER SOUTHERN STATES, South Carolina has failed to produce its share of outstanding novelists. The great novel about Charleston, a proud and complex city of graceful charm and a hint of wickedness, has yet to be written, but Josephine Pinckney's 1945 novel *3 O'Clock Dinner* remains worth reading. In the modern era, however, South Carolina has produced and become the home of both critically acclaimed and popular authors whose work has tended to deal with rural folkways, the pace of modernization, and the ongoing question of race.

James Dickey, a major American poet, literary critic, and novelist, taught for almost thirty years at the University of South Carolina until his death in 1997. His best-known works are his collection of poems *Buckdancer's Choice* (1965), winner of the National Book Award, and his 1970 novel, *Deliverance*. William Price Fox, who became a teacher in creative writing at the University of South Carolina, has tapped the rich vein of both North and South Carolina life in such books as *Southern Fried, Ruby Red* and *Lunatic Wind*.

Another well-known writer and teacher in the state is Bret Lott at the College of Charleston. Although after eighteen years he left for several years to become editor in chief of the *Southern Review*, he returned to the faculty in Charleston in 2007. His best-known book, *Jewel*, became a book-club selection on the Oprah Winfrey show after it had gone out of print. He recalled vividly, "The day she called, his book was ranked No. 1,069,713 on Amazon.com's sales ranks. By that evening, it was No. 1."[7] Lott's other works include *Reed's Beach, A Stranger's House, The Man Who Owned Vermont*, and the memoir *Fathers, Sons, and Brothers*.

The work of Pat Conroy, using the South Carolina lowcountry as a setting and backdrop, has reached a wide audience. Conroy's family followed his marine father to Beaufort, South Carolina. After high school there, he spent four years at the Citadel, an experience captured in his novel *The Lords of Discipline*. Conroy taught briefly at a small African American school on Daufuskie Island, an experience he novelized in the award-winning *The Water Is Wide*. Life with an often cruel and abusive father (with whom he eventually reconciled) and shaped also by the complexities and contradictions of the southern context informs his works *The Prince of Tides* and *The Great Santini.* Several of Conroy's works have become feature-length films.

Dori Sanders, an African American peach farmer from the town of Filbert near Rock Hill, wrote *Clover,* a well-received first novel in 1993 that won the Lillian Smith Award. The book develops, through the eyes of a child, a variety of complex themes ranging from interracial relationships to how modernization has changed the rural South. The granddaughter of a freed slave, Sanders continued to sell roadside peaches near her farm in York County on land purchased in 1915 by her sharecropper father. Sanders's other books include a second novel, *Her Own Place.* Her *Country Cooking* includes such exotica as "Miss Hattie's Hurricane Survival Fireplace Dinner." *Promise Land: A Farmer Remembers* is based on a presentation she made at the Southern Foodways Alliance in 2004, on the fortieth anniversary of the Civil Rights Act of 1964, that includes an account of growing up in a segregated society.

Charleston native Josephine Humphreys won the Ernest Hemingway Prize for a first novel with *Dreams of Sleep* (1984). Her second novel, *Rich in Love,* was adapted as a film released in 1993. Later books include *The Fireman's Fair* and *Nowhere Else on Earth,* her first historical novel.

Although he kept a low profile in the state, few writers have sold more books than Frank Morrison "Mickey" Spillane, who moved in 1953 to Murrells Inlet on the South Carolina coast and remained there until his death in 2006. He is best known for his thirteen books about hard-drinking detective Mike Hammer that always involved buxom women and vigilante justice. Although mainstream critics sniffed at his works, his power as a writer eventually won respect and recognition. His books have sold more than 140 million copies.

Anne Rivers Siddons is widely identified as a Georgia writer, but in the decade after moving to Charleston in 1998 she published four new novels: *Low Country, Islands, Sweetwater Creek,* and *Nora, Nora.* Her best known book, *Peachtree Road* (1988), sold more than a million copies. Native Chicagoan John Jakes, who moved to Hilton Head Island in the late 1980s and continued to write there, is the creator of the eight-volume *Kent Family Chronicles,* the *North and South* trilogy, and many historical novels. Three other women writers from the Charleston area deserve mention. Sue Monk Kidd, Dorothea Benton Frank, and Mary Alice Monroe have all developed readerships beyond the state's boundaries.

THE WIDESPREAD APPRECIATION of African American folk art in South Carolina represents another element in the cultural life of the state. In many respects this is a continuation of the celebration of African American life that began with the Charleston Renaissance. In other ways it represents a new direction. African American folk artists, rather than white interpreters, have received national and international attention.

The production and sale of sweetgrass baskets in the city of Charleston and along Highway 17 north toward Georgetown represent the coming together of three hundred years of sea grass baskets in South Carolina, African American folk art, and the entrepreneurial impulse. The craft of basket making flows from cultural roots deep in Angola, Senegal, and the Congo. As early as the seventeenth century, slaves produced coiled baskets made of strong bulrush bound with tough oak splits or palmetto butt. These baskets served practical purposes on lowcountry plantations, especially "fanner" baskets used in winnowing rice.

In the early twentieth century, beset by economic hardship and struggling in the bonds of tenant farming, blacks near Mount Pleasant began producing sweetgrass "show baskets" to sell to tourists. Their material became the more aesthetic marsh sweetgrass sewn with strips of palmetto leaf and adorned with longleaf pine needles. Over time the traditional craft won international acclaim. The Smithsonian Institution has long recognized and displayed the artistry of sweetgrass basket makers. The baskets and their makers are featured in Charleston's downtown market and along Meeting Street near Broad in front of the federal courthouse.[8]

Another folk artist, master ironworker Philip Simmons, further illustrates the contemporary celebration of traditional African American craftsmanship in South Carolina. Trained as a blacksmith, he moved into the specialized fields of ornamental iron in 1938. Simmons, who has produced more than five hundred works throughout Charleston—from gates and fences to window grills and balconies—has received national and state recognition. The Smithsonian Institution named him a "National Folk Treasure," and he received a National Heritage Fellowship from the National Endowment for the Arts. One of the artist's decorative gates is on permanent display at the Charleston International Airport and provides many visitors to Charleston with one of their first impressions of the city. In 2001 Simmons received the Elizabeth O'Neill Verner Governor's Award for lifetime achievement in the arts.

Jonathan Green, born in Garden's Corner near coastal Beaufort in 1955, has also received international acclaim for his paintings that portray Gullah life. Focusing on the images of everyday life in the tight Gullah farming community he observed as a child and recognizing its close cultural connection to Africa, Green has painted subjects ranging from the tossing of fishing nets to singing in the fields to powerful revival meetings, all portrayed in bright colors.

The first artist of Gullah heritage to receive formal training at a professional art school, the Art Institute of Chicago, he graduated in 1982 with a B.F.A. Although locating his studio in Florida, Green retained close connections to family in South Carolina. His much-reproduced work is known the world over as a heartfelt representation of African American heritage in South Carolina.

In 2005 Green and fellow African American artist Leo Twiggs of Orangeburg, the first black Ph.D. in fine arts from the University of Georgia, were featured at the Gibbes during Piccolo Spoleto. Twiggs, who also did postgraduate work at the Art Institute of Chicago as well as at New York University, entered the academic realm after getting his doctorate in 1970. His work in batik is extensive, and his use of the Confederate battle flag has intrigued many. *Myths and Metaphors*, the catalog for the Georgia Museum's 2004 retrospective of his work says, "The worn and tattered representations of the flag, almost disintegrating before the viewer, reveal a strong sense of shared history and unresolved conflict."[9]

Two earlier African American artists, Charleston native Edwin A. Harleston and William H. Johnson of Florence, deserve mention. Harleston, both a distinguished artist and civil rights leader, attended the School of the Museum of Fine Arts in Boston from 1906 to 1912. Founder of the Charleston NAACP in 1916, he moved to New York and became an active participant in the Harlem Renaissance. Portraiture became his primary mode of art, and he received portrait commissions from all over the United States. The Gibbes Museum purchased for its collection Harleston's painting of Aaron Douglas, one of the most significant African American artists of the twentieth century.

The Smithsonian Institution in Washington in 1971 sparked widespread interest with a major showing of the work of Johnson, who died the year before, after mental illness forced him to spend the last twenty-three years of his life in an institution. He studied for years in Boston and Europe, then drastically altered his style and returned to his native state to capture the simple way of life of African Americans in the South. After an arrest and harassment by local police, however, Johnson left the state again with bitterness. The Smithsonian American Art Museum in Washington and the Museum of Modern Art in New York own pieces by him, and in 2006 the Greenville County Museum of Art exhibited a collection of his works.

White artists from South Carolina include the husband and wife William Halsey and Corrie McCallum, who also studied at the School of the Museum of Fine Arts but returned to their native Charleston. Although Halsey exhibited in New York for several years and was told he should leave Charleston if he wanted to become a great artist, he decided, "I'd rather not be a great important artist."[10] Two contemporary coastal natives who did achieve recognition with art studios in New York are Sigmund Abeles and Brian Rutenberg. In an earlier period, South Carolina native Washington Allston (1779–1843) earned a national reputation as a romanticist.

South Carolina's African American cultural life has also found expression in music. By a wide margin, however, John Birks "Dizzy" Gillespie is the most significant musical artist from South Carolina. Born in Cheraw in 1917, trumpeter Gillespie, along with saxophonist Charlie Parker and pianist Thelonious Monk, invented the bebop tradition of modern jazz while also fusing African and Cuban styles into a new jazz. His hometown of Cheraw has erected a monument to Gillespie.

Although some native black artists, such as singer Eartha Kitt, for years looked back with bitterness on their South Carolina childhood, the town of North claimed her as one of their own with a special day honoring her during the 1990s, and she later performed in the state for the first time with a well-attended concert in Charleston.

African Americans in the upstate helped shape new musical styles that would be their gift to the cultural life of the nation. The Piedmont blues style, a tradition in twentieth-century American blues identified by a particular finger-picking technique, had two notable practitioners from South Carolina, Pink Anderson and Reverend Gary Davis, both born in Laurens.

Anderson, who began performing as a blues singer in the 1920s, became known for his creative combining of guitar and harmonica, but like many black bluesmen recorded little until after World War II, finally achieving prominence in the 1960s. Syd Barrett created the name of the classic British rock band Pink Floyd by combining Anderson's name with that of Floyd Council, another bluesman from the South Carolina Piedmont.

Davis, by far the most influential of the South Carolina Piedmont bluesmen, combined gospel music with blues in such songs of his as "Twelve Gates to the City" and "Death Don't Have No Mercy." In 1940 at age forty-four he moved to Harlem, where he became a street musician and a music teacher. Davis's work became well known at the Newport Folk Music Festival in the 1960s. His music and fingerpicking influenced such legends as Bob Dylan and the Grateful Dead.

Greenville native Josh White also emerged from the Piedmont blues and gospel traditions and gained attention as a New York singer and guitarist. In the 1930s and 1940s, he attracted a large following of whites and middle-class blacks and became active in the early civil rights movement. Probably his best-known song was "Jelly, Jelly." In 1998 the U.S. Postal Service issued a stamp with his likeness on it.

In *Folk Song in South Carolina,* historian and folklorist Charles W. Joyner emphasizes that "together, the black and white folk in South Carolina created a new folk music, a folk music neither African nor European, but partaking of elements of both." The tradition of South Carolina folk music, he said, "rooted in the real hungers, needs, and struggles of our ancestors, and embodying as it does their ideals, problems, frustrations, and anxieties would seem to be among the choicest heritages of the state."[11]

The development of religious hymns is deeply rooted in South Carolina. As early as 1737 John Wesley published his first hymns in Charleston. In the nineteenth century other songs developed in the camp meetings that symbolized the tide of religious revivalism. Folk tunes brought over by the Scots-Irish in the upcountry played a major influence. By the outbreak of the Civil War more than a half-million copies had been sold of *The Southern Harmony,* a hymnal published by "Singing Billy" Walker of Cross Anchor in Union County. It was rivaled in popularity by *The Sacred Harp,* published by Benjamin Franklin White, Walker's brother-in-law, who was born near Spartanburg. *The Sacred Harp* remains in use in the rural South. Both white and black Methodist campgrounds, some dating back two centuries, remain active in Dorchester County.

Many feel that no South Carolina musician left a greater legacy than James Brown, who was born in 1933 in a one-room shack in Barnwell. After his death on Christmas day 2006, a front-page obituary in the *New York Times* stated,

> Through the years, Mr. Brown did not only call himself "the hardest working man in show business." He also went by "Mr. Dynamite," "'Soul Brother No. 1," "the Minister of Super Heavy Funk" and "the Godfather of Soul," and he was all of those and more.
>
> His music was sweaty and complex, disciplined and wild, lusty and socially conscious. Beyond his dozens of hits, Mr. Brown forged an entire musical idiom that is now a foundation of pop worldwide.
>
> . . . Mr. Brown was a political force, especially during the 1960s; his 1968 song "Say It Loud—I'm Black and I'm Proud" changed America's racial vocabulary.[12]

Brown was scheduled to perform in Boston when the Reverend Martin Luther King Jr. was murdered. Instead of canceling his show, the *Times* reported, Brown had it televised. "Don't just react in a way that's going to destroy your community," he urged. Unlike many other cities, where riots occurred, Boston was quiet. Later in his half century as singer, songwriter, bandleader, and dancer, Brown bonded with Strom Thurmond and gave a lusty performance at the veteran senator's hundredth birthday party in 2002.

More reflective of change in South Carolina is the band Hootie and the Blowfish. Four former University of South Carolina students—three white and one black—propelled their pop-rock band into international recognition with *Cracked Rear View*, their first album. It sold sixteen million copies and was the best-selling album of 1995, their peak year of travel and attention.

By then Darius Rucker, Mark Bryan, Dean Felber, and Jim "Soni" Sonefeld had worked together for a decade since meeting as freshman at the University of South Carolina, not long after Bryan heard Rucker singing in a dormitory shower in the mid-1980s. They played frat parties and local clubs, working their way up the music ladder until their breakthrough in 1995. Rucker's combination of soulful pop and subtle wit became a hallmark for the group.

ALTHOUGH NUMEROUS CHANGES in South Carolina's relationship to the arts have occurred, Charleston still reigns as the state's cultural mecca. It is a city with more than 160 art galleries and dozens of aspiring young artists. Since 1977 the annual Spoleto Festival USA has placed Charleston on the international cultural map. Gian Carlo Menotti and Christopher Keene were the driving forces behind the beginning of the festival, a counterpart to their Festival of the Two Worlds in Spoleto, Italy.

They hoped to find a host city for the annual seventeen-day event that would combine the attractions of an American tourist destination with old-world charm. Charleston seemed perfect. A wealth of performance spaces, including the historic Dock Street Theatre, proved a decisive factor.

Mayor Joe Riley intervened in heated disagreements that almost caused Charleston to lose the festival, but Spoleto Festival USA opened as planned in May 1977. *Newsweek* praised the variety of performances and called Charleston a "Sleeping Beauty" that had just awakened. The magazine also praised Mayor Riley for his determined efforts to revive the cultural life of the city.[13]

For seventeen days and nights each spring, the city hosts about a hundred Spoleto festival performances in artistic disciplines ranging from opera and ballet to sketch comedy as well as the wide variety of inexpensive or free offerings of the companion Piccolo Spoleto. Since 1977 the festival has hosted numerous major premieres, including plays by Tennessee Williams and Arthur Miller. Visitors also discover the culinary attractions of Charleston, the pleasure of a great walking city, and a sense of history that lives.

ONE OF THE BEST KEPT SECRETS of cultural South Carolina, at least to many South Carolinians, is Brookgreen Gardens on the Grand Strand near Pawleys Island. Brookgreen became America's first sculpture garden in 1931 and now contains over nine hundred works. The nine-thousand-acre gardens emerged from the vision of sculptor Anna Hyatt Huntington and her husband, Archer Huntington, the adopted son of nineteenth-century intercontinental railroad magnate C. P. Huntington. The vision developed as they drove past thousands of acres of abandoned rice plantations between Georgetown and Myrtle Beach early in the Depression-era 1930s.

Huntington bought those ruins, as well more than two miles of oceanfront property (now Huntington Beach State Park) across Highway 17, then a dirt road. He hired architects and hundreds of unemployed men to work on creating what today is a national historic landmark. It includes gardens, a zoo, and a significant collection of figurative outdoor sculpture by American artists, including many pieces by Anna Hyatt Huntington. Her studio remains preserved in the state park that they deeded to South Carolina.

Located between Georgetown and Myrtle Beach, Brookgreen Gardens is one of South Carolina's hidden gems. Archer M. Huntington and his sculptor wife, Anna Hyatt Huntington, developed the estate from four abandoned rice plantations, built a studio for her there, and created one of the world's largest displays of outdoor statuary, much of it work by her. They also bequeathed to the state more than two miles of oceanfront property that now makes up Huntington Beach State Park. *History of South Carolina Slide Collection*, A-22

Culture and the arts in South Carolina have provided a good barometer for social and economic change in the Palmetto State. A state once seen as representative of southern cultural vapidity now attracts an international audience to Spoleto USA, and South Carolina artists are also known the world over for tapping the rich vein of native folk art. Even H. L. Mencken might be impressed.

13

THE CHANGING ECONOMY

The combination of social change wrought by the civil rights era in South Carolina and the state's response to it opened a new era of economic development. In outlawing racial discrimination in employment, the Civil Rights Act of 1964 provided new job opportunities for almost a third of the state's population. That in turn significantly increased the market for goods and services.

The 1964 Civil Rights Act with its equal employment section came at a time when the textile industry was facing a labor shortage. Blacks began to move rapidly into textile manufacturing jobs. By the end of the decade they held almost 25 percent of such jobs in the state. A virtual caste system, in which white manufacturing workers were assured of having no blacks in equal positions, and certainly not as supervisors, had crumbled.

Early in 1965 U.S. Attorney Terrell L. Glenn and Attorney General Daniel R. McLeod of South Carolina met with textile industry personnel managers, and later by teleconference with several thousand line foremen, to explain exactly what the Civil Rights Act would require. They removed many misconceptions. A psychological study conducted by the Technical Education Commission a few years later revealed that the new hiring policies had resulted in increased productivity, with white workers determined to show they could produce more and black workers determined to prove them wrong.

For many blacks, textile jobs offered opportunity for a full-time regular paycheck and an entry point that could lead to better-paying jobs in other industries. The technical education centers operated on a desegregated basis from the beginning. Although newer industry carried no historic memory of racial discrimination in employment, in the white-collar part of the plants, where hiring and promotion decisions were made, few black faces appeared.

With the new political and social freedoms and economic opportunities for African Americans, their out-migration from the state had essentially ended by 1970. Many returned home to retire near family and friends or simply find jobs and live near them. Despite a black middle class that expanded significantly in the next decades, blacks in the state overall remained far behind whites economically, a condition rooted in past discrimination and mostly hidden because of a black presence throughout the workforce.

THE FIRST PHASE of South Carolina's economic development, which ended with the Civil War, had depended almost exclusively on agriculture based overwhelmingly on slave labor. The second phase, which centered on cotton in agriculture and textiles in manufacturing, remained dominant until after World War II. In addition to cotton, Franklin Roosevelt's New Deal had rescued tobacco farmers from the Depression, restoring the Pee Dee region's economy through production controls and price supports. By 1970, in response to a new awareness of tobacco-related illnesses and other health risks, the crop had entered into a sharp decline. Phase three and the beginnings of industrial diversification followed the dramatic impact of World War II, which provided greatly expanded educational opportunities for veterans through the GI Bill and a backlog demand for goods and services that the entire country shared. The war mobilization effort in South Carolina also left behind an important deposit of new skills and continued the population shift from rural to urban.

At the end of World War II the coastal plain had barely developed beyond the seafood industry and forest products. The latter would develop statewide as a significant economic element.

Myrtle Beach renamed the sixty-mile stretch of wide, gently sloping beach that stretched north and south of the city the Grand Strand and launched a successful national advertising and promotion campaign that stretched into Canada. Steady growth, expanded tourism, and rising real estate prices followed.

In the 1950s twenty-seven-year-old Yale Law graduate Charles Fraser visualized more than trees and forests in the large chunk of Hilton Head Island his lumberman father had purchased. Fraser developed Sea Pines Plantation, preserving forest land as nature trails and natural habitat as part of a master plan that later would be replicated on a grander scale at Kiawah Island.

WITH THE ASSISTANCE of Senator Jimmy Byrnes in Washington, the barely active Charleston Naval Shipyard, which employed five thousand civilians at its peak in World War I, had gotten a boost in the mid-1930s. By the time the

United States entered World War II in December 1941, employment at the Navy Yard had expanded to ten thousand. It reached a peak of twenty-six thousand in 1944 that included significant numbers of women and blacks, whose lower pay compared to white males reflected national norms.

The influx of workers resulted in residential communities that would provide the basis for the city of North Charleston, the state's third largest city in 2006 (behind Columbia and Charleston). The payrolls for shipyard workers and U.S. Navy personnel provided a major boost to the economy of Charleston until deactivation of the shipyard and naval base in 1995.[1]

The most striking aspect of this third phase was the process by which a cluster of industries related to textiles (including apparel, chemicals, containers, trucking, and machinery) appeared on the scene. The wartime development of synthetic fibers brought in national companies such as DuPont and Celanese. Consolidations and mergers in the textile industry combined with mechanization and automation to increase efficiency rapidly in the industry. Dozens of new plants were built, and numerous antiquated plants were abandoned.

Meanwhile the textile industry continued to abandon New England, which subsequently concentrated on information technology and manufacturing more value-added products that paid better compensation to workers. Dyeing and finishing, carpets and knit goods, textile machinery, apparel, and even the woolen industry completed the migration to the South. Better-paying, more highly skilled jobs developed in the new synthetic fiber plants. From the textile base and chemical fiber plants, petrochemical fiber plants followed, all concentrated in the Piedmont.

The apparel industry moved into the state, attracted by low wages, the skill of farm women accustomed to needlework, and low-cost access to textile manufacturers. The apparel plants became a major market for the textile mills after World War II. In many smaller communities there had been no local work available before to generate cash income to supplement marginal farmers and submarginal farm laborers. A biracial workforce began to get jobs in these plants.

Textiles remained the dominant industry until well after World War II. In 1975, 137,300 South Carolinians were employed in textiles and another 41,400 in apparel and other finished products—a total of 178,700 textile-related jobs. Globalization, productivity gains through technology, and an end to protective tariffs, however, sent those numbers plunging 80 percent by the opening years of the twenty-first century. By 2003, fewer than 38,000 jobs remained, one-third fewer than two years earlier.

Meanwhile by the end of the century tobacco production fell by almost two-thirds from its peak of 197,000 pounds in 1955. The Pee Dee's hub city of Florence had become a regional center for health care and manufacturing, and strong leadership at Francis Marion University provided a stimulating institutional boost to the region's economy, which lagged behind that of the state as a whole.

The apparel industry, the principal end user for textile products, lost huge numbers of jobs—drawn away by subsistence wages overseas—and to many seemed a dead business in the state. But specialty apparel for bikers at Hincapie Sportswear in Greenville and Swadeshi designs made in Andrews for yoga enthusiasts provided examples of adaptive manufacturers. Stone International's direct online marketing to consumers proved sufficiently effective that despite the odds, CEO Eugene E. "Jack" Stone IV initiated in 2004 a formal South Carolina Apparel Cluster.[2]

Meanwhile the surviving textile industry was finding footholds with new niches and markets. One major report, compiled by Michael E. Porter and the Monitor Group, suggested expansion into such markets as automotive and industrial products, health-care products requiring superior quality, and military-related textile products that require production in the United States.[3]

Milliken in Spartanburg—dominated for decades by owner Roger Milliken, who was in his nineties when he turned over operations to a new chief executive officer in 2006—remained the nation's number-one textile company. The company, which maintains strict privacy about company matters and discloses little about its out-of-state operations, had developed a reputation for pioneering research and development of innovative new products. In contrast the state's venerable Springs Industries had transformed itself into Springs Global, with extensive overseas operations, including a partner company in Brazil. Only two of its manufacturing facilities remained in South Carolina in 2007. Much of its domestic production specialized in bed linens, bath products, window fashions, and items for babies and children and for home sewing. Smaller companies such as Alice Manufacturing and Inman Mills also became more specialized in high-end home furnishings and related items.

The record of the textile industry confirmed that the state could no longer compete as a low-wage location in a world economy.

THE END OF RACIAL CONFLICT in the South combined with the positive world attention the region received after the 1976 election of Georgia governor Jimmy Carter as president to attract a new wave of international as well as national corporate investment. For South Carolina it also attracted outside attention to the state's historic sites, natural beauty, sandy beaches, and other attractions for tourists and retirees.

Phase four quietly began in the early 1970s when Michelin opened its first tire plant in the South Carolina upcountry. Textile manufacturers initially objected to such companies, whose higher pay and benefits enabled them to recruit the best manufacturing workers from the textile industry. Michelin, and the other international corporations that followed, would never have located in South Carolina without the Port of Charleston.

The farsighted South Carolina Ports Authority has served as a major force in transforming the state economically. Whether it is the BMW manufacturing plant in Spartanburg (built on land owned by the South Carolina Ports Authority), which has created a major auto industry manufacturing and research cluster, the extensive expansion and presence of Michelin in the state, or the capital-intensive $1.3 billion Fuji research and manufacturing complex in Greenwood County—none would be in South Carolina without the Port of Charleston.[4] Nor would Global Aeronautica, the state's first major component for an aeronautics cluster; it opened a facility in North Charleston in 2007 to build the fuselage for the Boeing 787 passenger plane, using parts from dozens of countries. Since shortly after World War II, the port has provided the state with a major international transportation hub, ranking among the nation's top five in 2000.

From its initial South Carolina operation dating back to the early 1970s, long before BMW arrived, Michelin has greatly expanded its presence in the state. Its North American headquarters is located in Greenville, and in 2008 the company's operations included nine tire manufacturing and related facilities in Anderson, Lexington, Spartanburg, and Greenville counties with almost eight thousand employees. In 2007 and 2008 Michelin announced almost $450 million in expansions and updates at its nine facilities in the four counties. A list of the world's fifty most respected companies compiled for *Forbes* magazine in 2006 ranked Michelin fifth and BMW eighteenth.[5]

The special quality of the water at Lake Greenwood attracted Fuji, a low-profile facility in the state where assembly-line robots make every one of the disposable cameras it sells in the United States. The expansive Fuji facility includes significant research and manufacturing components for high-tech medical imaging and other equipment.

In addition to its access to international trade, the port is connected to the entire upstate industrial area by interstate highways. Less than an hour's drive west of Charleston, I-26 intersects I-95, the major artery for the entire East Coast. Another hour west and it links at Columbia with I-77 to Charlotte and the upper Midwest and then to I-20, which runs west through Atlanta to western Texas. Barely another hour, before extending to the Blue Ridge Mountains and the North Carolina border, it connects to I-85 near Greenville and Spartanburg. Locals call the hundred-mile stretch of I-85 in South Carolina "the autobahn." It links to Charlotte and North Carolina's Research Triangle to the northeast and to Atlanta to the southwest.

The twenty-first century opened with a rapidly expanding international market for the state's forest industry, which in 2004 was the third-largest sector in manufacturing. The market to China alone grew from two hundred thousand dollars in 1999 to more than seven million four years later. Forest products exported around the world through the Port of Charleston range from yellow pine lumber and fiberboard to packing materials, such as boxes and crates, for a rapidly expanding market.[6]

THE COMBINED STORY of German automaker BMW opening a plant in South Carolina and its participation in the Clemson University International Center for Automotive Research (CU-ICAR) is worth telling in some detail. Of all the elements of modern economic development in the state, none is more important.

Clemson officials had begun brainstorming in the early 1990s with the civic and business leadership of Greenville, thirty-five miles away, to develop some type of major research facility that would meet their mutual interests. Meanwhile Governor Carroll Campbell and his administration had begun negotiating with BMW officials about locating a planned North American manufacturing facility in South Carolina.

In the end Department of Commerce director John Warren, a retired president of the SCANA Corporation (parent company for South Carolina Electric and Gas) and a quiet man with an unerring sense of timing, voiced an earthy, barnyard expression to let BMW's top official know that the time had come to make a decision about whether to locate in South Carolina. The response sealed the deal. Other significant players included the ports authority and key legislative leaders such as then House Speaker David Wilkins, who had a special interest in his hometown of Greenville, and his successor as Speaker, Representative Robert W. "Bobby" Harrell of Charleston.

Campbell approved a $130 million incentives package that included $40 million for an I-85 interchange west of Spartanburg and a free fifty-year lease on a $45 million package of land and new site infrastructure on a 1,039-acre site owned by the South Carolina Ports Authority. (BMW can purchase it at original cost after fifty years.) The state's technical education system provided

$20 million to reimburse BMW for training a skilled workforce of two thousand at three of its upstate TEC campuses.

Ground breaking began in 1992, construction in 1993, and hiring and production in 1994. By 2006 the millionth car came off the assembly line. By 2007 more than $3.5 billion had been invested in the plant, and more than 5,400 full-time jobs existed on the BMW manufacturing site, roughly 30 percent of them held by African Americans or Hispanics. One-quarter of the employees were female. Weekly product value exceeded $210 million, and weekly payroll more than $30 million. BMW unit sales in the United States had increased fivefold, from 65,000 in 1994 to 335,000.

Average pay was roughly fifty thousand dollars a year. A majority of employees drove BMWs that the company leased at an attractive rate. Executives wanted the workers to identify with the high-performing luxury vehicles they were assembling. Those associates speak with demonstrable pride in their jobs coordinating with robots and computers to produce the cars, most of them custom made for specific buyers. The cars leave the automated assembly line untouched by human hands during less than a day and a half of production time.

The total economic impact was much larger, with fifty-two suppliers in seventeen counties—80 percent of them new companies—employing more than twelve thousand other workers, in addition to spawning new restaurants and expanding the market for other businesses in the Spartanburg area. In addition to BMW, South Carolina also had attracted a small cluster of auto-related plants—American-LaFrance fire truck and Daimler-Sprinter plants near Charleston, a Honda all-terrain vehicle plant near Florence, as well as a Cummings Engine plant near Charleston and four Bosch plants around the state. By 2007 the state's automotive cluster employed roughly fifty thousand people. A $750 million expansion that BMW announced in 2008 would increase annual production capacity by two-thirds, to 240,000 vehicles, by 2012, with expanded economic impact throughout the upcountry.

As a socially responsive corporate citizen, BMW has used job development credits from the state to fund a variety of innovative social service, cultural, and education programs. For example, the "Call Me Mister" programs at Clemson and some of the state's historically black colleges and universities support young black men in becoming elementary school teachers. Through 2007 more than $23 million was committed to community organizations throughout South Carolina.

In 2006 BMW was shipping roughly 60 percent of the new cars produced in South Carolina back to Europe through the Port of Charleston. They provided the core component (followed by textiles) for a 2003 report by the U.S. Department of Commerce showing South Carolina with $2.7 billion, second only to California's $3.5 billion, in state exports to Germany. Meanwhile some eight thousand shipping containers, primarily of engines and transmissions, were imported annually through the Port of Charleston from Germany. The South Carolina facility produced 17 percent of all BMW automobiles, whose worldwide sales had more than doubled to 1.2 million since the company moved into the state.

Within weeks after announcement of the BMW plant, corporate officials visited Clemson to explore a relationship parallel to one the company had in Germany with the University of Munich. In response Clemson officials visited BMW corporate headquarters in Munich. Top officials there rejected a proposal to help Clemson build a wind tunnel as a research tool for the $10 billion U.S. motor sports industry.

Instead they proposed joint development of a facility designed as a global center of academic and industry expertise in automobile manufacturing, safety, and power-train development—what became the International Center for Automotive Research. At lunch that day BMW's chief executive officer, Bernd Pischetsrieder, told the Clemson delegation, "We're going to plant an acorn today and plan a seventy-five-year relationship."[7]

As the process developed, Clemson University president James Barker recalled, it involved two different cultures—academic and corporate—coming together. "We were each fascinated by how the other works. They're separate and need to build a connector, and ICAR is the connector. It serves as a bridge."[8]

Before breaking ground on ICAR, Clemson officials and legislative leaders visited North Carolina's Research Triangle Park, which dates back to the 1960s, and the nearby North Carolina State University Centennial Campus, developed three decades later. Impressed, they returned with a vision of an advanced twenty-first-century facility, analogous to the proposal by Governor Hollings four decades earlier to establish the technical education program, which over time expanded to include a broad junior-college curriculum.

Robert "Bob" Geolas, the North Carolina-born director of the Centennial Campus, was hired as CU-ICAR director. His directive: develop a place where the quite different cultures of business and higher education could simultaneously operate both separately and together.

By the end of 2006 two major research and development facilities—one by BMW and the other by the Timken Company—with a combined total investment of more than forty million dollars, were fully operating on a carefully landscaped 250-acre site along I-85 in Greenville. The facilities incorporated up-to-date LEED, or green, standards for environmental protection.

Although Timken wasn't a supplier for BMW, it produces a specialized line of automotive products, and the broad concept of ICAR and the developing Clemson graduate campus appealed to them. They had recently acquired five manufacturing plants in the state to go with the one that they already operated, which meant close proximity between its research, development, and production facilities.

The Clemson graduate center, named for Governor Campbell, is designed to provide an academic anchor for ICAR. It is less than a three-minute walk from the Timken and BMW research facilities. The setting is designed to provide students and faculty access to knowledge of future trends, including marketing and management, in the auto industry, to create the intellectual capital that companies such as BMW need to compete globally.

The facility allows students to have access to corporate researchers and faculty-coordinated internships, as well as providing access for graduate students to information and trends that might become the subject for a master's thesis or Ph.D. dissertation. The curriculum is designed to integrate disciplines. Faculty get to share ideas with top corporate researchers in an environment designed to promote personal interaction, with common parking and places for interacting during lunch.

Those developing CU-ICAR shared large goals and aspirations. "This is not a sprint, but a marathon," Geolas observed a few weeks after the Timken facility opened, "and we need to see it that way."[9] He viewed the BMW and Timken facilities as important first steps for developing ICAR.

From BMW's perspective the Clemson graduate campus at ICAR also offers a needed nontraditional approach of systems analysis that integrates mechanical and electronic systems in training graduate engineering students. As the automotive systems become increasingly electronic, integrating information technology, whether for steering, braking, or improvements to driving safety, BMW will need engineers and managers trained in combining mechanical and electronic technology.

Clemson's long-term vision for ICAR extends to two overlapping industries, U.S. automotive manufacturing and the $25 billion worldwide motor sports industry. The latter encompasses NASCAR, Le Mans, and the full Formula 1 racing world. According to Chris Przirembel, vice president for research and economic development at Clemson University, roughly four thousand small and medium-sized engineering companies have Formula 1 racing as their primary customers, which opens broad opportunities for licensing new technology created at ICAR.

For the U.S. automotive industry, ICAR is physically closer than auto research centers near Detroit to a majority of what the trade calls original equipment manufacturers (OEMs). In addition to BMW in South Carolina, Honda, Nissan, Toyota, General Motors, Volkswagen, and Mercedes all had or were developing major auto plants in the Southeast.

IN USING FUNDS provided by the state as tax credits for new job creation, BMW adopted an idea proposed by Columbia activist Samuel Tenenbaum to create well-endowed chairs in higher education for outstanding researchers in science, medicine, and technology. BMW used job tax credits provided by the state to put ten million dollars into the endowed chairs program, two at Clemson, one for the School of Business at the University of South Carolina, and one in medicine at the Medical University of South Carolina. Michelin and Timken each provided an additional three million dollars for endowed chairs.

Meanwhile, partly in response to what legislative leaders learned in their North Carolina visit, the General Assembly in 2004 passed four acts related to economic development. President Barker of Clemson believed the established facilities in North Carolina reflected a datedness that this special legislation addressed. The first act draws money from the state lottery to fund Research Centers for Economic Excellence, which require matching funds from the private sector to fund the high-profile endowed chairs.

The second bill, the Life Sciences Act, is to build research infrastructure. A third is the Innovation Center Act, which is aimed at moving research developed in the state's universities to the marketplace with start-up companies. The fourth created a new venture capital fund for new companies.

Although glitz, glitter, and excitement flowed from the auto industry, total manufacturing jobs in the state had declined by 31 percent in the two decades ending in 2005.

THE MAJOR NATURAL resource of the state is water, an abundance of freshwater streams and rivers that feed more than a half-dozen large, man-made lakes covering well over a million acres. On a per capita basis no state exceeds South Carolina in the number of fishing licenses sold annually. Boating is for many a statewide pastime. However, mercury levels in many rivers and streams have increased to such a level that warnings have been issued in regard to eating fish caught in them. This is an another by-product of economic development.

The upcountry's hardwoods with their bright fall foliage and the region's easy access to the Appalachian Mountains, whose Blue Ridge dips into the state's western edge, add to its quality of life. The combination of water and abundant forests joins with the quiet, still beauty of lowcountry swamps and a 281-mile Atlantic coastline with well over a hundred thousand acres of accessible, protected tidal marsh and wetlands to create great natural beauty that has helped make the state an alluring destination for retirees.

The coast also provides for a localized seafood industry, based on oysters, shrimp, crabs, and commercial fishing. But white sand beaches, mild winters, and an explosion of golf courses combine to make tourism the coastal plain's major industry. The closing in 2006 of the legendary Pavilion in Myrtle Beach symbolized an end to six decades of nostalgic memories of native South Carolinians and other summer vacationers and a new commitment to attract high-end replacements to the Grand Strand beaches, seafood restaurants, and impressive golf courses. As the twenty-first century opened, the area's population also surged, propelled both by retirees and working families.

Beaufort County's 40 percent population growth in the 1990s was spurred primarily by Hilton Head Island and the Del Webb Sun City retirement development. The thousands of affluent newcomers provided sufficient cultural demand to anchor a thriving symphony orchestra in the county.

Charleston has become a major national and developing international tourist destination with its historic preservation, major Revolutionary and Civil War historic sites upgraded and staffed by the National Park Service, historic gardens unparalleled in America, emerging and significant art scene, and developing international slavery museum. An alluring city for walkers to soak up the merging of history into the present, its superior lowcountry cuisine is evidenced by a variety of quality restaurants. Its port has become both a point of arrival and departure for cruise ships. So much of the city's development is linked to the vision, leadership, and political skill of Mayor Joe Riley, elected in his mid-sixties to a ninth four-year term in 2007, that *Governing* magazine has called him "a living argument against term limits."[10]

The 2005 Porter report included tourism as one of four existing business clusters in the state (with automotive, textiles, and chemical products the others). As an element of economic development for the state, however, tourism provided few high-paying jobs, with average annual wages of $16,556. Throughout the coastal region, however, tourism spurred rapid growth in the finance, insurance, and real estate sectors. Except for the Charleston and Hilton Head areas, the state attracted comparatively few high-end visitors.

In a 2007 *Southern Living* survey, Charleston was voted readers' third favorite shopping destination, but swept the category of favorite southern city. Readers chose Myrtle Beach as their second favorite beach town/resort and second favorite family vacation spot. Beaufort ranked first as the readers' favorite small town.

The alluring beaches, however, face the perils of nature. The combination of storm erosion and changing sea currents can shift massive amounts of sand from one location to another, creating conditions that can be overcome only by hauling in sand for beach renourishment, an expensive and only temporary form of maintenance. Retired Duke University professor Orrin Pilkey, a widely recognized expert on beach erosion, calls beach renourishment financed by taxpayers "welfare for the rich." He further argues that replenishing the beach destroys the ecosystem, with a loss of pleasure for tourists who enjoy watching seabirds that will disappear when their food chain is gone.[11]

A competing view is that the increased property values created by beach renourishment, combined with the beach's value as a central attraction for tourists, justifies the cost—especially at Myrtle Beach.[12] The threat of global warming with its prospect for more powerful storms and a gradual rise in sea levels, however, creates long-term concerns about the coast's future. The vast costs of hurricane damage in the Gulf of Mexico states of Florida, Alabama, and Louisiana have resulted in skyrocketing insurance rates and policy cancellations, suggesting slower residential growth ahead in coastal areas.

ALTHOUGH CHEMICAL PRODUCTS are considered a cluster in the state, roughly half of the industry's twenty-five thousand employees early in the twenty-first century worked at the Savannah River Site near Aiken. The existing industrial sector had traditionally depended on the textile industry as major customers.

The Savannah River Site's half-century-old technical center was certified in 2004 by the U.S. Department of Energy as the Savannah River National Laboratory. The only site in the country to process and store plutonium, SRS's five decades of developing hydrogen and nuclear weapons capabilities provided a core of expertise.

The state's hydrogen development idea flows from a twenty-first-century collaborative initiative launched by University of South Carolina president Andrew Sorensen. During his first week as USC president in 2001, he visited Clemson University to see President Barker, who would recall it as the first visit there ever by a University of South Carolina president for a nonathletic event. Sorensen recalled walking out of the elevator outside Barker's office and facing a wall of newspaper and television reporters.

"I said, 'Jim, you must be expecting someone special,'" Sorensen recalled, "and he said, 'Yes, we are. You.'" Sorensen spoke of the need to keep their rivalry on the athletic field and work collaboratively to serve the state. They agreed to do an inventory of all the projects their faculties were working on together and were surprised to find twenty-one small projects involving joint faculty, but with no institutional oversight.[13]

To help create a statewide climate for the idea, Sorensen spoke to local chambers of commerce and Rotary clubs where USC's fifteen branch campuses are located across the state, preaching the virtues of collaboration across institutional boundaries. Meanwhile Medical University of South Carolina president Ray Greenberg enthusiastically joined the other two in the quest for collaboration. They began with the fledgling endowed chairs program. In one unique example of collaboration, a former cardiological scientist from Georgetown Medical Center accepted a primary faculty appointment at USC with his laboratory at MUSC in Charleston and with Clemson joining as a third research university, each making equal payments for his salary. USC and MUSC merged their schools of pharmacy, a national first, with an executive dean for both campuses. Each has the same curriculum, which allows incoming students to choose which one to attend—with plans for a third campus in Greenville.

The designation of a national science laboratory at the Savannah River Site followed a meeting Sorensen set with White House chief of staff (and USC graduate) Andrew Card, a former General Motors executive long interested in the idea of hydrogen-fueled automobiles, and the two top SRS officials. Senator Lindsey Graham and Fourth District congressman Bob Inglis helped secure more congressional funding for hydrogen research, and an endowed chair for hydrogen research was created at USC. House Speaker Bobby Harrell became an advocate for both the endowed chairs program and the hydrogen initiative.

To demonstrate the potential of hydrogen, USC developed a LEED-certified residence hall complex in which a hydrogen fuel cell provides some of the energy for the heating, air conditioning, and electricity the building uses. The fuel cell, located on a grass-covered roof that reflects away the sun's heat in the summer and keeps heat from escaping during the winter, did not save money because of the cost of hydrogen fuel, but it provides a model for how the future may look and will be a showpiece for hundreds of experts in hydrogen storage and manufacturing at the 2009 annual meeting of the National Hydrogen Association scheduled at USC.

SRNL works with researchers at USC, its university partner, in South Carolina's quest to move to the forefront of hydrogen fuel cell development. The state also has taken a leadership role in the Southeast in nuclear technology, with nuclear fuel produced by Westinghouse at a plant near Columbia and roughly half the state's electric power generated by seven nuclear plants. With two additional nuclear power stations scheduled to go online before 2020, the Savannah River National Laboratory quickly became involved in researching the potential for developing a nuclear reactor that can break molecules of water into hydrogen and oxygen during off-peak hours.

The Aiken County Center for Hydrogen Research opened in 2006. The building is owned by Aiken County, but half of its sixty thousand square feet of space was initially manned by fifty scientists and engineers from the Savannah River National Laboratory. Toyota Technical Center announced plans to lease space at the center for hydrogen research aimed at fueling cars.

In a related development the U.S. Department of Energy selected Clemson as one of four universities to receive $2 million research and development grants. Clemson's grant is to explore a method to filter impurities out of hydrogen as a step toward making it a viable alternative energy source. All of these developments, including links to ICAR, have led to South Carolina's becoming a center for hydrogen as a major fuel source.

Environmentalists and others express strong concerns, however, about long-term storage of plutonium and radioactive wastes in SRS facilities not designed for that purpose. They also have complained about limited access to library data in regard to radioactivity issues.

AS WITH SRS, except for some impact by its congressional delegation, the state has little influence in determining the location of military bases. Those decision are made by the Department of Defense.

The presence of military bases, however, continues to have significant economic impact, with such major facilities as Shaw Air Force Base near Sumter, the Parris Island Marine Corps Recruit Depot and Marine Corps Air Station near Beaufort, the army's infantry training center at Fort Jackson in Columbia, Charleston Air Force Base, and a cluster of navy facilities that remained after the closing of the Charleston Naval Base in 1995. The economic influence in Charleston, for example, is reflected by the almost eleven thousand active-duty air force and navy personnel and more than sixteen thousand civilian employees there in 2005, as well as the corresponding purchases from local suppliers. A report estimated total annual economic impact in the three-country area (Charleston, Dorchester, and Berkeley) at $3.5 billion.[14]

Numerous studies pointed to a need for greater public-private collaboration and recognition of the need to raise the prosperity of all South Carolinians.

With an implicit suggestion of Charleston serving as a primary point of contact, the Porter report said the attractions there can "add significant value to the state" by attracting talent and businesses to the state to help achieve that goal.[15]

A NEW VISION for downtown Columbia emerged after USC president Sorensen became concerned when, in shaking hands with hundreds of the 7,500 graduating seniors, he learned that many planned to leave the state and head for Charlotte or Atlanta or New York—not because they wanted to leave South Carolina, but because the state lacked high-paying, intellectually challenging, and fulfilling jobs. He approached members of the Guignard family—whose eighteenth-century ancestor was surveyor for the planned city of Columbia and arranged for hundreds of acres of land bordering the Congaree River to be held by his descendants. They gave a large tract of undeveloped land to the university and later sold it more. USC began establishing research facilities there with the idea of their becoming incubators for new products and jobs. The futuristic Innovista is planned as a long-range, large-scale development for Columbia that includes parks and biking trails, eateries, and modern high-rise condominiums with ground-floor boutiques. Land prices had skyrocketed before the 2008 economic recession.

Although the state entered the twenty-first century with the thrust of three decades of dynamic change, South Carolina economist specialist Harry W. Miley Jr. has asked whether the state had become two distinct economies. One economy comprised dynamic urban growth and expansion in fifteen metropolitan-area counties; the other is characterized by the rural stagnation that dominated the remaining thirty-one counties.

Those fifteen metro-growth counties accounted for 85 percent of the state's population, with an average per capita income of $23,538—almost 85 percent of the national average—25 percent greater than in the rural counties. Slow growth in both population and jobs characterized the rural counties, although none suffered a net population loss during the three-decade period.

A few hard facts: the state's population in those three decades grew by more than 50 percent, compared to 35 percent for the United States as a whole. Total personal income increased by 177 percent, adjusted for inflation, compared to 122 percent nationally. The total number of wage and salary workers increased by 925,000—almost 90 percent, compared to 74 percent nationally. Per capita income climbed from 73.5 percent of the national average to 82.5 percent.

South Carolina had suddenly become a place to move into rather than a place to leave. The population change reflected the most massive net migration into the state ever. In 1970 only one in ten South Carolina residents was born outside the state. In the next three decades net migration from other states and abroad added seven hundred thousand people—almost half during the 1990s. Growth in that decade came primarily from outside the South. The heaviest in-migration came from New York, New Jersey, Pennsylvania, Ohio, and California—in that order. The state's population topped four million for the first time.

The new migrants represented both retirees and younger families moving in as part of the state's economic expansion. The former group concentrated along the Atlantic coast, enjoying access to the beaches, lush greenery, lower costs of living, and a slower pace of life.

For the 1990s alone the Census Bureau reported official Hispanic population in the state more than tripled to 95,076. Although in 2004 the bureau estimated an increase in Hispanic population in the state to 130,000, an extensive University of South Carolina study estimated the actual number at more than 400,000. The USC Consortium for Latino Immigration Studies examined in-migration, school enrollment, birth rates, and death rates. The study also included interviews in Spanish with 381 immigrants from Mexico, the source of more than half the state's Latino population. Hard working and productive, in search of better economic opportunity, immigrants were concentrated in the construction, trade, and hospitality sectors, with agriculture trailing far behind. Most regularly sent money to family in their native country.[16]

The state's total population grew older, with the census median age in the state rising from 25 in 1970 to 35 in 2000 (average age for Hispanics was eight years younger). The largest age cohort also shifted dramatically in that period, from 10–14 to 35–39. The percentage of population over 65 almost doubled, from 7 percent to 12.

As the twenty-first century opened, native South Carolinians in six counties—Aiken, Beaufort, Berkeley, Dorchester, Horry, and York, with its spillover from neighboring Charlotte, North Carolina—found more than half their neighbors were born outside the state.

In contrast, during the 110 years before 1970 the state experienced a net out-migration of almost 2.8 million.[17] That number reflected not only the legacy of the Civil War's economic devastation among whites but also the loss of freedom by blacks after Reconstruction. By providing blacks greater freedom and economic opportunity, the civil rights era ended decades of massive net out-migration.

Between 1970 and 2000, African Americans fell from 30.5 percent to 29.5 percent of the state's population, but their numbers increased by almost

400,000 and included many who had returned after leaving the state earlier. Social change, more openness to new ideas, and improved economic opportunities also significantly reduced the brain drain among the best and brightest young blacks and whites.

The effects of past discrimination on African Americans in education and job opportunities, however, remained significant. In 1970 black per capita income in the state was 40.5 percent of that for whites. In 2000 it had improved only to barely half—$22,095 for whites and $11,776 for blacks. The number of majority-black counties in 2000 remained unchanged at twelve. All were rural. Per capita income for blacks in these counties fell well below the group's state average. But urban Richland County (Columbia), at 50.3 percent white in 2000, appeared headed toward rapidly becoming a black-majority metro county. Black per capita income there topped the group's state average by almost $2,200.

Home ownership in South Carolina ranked twelfth in the nation in 2000, but 20.3 percent— a total of 326,457—of these homes were mobile homes. The number in some rural counties approached 40 percent.

Although virtually any drive in the state beyond the metro suburbs soon rolls into countryside that shows evidence of the state's once-dominant agricultural economy, traditional farming itself played only a tiny economic role as South Carolina moved into the twenty-first century. In 1999 farm income represented 0.4 percent of the state's total income, less than the national average. Even in the rural counties it represented only 1.3 percent of total income.

Statewide, the percentage of farmworkers had plummeted between 1950 and 1999 from 21.1 percent of all males and 4.7 of all females to 0.5 percent of all male workers and a barely visible 0.1 percent of females—one of every thousand. The once-dominant farm economy has eroded almost to memory and imagination except for cotton fields that depended on federal price supports, a greatly reduced tobacco crop, and scattered patches marked by roadside stands of peaches, berries, and vegetables that continue to attract passing motorists, as well as the inviting offerings such as found at McLeod Farms in the Pee Dee and a scattering of similar sites.

MORE THAN A CENTURY after William Gregg expressed his philosophy— extended to include poor blacks as well as whites—it came to prevail through the work of a succession of progressive governors who provided the leadership to stop doing things the old way and to begin to combat the cycle of ignorance, poverty, and illiteracy that long had blighted a proud state. Despite much progress, the battle to develop and maintain a fully funded comprehensive system of education that is competitive with other states remains to be won. What remains unchanged is the conclusion of a report in 2000 on South Carolina's economy that "a major obstacle is the need for . . . providing its population with the education and skills necessary to match the needs of employers."[17] In an apparent response to Gov. James "Jim" Hodges's success following his 1998 election in establishing a statewide lottery to fund scholarships for graduating high school seniors, the percentage of high school graduates going to college jumped from 44 percent in 1992 to 65 percent in 2002.[19]

Perhaps no modern South Carolinian can match the record of accomplishment of Charles H. Townes. A Greenville County native who graduated summa cum laude at age nineteen from Furman University, Townes helped develop radar bombing techniques for the United States during World War II. However, he is best known for his work in inventing the laser. Its impact has revolutionized industry and medicine, and it earned him a share of the Nobel Prize for Physics in 1964. In 2005 he also received the $1.5 million Templeton Prize for his writings about the interrelationship of science and religion. "Science is an attempt to understand how our universe works," he said in an interview, and religion is "an attempt to under the purpose and meaning of that universe. . . . The two have to come together. So studying either one should teach us something about the other."[20] Although he left South Carolina permanently after college, he has served for many years as a Furman trustee. Both Furman and Clemson universities have named twenty-first-century campus science centers for Townes, and a statue of him at a new Greenville park was designed with the idea of inspiring children to believe in their capacity for creative achievement.

After more than three decades of impressive growth, however, the transformed economy of South Carolina shared fully in the economic crisis the nation faced in the final months of 2008. The economic recession brought a steep drop in state tax revenues—exacerbated by recent legislative zeal for substituting sales taxes for property and income taxes—that reverberated through the state's budget: not even education was spared in the cuts that ensued. The economic future appeared clouded with uncertainty.

14

CHANGE AND CONTINUITY

Life in South Carolina has changed more since World War II than in any other period of the state's history, except for the brief era of Reconstruction. The twin forces of transformation flow from the interconnected federally mandated collapse of segregation and the pace of economic modernization. Yet the state retains a strong sense of continuity with its past.

Continuity with the past also remains strong as southern identity continues to assert itself, especially the deeply embedded sense of place. That cultural identity—much of it linked to the little-recognized melding of western European and African influences—is found in food, music, and religion. From grits and collard greens to sweetened iced tea and pecan pie, natives of the state take for granted much of what they eat and how it is prepared. The official state dance, the shag, emerged from white teenagers in the 1950s learning the steps from blacks and the folk transformation of the beat from rhythm and blues to beach music. And there's the role of religion, with its message of brotherhood that significantly underlaid the relative ease of transition into a multicultural society.

As South Carolina moves fully into the twenty-first century, however, its future may be shaped as never before by the actions of an increasingly diverse population, including in-migrants and a generation of natives who have grown up mostly attending integrated public schools.

Under almost total Republican control, however, state government in the first decade of the twenty-first century drifted from the previous half century's focus on improving public education at all levels as the engine driving economic development. Much more attention was paid to keeping taxes low and shifting the tax burden away from those better off than to grappling with the issues related to developing a healthy and well-educated workforce to complement business-friendly government.

On the surface, public life in contemporary South Carolina shows little outward evidence of the withering hand of Jim Crow. Below the surface, however, the effects and residue of past discrimination remain fully present in terms of racial disparities in health, education, and income.

The signs of significant growth in prosperity remained offset by the less visible reality of enduring poverty for many. More than a half-million South Carolinians lived below the poverty level in 2005. The almost identical rates of poverty among African Americans and those of Hispanic origin tripled that of whites' (26.4 percent among blacks and 8.6 percent among whites). Rates of unemployment and personal income further reflected these racial differences. White unemployment was 6.9 percent in 2004, compared to 10.2 percent—almost 50 percent higher—among blacks. Black per capita income in the state amounted to 53 percent of that for whites—$11,776 and $22,095, respectively.[1]

Measured differences in racial attitudes disclose a range of difference in perception between white and black South Carolinians. A 2000 survey on racial attitudes conducted for the Palmetto Project, a private nonprofit initiative (funded in part by corporations) to put new and creative ideas to work in South Carolina, measured such differences. Fifteen percent of whites and 37 percent of blacks called race relations "the most important" problem facing the state.

Blacks also believed far more than whites that "a white child in South Carolina has a much better chance of achieving financial success." Half of all blacks agreed with the statement, but only nineteen percent of whites. On a different question, whether a nonwhite person in South Carolina has "as good a chance as a white person at getting a job for which he or she is qualified," the level of disagreement narrowed. Among whites, 37 percent strongly agreed and 14 percent somewhat, compared to 24 percent strongly agreeing and 18 percent somewhat by blacks.

The greatest disagreement came in response to the state's system of criminal justice. When asked in 2000 if it treats nonwhites "more harshly than whites," 58 percent of blacks strongly agreed, but only 12 percent of whites did. That perception may well have changed after videotapes surfaced of a series of incidents depicting racially abusive treatment by several highway patrolmen, who were only minimally reprimanded. Legislative hearings followed in 2008, resulting in resignations by the State Highway Patrol's two top officials.

A lack of white awareness of the factual disparity may well have accounted for much of the white perception in the 2000 survey. In 2004 more than twice as many black men as white men received state prison sentences—8,098 blacks and 3,797 whites. The average sentence length, however, was almost identical —an indication that the state's judiciary was evenhanded even if racial disparities appeared to reign within the larger system.

Whites outnumbered blacks in 2004 by 15 percent in total arrests, by more than two to one on violations for drunkenness, prostitution, and liquor law violations, and by more than three to one for driving under the influence. Blacks outnumbered whites more than three to one in arrests for robbery and more than two to one for murder (202 to 83). Most murder victims were also black (among murder victims, blacks outnumbered whites, 182 to 105).

The number of drug arrests in 2004 included 11,748 white men and 14,839 black men. Among females, whites arrested for drug offenses outnumbered blacks 3,583 to 2,031. For regular cocaine possession, 669 whites and 777 blacks were arrested. But arrests for crack cocaine possession, which carried harsher penalties, were more numerous for blacks regardless of age or gender—a total of 1,902 blacks and 208 whites.

On matters of parole, however, the statistics reflect a greater degree of equity. For many years a voice of moral clarity on the biracial Probation, Pardon, and Parole Board was Rhett Jackson, a sensitive white businessman who played a key role as a United Methodist Church layman in developing denominational policy for integrating church functions in the state. The pattern that developed for parole reflected a sense of racial parity reflecting the pattern for arrests. The 2,266 paroles granted in 2005 went to 1,499 blacks and 732 whites.[2]

The Palmetto Project survey also indicated strong interest among whites and blacks in the potential for religious institutions to become actively involved in improving race relations. When asked whether they would attend such a meeting at their church, 81 percent of blacks and 87 percent of whites said they would.

Organized religion played a significant role in the 1960s and 1970s in easing the transition from segregation. The Columbia-based Christian Action Council (representing seventeen denominations ranging from the Catholic Church to the Church of God) worked statewide to develop interfaith and interracial efforts to advance the transition to a society based on their bedrock principles of brotherhood and the Golden Rule. Catholics provided leadership through the integration of their parochial schools, beginning as early as 1954 at St. Anne's School in Rock Hill, well ahead of the public schools.

The state's United Methodist Conference in 1972 combined its separate black and white divisions into one, made cross-racial assignments of pastors, and signaled its support for interracial congregations. Most blacks remained in their traditional churches, which had always served as a primary outlet for institutional support that transcended worship. Also, they were assured of the opportunity for leadership roles there. Many of their clergy and those in other fellowships continued their historic role in exerting community leadership.

The twenty-first century opened, however, with more divisiveness on such issues as biblical interpretation and homosexuality. The state's two Episcopal dioceses, that of South Carolina (the lowcountry) and that of Upper South Carolina, appeared divided. At one point some clerical leaders in the Charleston-based Diocese of South Carolina advocated leaving the Episcopal Church USA and seeking oversight from a province in the worldwide Anglican Communion outside the United States. The Columbia-headquartered Diocese of Upper South Carolina, however, remained more committed to accepting change. Both remained within the Episcopal Church.

During the era of civil rights transition, Episcopalians—many of them descendants of prominent families in the state and many in positions of influence as executives in media, banks, commerce, and the bar—had played a significant role in accepting the changing social structure.

The overwhelming majority of South Carolina churchgoers, however, would be broadly classified as evangelical Christian. Most are Baptists, including 928,000 (almost all white) Southern Baptists, 175,000 (virtually all black) National Baptists, and 7,583 Freewill Baptists.

According to Association of Religious Data Archives and the Hartford Survey of Religious Data, membership totals for other denominations in South Carolina in 2007 included United Methodist, 302,000; African Methodist Episcopal, 300,000; Roman Catholic, 132,000; Presbyterian USA, 104,000; African Methodist Episcopal Zion, 65,000; Lutheran, 61,300; Church of God, 57,000; Episcopal, 52,000; Pentecostal Holiness, 33,820; Church of Jesus Christ of Latter Day Saints (Mormon), 20,424; Charismatic (Independent), 13,600; Jews, 11,000; Muslims, 5,761; Greek Orthodox, 3,867; and Unitarians, 1,519.[3]

The Southern Baptist Convention has remained the largest and most politically and socially conservative Protestant denomination in America, but it has shown progressive tendencies in regard to racial issues. Many white evangelicals, activated politically by born-again Christian Jimmy Carter's successful run for president in 1976, became disenchanted with his Internal Revenue Service director's denial of a tax exemption for then-segregated private schools created by church groups in the South. A few years later a biographer of Jesse Helms, the archconservative Republican senator from North Carolina, wrote, "Helms's allies are infiltrating the national leadership of the Southern Baptist Convention."[4] Evangelicals in South Carolina, like those elsewhere in

America, have since exercised a wide influence on public opinion, especially with regard to contested social issues such as abortion and same-sex marriage.

South Carolina also has been significantly influenced by the megachurch movement that late in the twentieth century emerged nationally. These churches are generally classified as having more than 2,500 people in attendance each Sunday, an authoritative or charismatic religious leader, and a variety of weekly activities ranging from traditional Bible studies to exercise classes and bowling nights. By 2008 at least twenty-four of these congregations existed in South Carolina.[5]

With their emphasis on informality in worship combined with youth- and family-oriented programs and services such as daycare, these new forms of religious expression reach out to suburban, culturally conservative whites with young children. These churches sometimes package and franchise themselves. In South Carolina the nondenominational Seacoast Church best fits this pattern, with seven locations regularly attracting thousands for Sunday church services. Although congregations such as Seacoast reject theological labels, their message of "following Christ alone," combined with a literal reading of the Bible, aligns them with more traditional evangelical denominations.

The influence of the evangelicals is most visible in politics. Oren Smith of the Palmetto Family Council helped galvanize evangelical voters in 2006 to adopt the so-called Marriage Amendment to the state constitution. The amendment banned marriages for same-sex couples.

South Carolina politics has long been influenced by a conservative vision of religious faith. James McBride Dabbs, writing of the resurgence of religion in the South after the Civil War, noted that white southerners believed themselves defeated in that conflict by man, but not by God. Dabbs saw this as part of the South's problem, its refusal to humble itself before God. He observed, "Where freedom is, God is. . . . the South has stressed order too much and freedom too little."[6]

DESPITE THEIR SMALL NUMBERS, Jews have been elected to a significant number of mayoral and legislative positions from the nineteenth century forward. Solomon Blatt of Barnwell, son of a small-town Jewish immigrant merchant, retired in 1973 after thirty-three years as Speaker of the South Carolina House of Representatives—one of the most powerful positions in state government —the longest tenure of anyone in that position in any state. In 2004 Representative Joel Lourie of Columbia won election to the S.C. Senate, following the path of his father, Isadore Lourie, who earlier also had served in both legislative bodies.

Political anti-Semitism was a rare occurrence. Blatt lost his first race for the S.C. House in the 1920s, when the Ku Klux Klan made one of its periodic revivals, but the local white establishment in Barnwell recognized his leadership capabilities, persuaded him to run again, and he was thereafter unbeatable.

In traditionalist South Carolina, women have been slow in gaining positions of power in religion or politics. Although women made up 53 percent of the state's registered voters at the beginning of the twenty-first century, in 2007 they held only 8.8 percent of the seats in the legislature, the lowest in the country and barely a third of the national average of 23.5 percent. No women served in the forty-six-member S.C. Senate in 2007.

Only three women had ever been elected to constitutional office: Nancy Stevenson as lieutenant governor and Barbara Nielsen and Inez Tenenbaum as state superintendent of education. Seven-term state representative Jean Toal of Columbia, however, shattered the glass ceiling when the legislature elected her in 1988—as the first woman and first Roman Catholic—to the South Carolina Supreme Court. She won election in 1999 as chief justice.

THE SPOUSE FROM "off" who married a white South Carolina native and moved into the state might well agree that it's "one great big small town."

In 1988 Jean Hoefer Toal (right) became the first woman to sit on the state supreme court. She also became the first Roman Catholic to serve on the state's highest court. *History of South Carolina Slide Collection*, B-215

The state's physical compactness and traditionally homogeneous population—where a few decades ago in the upcountry a textile mill owner would likely have a cousin working for him as a loom fixer—helps explain why. A transplanted New England Irishman exclaimed years after meeting his wife's myriad kinfolks, "I didn't realize I was going to marry the whole state!"

Among traditional white South Carolinians, social acceptability is measured and reflected by the customary initial questions asked when two people from different towns or cities meet for the first time. To determine another's connections subtly, one might ask, "Who do you know?" As one perceptive native explained several decades ago, "If you know the right people, you're quite nice, and it doesn't make a damn whether you're done anything or not. . . . The aristocratic tradition amounts to learning the technique of it."[7]

Among the papers left several decades ago by an octogenarian historian was the following poem, which the editor of a monthly publication of the South Carolina State Library printed as a worthy contribution to Caroliniana:

CONFLICT IN THE HOLY CITY

I thank thee, Lord, on bended knee
I'm half Porcher and half Huger.

With holy pride my heart doth beat,
I live at nineteen Lamboll Street,
With grateful tears my eyes are wet,
My uncle's J. Le Boutillier Rhett.

For other blessing thank thee, too—
My grandma was a Petigru;
Simons and Waring and Legare
Appear upon my family tree.

Dear Lord, look down on those in pity
Who dwell outside the Holy City.
And when I die, save me from hell—
I go to church at St. Mich-a-el—

I thank thee, Lord, on bended knee
I'm not half Porcher nor half Huger.

With holy pride my heart doth beat,
That I don't live on Lamboll Street.
With grateful tears my eyes are wet
That I'm not kin to any Rhett.

For other blessings thank thee, too—
My grandma was no Petigru;
Simons and Waring and Legare
Don't adorn my family tree.

My grandma by the name of Brown,
Was born on some street way up Town;
My dad was Smith of lowly rank
Who lost money in the Peoples' bank.

Dear Lord, look down on those in pity,
Who think this is the only city.
And when I die, save me from hell;
So I won't meet the elite of St. Mich-a-el![8]

The following bit of doggerel offers a more up-to-date response:

Here I am, a migrant from "off,"
Thank you, God, that I came not soft.
The food at times is oh so quaint;
those grits, which like cream of wheat ain't.

I've learned even if I get tight,
I'm still supposed to be polite.
And here the beaches still are free,
and there's the mountains to see.

I'm getting it that they don't holler
when getting that Yankee dollar.
They talk strange, in syllables of two,
that I sometimes miss quite a few.

I've quit ticking like a time bomb
when my children call me "Ma-om."
The livin' is easy, I'm turning gray,
and it looks like I'm here to stay.[9]

In 2003, forty years after enrolling at Clemson, Harvey Gantt addressed the annual awards dinner of the Greater Columbia Community Relations Council, an arm of the area's forward-looking chamber of commerce. Now a former mayor of Charlotte, a two-time Democratic candidate for the U.S. Senate, and a successful architect, he observed, "South Carolina has come a long way since 1960," but added, "Race is still too much a factor."

He continued, "For me, the central idea is the *promise* in the Constitution that every citizen has the opportunity to move upward in the social and economic ladder, free from any limitations a government might impose due to race, ethnicity, gender, religion, or natural origins. It is that promise that inspires hope and the desire to succeed in the heart of ordinary citizens." Gantt acknowledged progress had occurred, but said, "Clearly, from my vantage point, we have much to do. I believe most of you here will agree with me."

The planners of the event had clearly made contact with Clio, the muse of history. Gantt was introduced by chief U.S. District Court Judge Matthew J. Perry, Gantt's lawyer in gaining enrollment at Clemson. (Not long thereafter, Judge Perry's name went on the front of the new U.S. District Courthouse in Columbia, and the USC School of Law hosted a special event honoring him and his career.) The honoree that night was none other than Cleveland Sellers, the survivor of a gunshot wound during the Orangeburg Massacre who had been imprisoned and then pardoned. A popular and respected faculty member and director of the African American Studies Program at the University of South Carolina, he was warmly introduced by Community Relations Council chair Betsy Boineau. Her late husband, businessman Charles Boineau, won a special election in 1961 to become the state's first Republican legislator since 1902.

Sellers mentioned growing up in a black middle-class family in the town of Denmark, as "an Eagle Scout, an athlete, a member of the student government, and an [Episcopal] acolyte." He noted South Carolina's "tradition of silence" and announced he had chosen that evening "to violate that tradition."

He addressed the way history had been written, and he quoted from his eighth-grade history book, written by Mary C. Simms Oliphant, granddaughter of the novelist William Gilmore Simms. A chapter titled "The Greatest Problem" gave this overview of the period following the Civil War: "There were so many more Negroes than whites that they would have been in control if they had been allowed to vote. They had nearly ruined the State during the years they voted. The whites were determined that this should not happen again. Regulations were made which prevented the Negroes from voting, and to this day South Carolina has a white man's government. The welfare of two races living in one small state is a problem you will have to face when you become citizens."[10] In a section titled "Fighting Fire with Fire," Oliphant wrote, "Whenever the Negroes gave trouble, the Ku Klux Klan dressed in long white robes and caps and, mounted on fast horses, galloped through the darkness, frightening the superstitious blacks into submission."[11]

Sellers contrasted that version of history, instilled in a generation of South Carolina's white and black pupils, with the one presented at a major symposium on South Carolina and civil rights at the Citadel in 2003, "where we were able to address the heroic and courageous struggle of ordinary blacks in overcoming segregation." He also addressed the Orangeburg Massacre, contending, "A veil of secrecy and a cloak of silence" had served as the "methods employed to avoid responsibility or culpability."

He quoted James McBride Dabbs: "As a general thing, the Southerner is burdened by his unhappy past; he doesn't understand it, and he finds it hard to accept. The white Southerner is further confused by the myth of a splendid past, a myth woven during the dark decades from 1865 to 1900, and now, though our minds begin to warn us, still believed in our hearts. Believed in and desired. According to this myth, the South was once a complete, perhaps perfect creation, envied by the North, and out of envy attacked, defeated, and crippled. The trouble with this picture is that it is not so." Sellers concluded with a call for ending polite silence, adding, "The Palmetto State is still haunted by the ghost of Jim Crow. . . . Let us begin the difficult but necessary work of reconciliation."[12]

Those remarks by Gantt and Sellers to Columbia's predominantly white business and civic leaders reflected movement toward the call by Sellers that day "to speak truth to power." Three years earlier Mayor Joseph P. Riley Jr. of Charleston had marched to Columbia (his police chief insisted that he wear a bulletproof vest) to dramatize support for removing the Confederate battle flag from the State House dome. In a speech at the State House, Riley recognized the presence of Sellers and referred to him as "an outstanding civil rights leader in our state . . . and a hero to my son."

In 2006 Sellers's youngest son, Bakari, defeated a white twenty-four-year incumbent to become at age twenty-two the youngest member of the South Carolina legislature. He met several months later with Pete Strom Jr., son of the SLED chief who had arrested Cleveland Sellers thirty-nine years earlier on the night of the Orangeburg Massacre. Bakari Sellers had quickly begun to gain recognition in the legislature for his keen political instincts and early display of leadership. Young Strom, a well-regarded trial lawyer in his late forties with a practice in Columbia, had attended integrated public schools there. He offered the second-year law student and freshman legislator a summer internship in his law firm. Both men were quietly aware of the interaction between their respective fathers. Bakari Sellers accepted the offer.

That exchange provided powerful symbolism for a promise of reconciliation generated by emerging generations of native South Carolinians. The end of enforced racial segregation opened a new era in social relations that continues to evolve. The first generation of children who attended integrated public schools have become parents of schoolchildren. Interracial marriages are not common in South Carolina, but they happen. When they do, most families adjust to the new realities, especially after children are born.

In telling the story of one of the state's oldest and most deeply rooted plantation families, Edward Ball's award-winning book, *Slaves in the Family,* helped launch dialogue about black-white family relationships. The book's story involves a dozen families, only two of which were interracial. Family members divided in their response to the book, but curiosity tended to replace initial fear among whites and sarcasm among blacks after the taboo of silence was broken—and then came the question, "Can we talk to them?" "Dozens of times at book signings," Ball recalls, "it happened that people said they had suspicions of black relatives and, after the book, it would be easier and less dangerous to confront."[13]

The announcement in December 2003 by seventy-eight-year-old Essie Mae Washington-Williams—six months after Strom Thurmond's death—that she is his biracial daughter, and the Thurmond family's graceful acknowledgment of her claim, created a buzz throughout the state. Whites found it "interesting," and many blacks felt vindication in the story, well known in their community but new to many whites, being acknowledged by all. After hearing Washington-Williams speak in Charleston, a black man said, "She just makes me feel so good." A college-educated black woman, however, said, "So what? I know a hundred stories like that." In one upstate community a black man surprised a white with the same surname whom he knew well by asking, "When is the family reunion?" It got cancelled that year.[14]

The Thurmond family saga, however, played out in the public arena. After her name was added to those of his four other children on the statue of him on the State House grounds, the *Charleston Post and Courier* noted in an editorial, "What also should be recorded for posterity is what a remarkable woman Essie Mae Washington-Williams is in her own right." Calling her "a model of decorum," the newspaper added, "Mrs. Williams hasn't refused the spotlight, but she has chosen her appearances and her words carefully. She has been so impressive that the Legislature's endorsement of the proposal to add her name to the Thurmond monument was a foregone conclusion. It was, of course, her due. But her fine character has made it a particularly satisfying event."[15]

On a subsequent visit by Washington-Williams to Edgefield, Thurmond's hometown, both weekly newspapers trumpeted front-page celebrity stories. Two of her children attended and received a warm reception at the extended Thurmond family reunion held in Edgefield County. She said later, "The outreach of the public has amazed me."[16] In 2007 a quartet of other black relatives quietly showed up at the reunion, where one observer said afterward, "Overall, they were well-received."[17] Strom Thurmond, the South's leading symbol of segregationist resistance for more than two decades after his 1948 Dixiecrat campaign, privately knew that when it came out, this story about him and his black daughter would be bigger than anything in his life.

Sociologist Herbert Blumer, in an essay published in 1965, "The Future of the Color Line," discussed the "inner" line of separation, the question of equal social status. Writing about it as a national issue at the peak of the civil rights movement, Blumer said, "Its presence can be noted most clearly among the whites who are willing to accept Negroes as having equal social status yet who are not disposed to admit them into intimate and private circles, represented by social sets, cliques, private clubs, friendship sets, family circles, courtship, and marriage."[18] But even that inner circle has begun to crack.

THE DISTINCTIVE PAST that traditional South Carolinians still feel in their bones clearly includes foremost the element of race that dates to the state's first permanent European settlers and their bringing with them chattel slavery —an almost benign term for a system in which one human literally *owned* another. As France, England, and other parts of the world rejected slavery as morally repugnant, South Carolina evolved as a society of planter dominance and the slave-based cotton kingdom. Slavery led to the Civil War, total defeat, and economic devastation. That experience led to the myths of Reconstruction and the romanticism of the Lost Cause.

The legally designated inferiority and disenfranchisement of African Americans that followed sparked an out-migration of hundreds of thousands of South Carolinians (mostly African Americans) that accelerated during the Great Depression. Support from the New Deal and federal defense spending during World War II revived the economy. The civil rights era had a transforming impact on opening new opportunities for African Americans, expanding both the workforce and the market for goods and services, and also opening the state to new ideas. And it also ended the brain drain of many of the brightest young people who had sought economic opportunity and a more open society elsewhere. These changes, combined with the attraction of the state's natural beauty and its developing cultural attractions, also attracted new residents who added spice to the cultural mix.

Yet William Faulkner's observation still stands. The past remains the lens through which the southerner looks to navigate the future.

A SOUTH CAROLINA CHRONOLOGY

1526   The first European settlement in what is today South Carolina is established by Spanish explorer Lucas Allyon near Georgetown. This settlement becomes the site of the first North American slave revolt. African slaves and native peoples band together against the Spanish, who abandon the settlement the following year.

1660   Charles II is restored to the English throne. Three years later, he grants the territory that today includes South Carolina to eight English nobles who supported him. Anthony Ashley Cooper takes the lead in organizing the colonial venture by the Lords Proprietors.

1670   The first boatload of settlers arrives in Carolina and settles on a tidal swamp above the entrance to the Ashley River. At year's end African slaves arrive. The population of the colony is about 155 people, of whom 15 are African slaves. The native population is somewhere between 20,000 and 50,000 people.

1680   The settlement moves to Oyster Point, today's Charleston Peninsula. The population of the colony, excluding natives, is roughly 1,200, including 200 enslaved Africans.

1696   South Carolina enacts its first slave code, modeled on the Barbadian code that gives masters absolute authority over their slaves.

1700   The Colonial Assembly votes funds for what would become the first library in the colony, a private lending library for the city elite. The colony's population includes 5,500 whites and perhaps as many as 2,000 Africans.

1708   South Carolina's population exceeds 8,000, being almost evenly divided between whites and black slaves with roughly 4,100 Africans and 4,080 white settlers.

1715   The English colony in Carolina faces near extinction due to the Yamassee War. Settlers fight and defeat a large alliance of native tribes led by the Yamassee.

1720   The population continues to grow with the import of African slaves; of it's 18,500 people, roughly 12,000 are slaves.

1730   The colony becomes free of proprietary rule as a royal colony directly under the oversight of the monarchy. The population has grown to 30,000 people, over two-thirds of whom are African.

1740   Slave imports occasioned by the rice boom have boosted the population to 60,000, two-thirds of whom are Africans. The Stono Rebellion in 1739, the major slave rebellion in South Carolina history, has shaken the colony and leads to the execution of forty slaves and to a more stringent slave code.

1749   Congregation Beth Elohim is organized by Sephardic Jews who had been arriving in South Carolina since the 1690s. Slave imports slowed after 1740. The total population of the colony stands at 65,000.

1760   South Carolina is in the midst of a war with the Cherokees that ends in 1761 with an English victory and drives the Cherokees into the northeast corner of what is today South Carolina. The white population of the colony has risen with the opening of the South Carolina backcountry to immigrants, who are largely Scots-Irish. Population is roughly 80,000 in the colony; 65 percent are African slaves.

1770   After several tumultuous years, Charleston's political leadership symbolically challenges royal British authority by placing a statue of William Pitt at the crossroads of Meeting and Broad streets. Pitt, an English parliamentarian, has been an outspoken opponent of the king's imperial policy. The population of the colony stands now at 130,000, including 80,000 African slaves.

1780   Charleston falls to British forces after a month long siege. By the end of the year, South Carolina partisans are waging a guerrilla campaign that will upset the British "Southern strategy" and help lead to their eventual defeat. In 1780 the state's population of 180,000 includes 100,000 African slaves. The white population in the upcountry continues to grow. Over the next three years the Cherokee will be driven out of South Carolina entirely.

1791 French sugar planters arrive in Charleston, fleeing the Haitian revolution. These planters become the core of St. Mary's Church of Charleston, the first Roman Catholic parish in South Carolina, North Carolina, or Georgia. The 1790 census reflects a new white majority in the state, with 140,178 white residents, 107,094 slaves and 1,801 free blacks.

1800 The state legislature passes a law making it difficult to manumit slaves through will or deed. This move reflects concern about the number of masters, especially in Charleston, who are freeing slaves at the time of their death. Many are the biracial children of the planter class. The U.S. Census reports a population of 196,255 whites, 146,151 slaves, and 3,185 free blacks.

1810 The census reports 214,196 whites, 196,365 enslaved Africans, and 4,554 free people of color. It also reveals that slavery has spread to every county in the state. The previous year saw the publication of David Ramsey's two-volume *The History of South Carolina: From Its First Settlement in 1670 to the Year 1808,* the first major history of South Carolina.

1820 The growth of slavery in all parts of the state once again creates a black majority. South Carolina now has 258,475 slaves, 6,826 free people and 237, 440 whites. The state legislature, concerned about the number of free blacks, ratifies a new law that prevents free people of color from entering the state and allows masters to free slaves only with the consent of the legislature.

1830 The federal census shows 323,322 African-Americans and 257,863 whites. No numbers exist in this year for free people of color.

1840 The library of South Carolina College, designed by South Carolina native Robert Mills who also designed the Washington Monument, is completed. It is the first free standing library building in the United States. The census shows the state with 327,038 enslaved people, 259,084 whites, and 8,276 free people of color (almost all living in Charleston).

1850 John C. Calhoun dies almost one month after delivering a speech warning the North that the Union might be sundered unless it ceased "agitating" against slavery. The census shows that South Carolina has a growing slave population of 393,944 with 274,563 whites (statistics unavailable for free people of color).

1860 In the year of Abraham Lincoln's election (and the subsequent secession by South Carolina) the slave population of South Carolina is at an all-time high of 402,406 people. The census includes 291,300 whites and 9,914 free people of color.

1870 Three years into Radical Reconstruction Joseph H. Rainey of Georgetown becomes the first black South Carolinian to become a member of Congress. Alonzo J. Ransier becomes the first African American to serve as the state's lieutenant governor. The population stands at 415,814 African Americans and 289,667 whites.

1880 The collapse of Reconstruction leads to restrictions on black voting and office-holding. The African American population in South Carolina by percentage reaches its historical high: 60.7 percent, with 604,332 African Americans and 391,105 whites.

1890 Benjamin Ryan Tillman becomes governor of South Carolina, transforming South Carolina politics. As his influence grows, Tillman engineers the 1895 constitutional convention that formally disenfranchises African Americans. The U.S. Census reports 462,008 whites and 688,934 African Americans.

1900 The first census of the twentieth century shows South Carolina with a population of 1,340,316, with a 58.4 percent black majority: 782,321 to 557,807 white (and 188 "other"). The "fusion" system, in which political offices in some counties were divided between white and blacks, ends with a race riot in Georgetown where the system lasted longer than anywhere else in the state.

1910 Coleman L. "Coley" Blease is elected governor on a platform of extreme racism and class antagonism aimed at the white gentry. Dillon County is carved out from Marion County.

1920 After adoption of the Nineteenth Amendment, women in South Carolina vote for the first time. Community leaders in Charleston hold the organizational meeting of the Society for the Preservation of Old Dwellings (now the Preservation Society of Charleston), which is a pioneer in historic preservation.

1930 During the Depression tens of thousands of black South Carolinians seek better opportunities in the North; the census counts a white majority for the first time since 1800, with 944,049 white and 793,681 black residents. WCSC in Charleston, the state's first radio station, begins broadcasting.

1940 A hurricane sweeps through Beaufort, Edisto Island, and Charleston, leaving forty people dead.

1950 South Carolina's population exceeds two million for the first time, with a total count of 2,117,027 and a 61.1 percent white majority. The Atomic Energy Commission and DuPont chose a 250,000-acre site in Aiken and Barnwell counties for the Savannah River Plant, which will produce elements for nuclear weapons.

1960 Weeks after the Clemson Tigers defeat the USC Gamecocks 27–0 in the final Big Thursday football game, the state's first modern civil rights demonstration takes place in Greenville on New Year's Day 1960 with an organized march to the Greenville Airport to protest the threatened arrest of baseball star Jackie Robinson for entering the airport's "white" waiting room several months earlier.

1970 The racial breakdown of the population has changed to 69.3 percent white and 30.7 percent black. As part of the state's tricentennial celebrations, Gershwin's *Porgy and Bess* is performed for the first time in the state in which it is set.

1980 The population tops three million. The Governor's School for the Arts opens in Greenville.

1990 White/black population ratio remains at roughly 70/30, but 30,551 South Carolinians list their identity as "Hispanic Origin." Gov. Carroll A. Campbell becomes the state's first Republican governor elected to a second four-year term.

2000 Census population reaches 4,012,012. The official number of South Carolinians of "Hispanic Origin" more than triples, climbing to 96,288, but state demographers deem that a significant undercount. The state votes Republican in the presidential election for the fifth time in a row.

Source: Adapted from George C. Rogers Jr. and C. James Taylor, *A South Carolina Chronology, 1497–1992*, 2nd ed. (Columbia: University of South Carolina Press, 1994).

NOTES

Introduction

1. Quoted in Jack Bass, *Porgy Comes Home: South Carolina after Three Hundred Years* (Columbia, S.C.: R. L. Bryan, 1972), 3.

2. Charles W. Joyner, "Shared Traditions: South Carolina as a Folk Culture," in *Proceedings of the South Carolina Historical Association, 2006,* ed. Robert Figueira and Stephen Lowe (Columbia: South Carolina Historical Association, 2006), 9.

3. Quoted in Bass, *Porgy Comes Home,* 3–4.

4. Ibid., 4.

5. Ibid., 4–5.

6. James McBride Dabbs, *Who Speaks for the South?* (New York: Funk and Wagnalls, 1964), 364.

7. Quoted in Walter Edgar, *South Carolina: A History* (Columbia: University of South Carolina Press, 1998), 538.

8. Ibid, 8.

9. Ibid., 6.

10. Dan Carter, "Civil Rights and Politics in South Carolina," in *Toward the Meeting of the Waters: Currents in the Civil Rights Movement of South Carolina during the Twentieth Century,* ed. Winfred B. Moore Jr. and Orville Vernon Burton (Columbia: University of South Carolina Press, 2008), 420n24.

11. Joyner, "Shared Traditions," 10.

1. The Beginning

1. Stephen Bull, letter to Lord Ashley, September 12, 1670, in *The Shaftesbury Papers,* ed. Langdon Cheves (Charleston, S.C.: Tempus, 2000), 5:193.

2. Peter Wood, *Black Majority: Negroes in South Carolina from 1670 through the Stono Rebellion* (New York: Norton, 1975), 13–34.

3. Robert M. Weir, *Colonial South Carolina: A History* (Columbia: University of South Carolina Press, 1997), 273.

4. Robert Olwell, *Masters, Slaves, and Subjects: The Culture of Power in the South Carolina Low Country, 1740–1790* (Ithaca, N.Y.: Cornell University Press, 1998), 228–30.

5. Ibid., 228–29.

2. The American Revolution

1. Cornwallis quoted in Walter Edgar, *South Carolina: A History* (Columbia: University of South Carolina Press, 1998), 234.

2. Quoted in Walter J. Fraser, *Charleston! Charleston! The History of a Southern City* (Columbia: University of South Carolina Press, 1989), 169.

3. Thomas B. Horton, "Willington Academy," in *The South Carolina Encyclopedia*, ed. Walter Edgar (Columbia: University of South Carolina Press, 2006), 1032–33.

4. Both quoted in Jack Bass, *Porgy Comes Home: South Carolina after Three Hundred Years* (Columbia, S.C.: R. L. Bryan, 1972), 19.

3. An Era of Decline

1. Frances Anne "Fanny" Kemble, *Journal of a Residence on a Georgian Plantation in 1838–1839*, Brown Thrasher edition (Athens: University of Georgia Press, 1984), 37.

2. James Haw, "The Problem of South Carolina Reexamined: A Review Essay," *South Carolina Historical Magazine*, January 2006, 20.

3. Ira Berlin, *Many Thousands Gone: The First Two Centuries of Slavery in North America* (Cambridge, Mass.: Belknap Press of Harvard University Press, 2000), 142.

4. Harriet Martineau, *Retrospect of Western Travel* (1838; abr. repr., Armonk, N.Y.: M. E. Sharpe, 2000), 98.

5. Fox Butterfield,. *All God's Children: The Bosket Family and the American Tradition of Violence* (New York: Alfred A. Knopf. 1995), 20–21, citing Charles Ball, *Slavery in the United States: A Narrative of the Life and Adventures of Charles Ball, a Black Man* (New York: Kraus Reprint Company. 1969), 37.

6. G. D. Bernheim, *History of the German Settlements and of the Lutheran Church in North and South Carolina* (1872; repr., Spartanburg, S.C.: The Reprint Co., 1972), 352.

7. Dumas Malone, *The Public Life of Thomas Cooper, 1783–1839* (Columbia: University of South Carolina Press, 1961), 307.

8. Andrew Jackson's mother, Elizabeth, who died in November 1781 while nursing wounded Patriot soldiers in the Revolutionary War, has on her tombstone, located on the College of Charleston campus, these words of advice to her son: "Andy, never tell a lie, nor take what is not your own, nor sue for slander; settle those cases yourself."

9. Quoted in Walter Edgar, *South Carolina: A History* (Columbia: University of South Carolina Press, 1998), 336.

10. Martineau, *Retrospect of Western Travel*, 26.

11. Mark O. Hatfield, *Vice Presidents of the United States, 1789–1993* (Washington, D.C.: U.S. Government Printing Office, 1997).

12. *Dred Scott v. Sandford*, 60 U.S. 393, 407 (1857).

13. Both quoted in Bruce Catton, *The Coming Fury* (Garden City, N.Y.: Doubleday, 1961), 158–59.

4. Civil War and Reconstruction

1. Willie Lee Rose, *Rehearsal for Reconstruction: The Port Royal Experiment* (1964; repr., Athens: University of Georgia Press, 1999).

2. Robert K. Krick, "Maxcy Gregg: Political Extremist and Confederate General," *Civil War History* 19 (December 1973): 313.

3. William Tecumseh Sherman, *Memoirs of General W. T. Sherman* (New York: Library of America, 1990), 760–68.

4. William J. Cooper, *The Conservative Regime: South Carolina, 1877–1890* (Baton Rouge: Louisiana State University Press, 1991), 89–93.

5. See J. Tracy Power, "Civil War," in *The South Carolina Encyclopedia*, ed. Walter Edgar (Columbia: University of South Carolina Press, 2006), 183.

6. "Petition of Unionville Citizens, August 22 1865," Norris Crossman Papers, Ca. 1833, Papers 1837–1926, (233.0), South Carolina Historical Society, Charleston; Louise Vandiver, *Traditions and History of Anderson County* (Atlanta: Ruralist Press, 1928), 249.

7. Henry Orlando Marcy, March 22, 1865, "Diary of a Surgeon, U.S. Army, 1864–1899," South Carolina Historical Society, Charleston; Charles Tyler Trowbridge, Charles T. Trowbridge reminiscences, ca. 1892, (43/2094) South Carolina Historical Society, Charleston.

8. Julie Saville, *The Work of Reconstruction: From Slave to Wage Laborer in South Carolina, 1860–1870* (Cambridge: Cambridge University Press, 1996), 166–68.

9. Biographical Directory of the United States Congress, http://bioguide.congress.gov/biosearch/biosearch.asp (accessed August 27, 2008).

10. Robert J. Kaczorowski, *The Politics of Judicial Interpretation: The Federal Courts, Department of Justice and Civil Rights, 1866-1876* (1985; repr., New York: Fordham University Press, 2005), 43.

11. William Arthur Sheppard, *Red Shirts Remembered: Southern Brigades of the Reconstruction Period* (Athens, Ga.: Ruralist Press, 1940), 102.

12. Orville Vernon Burton, *In My Father's House Are Many Mansions: Family and Community in Edgefield, South Carolina* (Chapel Hill: University of North Carolina Press, 1985), 290.

13. "Plan of Campaign," 1876, Gary Papers, South Caroliniana Library, University of South Carolina, Columbia; reprinted in Francis Butler Simkins and Robert Hilliard Woody, *South Carolina during Reconstruction* (Chapel Hill: University of North Carolina Press, 1932), 566.

5. The Tillman Era

1. Francis Butler Simkins, *Pitchfork Ben Tillman* (1944; repr., Columbia: University of South Carolina Press, 2002), 315.

2. Quoted in Orville Vernon Burton, *In My Father's House Are Many Mansions* (Chapel Hill: University of North Carolina Press, 1985), 227.

3. Quoted in Richard Pearce, "Marketing Princes," *APF Reporter*, September 9, 1975, 8.

4. Montgomery Family Papers, South Caroliniana Library, University of South Carolina, Columbia.

5. Simkins, *Pitchfork Ben Tillman*, 295.

6. Edward A. Miller Jr., *Gullah Statesman: Robert Smalls from Slavery to Congress, 1839–1915* (Columbia: University of South Carolina Press, 1995), 211.

7. Edward Ayers, *The Promise of the New South* (New York: Oxford University Press, 1992), 289.

8. George B. Tindall, *South Carolina Negroes, 1877–1900* (Columbia: University of South Carolina Press, 1952), 299.

9. Ibid.

10. Jack Bass, telephone interview with William Hine, June 4, 2008.

11. William V. Moore, "Blease, Coleman Livingston," in *The South Carolina Encyclopedia*, ed. Walter Edgar (Columbia: University of South Carolina Press), 80.

12. Robert Botsch, "South Carolina Council on Human Relations," paper presented at the Citadel Conference on Civil Rights in South Carolina, Charleston, March 5–8, 2003; Jack Bass and Walter De Vries, *The Transformation of Southern Politics* (1976; Athens: University of Georgia Press, 1995), 501.

6. World Wars and the Depression

1. David Robertson, *Sly and Able: A Political Biography of James F. Byrnes* (New York: Norton, 1994), 175–77.

2. Ibid., 176–77; quotation from Jacquelyn Dowd Hall et al., *Like a Family: The Making of a Southern Cotton Mill World* (Chapel Hill: University of North Carolina Press, 1987), 339–40.

3. Daniel W. Hollis, "'Cotton Ed' Smith—Showman or Statesman?" *South Carolina Historical Magazine* 71 (October 1970): 251.

7. Civil Rights Era

1. Peter F. Lau, "'Mr. NAACP': Levi G. Byrd and the Re-Making of the NAACP in State and Nation, 1917–1960," in *Toward the Meeting of the Waters: Currents in the Civil Rights Movement of South Carolina during the Twentieth Century,* ed. Winfred B. Moore Jr. and Orville Vernon Burton (Columbia: University of South Carolina Press, 2008), 148.

2. Marcia G. Synott, "Feminists or Maternalists? White Women Civil Rights Activists in South Carolina," paper presented at the Citadel Conference on Civil Rights in South Carolina, Charleston, March 5–8, 2003.

3. Jack Irby Hayes Jr., *South Carolina and the New Deal* (Columbia: University of South Carolina Press, 2001), 176–77.

4. Patricia Sullivan, *Days of Hope: Race and Democracy in the New Deal Era* (Chapel Hill: University of North Carolina Press, 1996), 196–97.

5. James Clyburn, interview with Jack Bass, Columbia, S.C., December 1, 2006.

6. Cited in Kari Frederickson, "'The Slowest State' and 'Most Backward Community': Racial Violence in South Carolina and Federal Civil-Rights Legislation, 1946–1948," *South Carolina Historical Magazine,* April 1997, 184.

7. *Elmore v. Rice,* 72 F. Supp. 516 (D.C.S.C. 1947).

8. Jack Greenberg, interview with Jack Bass, Raleigh, N.C., May 17, 2004.

9. Although *Briggs v. Elliott* was of the first of the four cases decided in the lower courts, the Kansas case was listed first when they reached the U.S. Supreme Court. As a young lawyer Fritz Hollings assisted Robert Figg and John W. Davis, who was considered the nation's top appellate lawyer, in preparing the South Carolina case; he says the Kansas case was listed first because of maneuvering on the eve of the Supreme Court hearing. Initially the *Brown* case from Topeka was to be presented only as a written brief. (Byrnes had persuaded Kansas officials to appeal their case, but with a written brief and no oral argument.) Hollings said that Roy Wilkins, national executive director for the NAACP, had a longtime friendship with Solicitor General Simon Sobeloff and persuaded him to take action that resulted in the *Brown* case being argued orally before the Supreme Court and being listed first on the docket, thus giving emphasis that the issue was urban and national rather than rural and regional. Hollings said he and Figg helped prepare the Kansas attorney general, Harold Fatzer, the night before oral argument. Hollings, interview with Jack Bass, Charleston, S.C., January 30, 2006.

10. C. Vann Woodward, *The Strange Career of Jim Crow,* commemorative ed. (New York: Oxford University Press, 2002), 154–55.

11. William Gordon, "Boycotts Can Cut Two Ways," *New South,* April 1956, 5–10.

12. Neil R. McMillen, *The Citizens' Council: Organized Resistance to the Second Reconstruction, 1954–64* (Urbana: University of Illinois Press, 1994), 73.

13. John W. White, "The White Citizens' Councils of Orangeburg County, South Carolina," in Moore and Burton, *Toward the Meeting of the Waters*, 261–71.

14. Guy and Candie Carawan Collection, Manuscripts Department, Southern Folklore Collection, Wilson Library, University of North Carolina, Chapel Hill.

15. Derek Charles Catsam, "Into the Maw of Dixie: The Freedom Rides, the Civil Rights Movement, and the Politics of Race in South Carolina," in *Proceedings of the South Carolina Historical Association, 2006*, ed. Robert Figueira and Stephen Lowe (Columbia: South Carolina Historical Association, 2005), 5.

16. Ibid., 6.

17. Quoted in Douglas Martin, "Robert L. McCullough, 64, Dies; Civil Rights Innovator," *New York Times*, August 11, 2006.

18. John Lewis and Michael D'Orso, *Walking with the Wind: A Memoir of the Movement* (New York: Harcourt, 1999), 138.

19. Ibid.

20. *Rock Hill Herald*, January 22, 2008.

21. Ernest F. Hollings, interview with Jack Bass, January 30, 2007.

22. *Edwards v. South Carolina*, 372 U.S. 229 (1963), 236.

23. Quoted in Walter Edgar, *South Carolina: A History* (Columbia: University of South Carolina Press, 1998), 538.

24. John C. West, panel discussion at the Citadel Conference on Civil Rights in South Carolina, Charleston, March 5–8, 2003.

25. Jack Bass and Marilyn Thompson, *Strom: The Complicated Personal and Political Life of Strom Thurmond* (New York: Public Affairs Press, 2005), 177–78; *Iowa State Daily*, September 27, 1962 (quoted in Peter Wallenstein, "Higher Education and Civil Rights—South Carolina, 1890–1967," paper presented at the Citadel Conference on Civil Rights in South Carolina, Charleston, March 5–8, 2003).

8. Politics of Transition

1. Quoted in Jack Bass and Marilyn Thompson, *Strom: The Complicated Personal and Political Life of Strom Thurmond* (New York: Public Affairs Press, 2005), 86.

2. V. O. Key Jr., *Southern Politics in State and Nation* (Knoxville: University of Tennessee Press, 1984), 131.

3. Bass and Thompson, *Strom*, 117.

4. Ibid., 134.

5. David Robertson, *Sly and Able: A Political Biography of James F. Byrnes* (New York: Norton, 1994), 497–98, 501–2.

6. Tony Badger, "From Defiance to Moderation: South Carolina Governors and Racial Change," in *Toward the Meeting of the Waters: Currents in the Civil Rights Movement of South Carolina during the Twentieth Century*, ed. Winfred B. Moore Jr. and Orville Vernon Burton (Columbia: University of South Carolina Press, 2008), 7.

7. James F. Byrnes, *All in One Lifetime* (New York: Harper and Brothers, 1958), 407.

8. *Charleston News and Courier*, January 12, 1950.

9. "The Man They Love to Hate," *Time*, August 23, 1948, 17 (quoted in Christopher W. Schmidt, "Judge Waring's Battle with Southern Liberalism," paper presented at the Citadel Conference on Civil Rights in South Carolina, Charleston, March 5–8, 2003).

10. Robertson, *Sly and Able*, 521.

11. 132 F. Supp. 776–777 (1955).

12. See Jack Bass, *Unlikely Heroes* (1981; Tuscaloosa: University of Alabama Press, 1990), 298.

9. A New Era Evolves

1. Ernest F. Hollings, speaking to Wofford College students, January 2005, Charleston, S.C.

2. "The 1963 Inaugural Address of Governor George C. Wallace," January 14, 1963, Alabama Department of Archives and History, http://www.archives.state.al.us/govs_list/inauguralspeech.html (accessed 28 August 2008).

3. James C. Cobb, *The Selling of the South: The Southern Crusade for Industrial Development, 1936–1980* (Baton Rouge: Louisiana University Press, 1982), 166–67.

4. Jack Bass and Walter De Vries, *The Transformation of Southern Politics* (1976; Athens: University of Georgia Press, 1995), 27.

5. Ibid., 97.

6. Thomas F. Pettigrew, presentation to the class of Nieman Fellows, Harvard University, 1966.

7. J. C. Coleman, interview with Jack Bass, January 1970. Coleman was South Carolina deputy attorney general and chief defense counsel for the nine patrolmen tried and acquitted in federal court on charges of imposing summary punishment without due process of law.

8. Jack Bass and Jack Nelson, *The Orangeburg Massacre* (1970; Macon, Ga.: Mercer University Press, 2002), 81.

9. Ibid., 197.

10. Jack Bass and Walter De Vries, *The Transformation of Southern Politics* (1976; Athens: University of Georgia Press, 1995), 248.

11. Bill Barley, interview with Jack Bass, February 7, 2008. Barley was staff photographer for McNair in 1968.

12. Bass and Nelson, *Orangeburg Massacre,* 137.

13. Ibid., 208.

14. Ibid., 208.

15. William Saunders, telephone interview with Jack Bass, October 2006.

16. Jack Bass, *Porgy Comes Home: South Carolina after Three Hundred Years* (Columbia, S.C.: R. L. Bryan, 1972), 117.

17. Ibid., 115, 117.

18. Ibid., 117.

19. "South Carolina Governor to Obey Court on Schools," *New York Times,* January 27, 1970.

20. Bass and De Vries, *Transformation of Southern Politics,* 262.

21. Bass, *Porgy Comes Home,* 120.

22. James Clyburn, interview with Jack Bass, December 1, 2006.

23. Ibid.

24. Bass telephone interview with M. Hayes Mizell, January 13, 2007.

25. M. Hayes Mizell, speech at St. Andrews Presbyterian College, Laurinburg, N.C., July 4, 1969.

26. Victoria DeLee, telephone interview with Jack Bass, March 7, 2007.

27. Tom McCain, telephone interview with Jack Bass, March 7, 2007.

28. Strom Thurmond in "Rise of the Republican Party," episode 9 in *The American South Comes of Age,* South Carolina Educational Television, 1986.

29. Ira Katznelson, *When Affirmative Action Was White: An Untold History of Racial Inequality in Twentieth-Century America* (New York: Norton, 2005), 42–46.

30. I. DeQuincey Newman in "Rise of the Republican Party."

31. Tom Turnipseed, quoted in Jack Bass and Marilyn Thompson, *Strom: The Complicated Personal and Political Life of Strom Thurmond* (New York: Public Affairs Press, 2005), 209.

32. Cited in "Thurmond Image Seen as Changing," *New York Times*, October 17, 1971.

33. W. T. Cash, *The Mind of the South* (New York: Alfred A. Knopf, 1941), 429.

34. Quoted in Bass and Thompson, *Strom,* 298.

10. Popular Culture

1. Frank Beacham, "This Magic Moment: When the Ku Klux Klan Tried to Kill Rhythm and Blues Music in South Carolina," in *Toward the Meeting of the Waters: Currents in the Civil Rights Movement of South Carolina during the Twentieth Century,* ed. Winfred B. Moore Jr. and Orville Vernon Burton (Columbia: University of South Carolina Press, 2008), 126.

2. Ibid, 140.

3. Will Moredock, *Banana Republic: A Year in the Heart of Myrtle Beach* (Charleston, S.C.: Frontline Press, 2003), 12.

11. The Republican Rise

1. Jack Bass and Walter De Vries, *The Transformation of Southern Politics* (1976; Athens: University of Georgia Press, 1995), 267.

2. Bass and De Vries, *Transformation of Southern Politics,* 269–70.

3. Earl Black and Merle Black, *The Rise of Southern Republicans* (Belknap Press for Harvard University Press, 2002), 330.

4. Alexander P. Lamis, ed., *Southern Politics in the 1990s* (Baton Rouge: Louisiana State University Press, 1999), 8.

5. BMW executive Carl Fleischer, interview with Jack Bass, Greer, S.C., August 14, 2003.

6. Warren Tompkins, interview with Jack Bass, Columbia, S.C., June 4, 2003.

7. 956 F. Supp. 622 (D.S.C.); 163 F. 2nd 799 (4th Cir. 1999).

8. Lamis, *Southern Politics in the 1990s,* 70.

9. Phil Gailey, "Bigotry Issue in Carolina Campaign," *New York Times,* September 24, 1986.

10. Ibid.

11. Phil Gailey, "Talking Politics: Aplogy by Atwater," *New York Times,* October 10, 1986.

12. Marvin Chernoff, telephone interview with Jack Bass, October 7, 2006.

13. Robert McAlister, telephone interview with Jack Bass, December 4, 2006.

14. Samuel Tenenbaum, interview with Jack Bass, Columbia, S.C., October 7, 2006.

15. Peter Carlson, "The Nitty-Gritty Senator," *Washington Post,* October 14, 2004.

12. Beyond the Bozart

1. Mencken quoted in James M. Hutchisson, *DuBose Heyward: A Charleston Gentleman and the World of Porgy and Bess* (Jackson: University Press of Mississippi, 2000), 24–25.

2. Arnold T. Toynbee, *A Study of History* (New York: Oxford University Press, 1947), 1:315–16.

3. Donald W. Shriver, "He Made You Feel Like Somebody," *Christian Century,* July 15, 1970, 866–68.

4. Jack Bass, *Porgy Comes Home: South Carolina after Three Hundred Years* (Columbia, S.C.: R. L. Bryan, 1972), 126.

5. Ibid., 123–25.

6. Kirk Varnedoe, *Jasper Johns: A Retrospective* (New York: New York Museum of Modern Art, 1996), 112.

7. "Celebrated Author Takes Over Editorship of Historic Literary Publication," *LSU Highlights*, Fall 2004, http://www.lsu.edu/highlights/043/lott.html (accessed August 18, 2008).

8. Dale Rosengarten, *Row upon Row: Seagrass Baskets of the South Carolina Lowcountry* (Columbia: McKissick Museum, University of South Carolina, 1994), 10–11.

9. Marilyn Laufer and Frank Martin, *Myths and Metaphors: The Art of Leo Twiggs* (Athens, Ga.: Georgia Museum of Art, 2004).

10. Quoted in Bass, *Porgy Comes Home*, 128.

11. Charles W. Joyner, *Folk Song in South Carolina* (Columbia, Published for the South Carolina Tricentennial Commission by the University of South Carolina Press, 1971), 2.

12. Jon Pareles, "James Brown, the 'Godfather of Soul,' Dies at 73," *New York Times*, December 26, 2006.

13. Quoted in Fraser, *Charleston! Charleston!* 431.

13. The Changing Economy

1. Fritz Hamer, "Charleston Naval Shipyard," in *The South Carolina Encyclopedia*, ed. Walter Edgar (Columbia: University of South Carolina Press, 2006), 154–55.

2. Eugene E. "Jack" Stone IV, "Working to Revive South Carolina's Apparel Industry," *Business and Economic Review*, July–September 2005, 3–7.

3. Michael E. Porter and the Monitor Group, *South Carolina Competitiveness Initiative: A Strategic Plan for South Carolina* (Columbia: South Carolina Council on Competitiveness, 2005), 43–46.

4. Jack Bass, interviews with executives of all three companies, 2003.

5. Hannah Clark, "The World's Most Respected Companies," Forbes, November 21, 2006.; available online at http://www.reputationinstitute.com/press/21Nov2006FORBES WorldsMostRespectedCompanies.pdf (accessed August 27, 2008).

6. Maureen Taylor, "Forest Products: A Cluster That's Working," *Business and Economic Review*, April–June 2005, 8.

7. Quote provided by Chris Przirembel, vice president for research and economic development at Clemson University, interview with Jack Bass, Clemson, S.C., November 1, 2006.

8. Robert Barker, interview with Jack Bass, November 1, 2006.

9. Bob Geolas, interview with Jack Bass, November 7, 2006.

10. Christopher Swope, "Master of the Public Realm: Leveraging the Power of Urban Design and Civic Space," *Governing*, November 2003, 36.

11. Orrin Pilkey, "Beach Nourishment: Not the Answer," *Business and Economic Review*, January–March 2007, 7–8; also available online at http://findarticles.com/p/articles/mi_qa5313/is_200701/ai_n21281201 (accessed 22 August 2008).

12. Timony W. Kana, "(Myrtle) Beach Restoration: A Success Story?" *Business and Economic Review*, July–September 2006, http://findarticles.com/p/articles/mi_qa5313/is_200607/ai_n21392981?tag=artBody;col1 (accessed 22 August 2008).

13. Sorensen quote.

14. Report by Trident Chamber of Commerce.

15. Porter, *South Carolina Competitiveness Initiative*, 49.

16. Douglas P. Woodward, "The New Face of South Carolina's Force," *Business and Economic Review,* July–September 2006.

17. Net out-migration equals the difference between natural increase—number of births over deaths—and net change in population.

18. Donald Schunk and Douglas Woodward, *A Profile of the Diversified South Carolina Economy* (Columbia: Division of Research, Darla Moore School of Business, University of South Carolina, 2000), 32.

19. *Columbia State,* April 19, 2007, citing a report of the Southern Regional Education Board.

20. Tim Radford, "Bringer of Light," *Guardian* (London), May 5, 2005.

14. Change and Continuity

1. 2006 Statistical Abstract of South Carolina, S.C. Budget and Control Board, Office of Research and Statistics.

2. Ibid.

3. Association of Religious Data Archives, 2007, www.thearda.com (accessed October 17, 2007).

4. Ernest B. Furgurson, *Hard Right: The Rise of Jesse Helms* (New York: Norton, 1986), 28.

5. Hartford Institute for Religious Research, "Database of Megachurches in the U.S.," http://www.hartfordinstitute.org/megachurch/database.html (accessed August 22, 2008).

6. James McBride Dabbs, *Haunted by God: The Cultural and Religious Experience of the South* (Richmond: John Knox Press, 1972), 180.

7. Jack Bass, *Porgy Comes Home: South Carolina after Three Hundred Years* (Columbia, S.C.: R. L. Bryan, 1972), 61.

8. Quoted from ibid, 62.

9. A twenty-first-century bit of doggerel verse by Jack Bass.

10. Mary C. Simms Oliphant, *The New Simms History of South Carolina,* Centennial Edition (Columbia, S.C.: State Company, 1940), 265.

11. Ibid., 257.

12. Cleveland L. Sellers, acceptance of Columbia Community Relations Committee Award, June 11, 2003.

13. Jack Bass and Marilyn Thompson, *Strom: The Complicated Personal and Political Life of Strom Thurmond* (New York: Public Affairs Press, 2005), 365.

14. Jack Bass, confidential sources.

15. "Monument Admirable Addition," *Charleston Post and Courier,* July 3, 2004.

16. Bass and Thompson, *Strom,* 365.

17. Jack Bass, confidential source.

18. Herbert Blumer, "The Future of the Color Line," in *The South in Continuity and Change,* ed. John C. McKinney and Edgar T. Thompson (Durham, N.C.: Duke University Press, 1965), 336.

INDEX

Nielsen, Barbara, 200
Nissan, 186
Nixon, Richard, 124, 126, 136; defeated in 1960 in South Carolina, 132; guidelines for Civil Rights Act and, 129; Thurmond's support for in 1968, 133
North Charleston, S.C., 179, 181
Nullification Crisis, 38–39. *See also* Calhoun, John C.; Turnbull, Robert J.

Ocean Forest Hotel (Myrtle Beach), 142
"Operation Lost Trust," 152
Orangeburg, S.C., 10, 72; civil rights movement and, 91, 93–95, 98
Orangeburg Massacre, 116–19, 157; McNair's hopes of vice presidency dashed because of, 121; victims of, 116, 125

palmetto, 15, 50
Palmetto Family Council, 199
Parris Island, S.C., 190
Pavilion (Myrtle Beach), 143, 187; closing of, 145
Pee Dee (region), 79, 80, 143; economic development and, 178–80, 193
Penn Center (St. Helena Island), 45
Perry, Matthew J., 202
Peterkin, Julia, 161
Petigru, James Louis, 42, 47
Pettigrew, Thomas F., 116
Piccolo Spoleto, 174
Pickens, Andrew, 17
Pickens, Francis W., 44, 49, 58
Pickens County, 40, 42, 80, 90
Pickens District. *See* Pickens County
Pilkey, Orrin, 187
Pinckney, Charles Cotesworth, 154
Pinckney, Josephine, 168
piracy, 8
Pischetsrieder, Bernd, 184
Plessy v. Ferguson, 108
Poetry Society of South Carolina, 158, 161–62
Pollitzer sisters, 75
Porgy and Bess (Gershwin and Heyward), 159, 164; performed in Charleston, 123
Port of Charleston, 181–84

Port Royal experiment, 45
Porter report, 187, 191
Presbyterians, 22, 29
Przirembel, Chris, 185

Quakers, 3, 6

race, 58, 88; contemporary attitudes concerning, xi, 196–97, 202, 205–6; politics and, 65, 66, 93, 104–5, 110, 115–16, 132, 134, 137, 147, 150; slavery and, 49, 127–28; southern culture and, xv, 138, 140–41
Rainey, James, 56
Rainey, Joseph H., 55
Ransier, Alonzo, 55
Ravenel, Charles D. "Pug," 146–47
Reagan, Ronald, 147, 149
Reconstruction, xv, 26, 44, 70, 88, 128, 192, 195; African American voting rights and, 53–55; beginnings of, 45, 53; outcome of, 70–71, 115; white resistance to, 56–58, 60; Reconstruction Acts, 53–54
Reedy River, 168
religion, xv, 3, 138, 153–54, 195, 197, 202; contemporary statistics, 198; race relations and, 138, 140; slavery and, 23–24, 29–30. *See also* African Methodist Episcopal Church; Judaism; Methodists; Presbyterians; Roman Catholics; Baptists, Southern
Republican Party, 148; growing strength in South Carolina, 134, 195; leader's attempt to distance party from racism, 157; origins of modern party in South Carolina, 132; race and contemporary version of, 131–33, 149–50
Research Centers for Economic Excellence, 186
Revolutionary War. *See* American Revolution
Rex, Jim, 157
Rhett, Robert Barnwell, 40, 42
Ribaut, Jean, 2
rice, 13, 50, 70, 163, 170, 175; origins in South Carolina, 7–8; slavery and, xv, 21, 28, 45, 49
Richardson, John P., 64

ABOUT THE AUTHORS

JACK BASS, director of the Citadel Alumni World War II Oral History Project, is a professor emeritus of humanities and social sciences at the College of Charleston. He has a Ph.D. in American studies from Emory University and is the author or coauthor of seven other books about the American South, including *Strom: The Complicated Personal and Political Life of Strom Thurmond*, *The Orangeburg Massacre*, *The Transformation of Southern Politics*, and *Taming the Storm*, a biography of Judge Frank M. Johnson Jr. that won the 1994 Robert F. Kennedy Book Award. Bass served as executive editor for *The American South Comes of Age*, a fourteen-part series for South Carolina Educational Television. He was twice named South Carolina Journalist of the Year and was a Nieman Fellow at Harvard University.

W. SCOTT POOLE is an associate professor of history and the director of the master's program in history at the College of Charleston. A graduate of Harvard University and the University of Mississippi, Poole is the author of three previous works on the American South. His first book, *Never Surrender*, won the 2004 George C. Rogers Jr. Book Award of the South Carolina Historical Society. He served as a contributing historian for the History Channel series *The States* and the PBS series *Slavery in the Making of America*.